More praise for *Voting*

"Jim Geraghty is one of the most insightful and winsome voices writing on politics today. When he pronounces, you had best take note. All during the 2004 election, Jim Geraghty had it right, in a triumph of reporting and intuition. He now illuminates the landscape of American politics in an important new book."
—Rich Lowry, *National Review*

"No one in 1963 could have dreamed that a scant ten years later the Democrats would have trashed their own bona fides as the national warrior party, but the party, alas, was down to the challenge and many years later is still going weak: voting for war, before voting against it, refusing to vote for its own resolutions, lamenting its tag as the wobbly and rubber-kneed party, while doing all it can to make this tag even more accurate. This is good for Republicans, but bad for the country, which badly needs a responsible opposite party. Everyone who cares about politics should read *Voting to Kill* to find out why it happened; Democrats should read it and try to recover. In the last case, they probably won't."
—Noemie Emery, *The Weekly Standard*

"Republicans and conservatives will want to buy *Voting to Kill* to keep it out of the Democrat's hands. Democrats will want it if they want a clue. And anyone interested in the politics of the next thirty months will want it as a map of the terrain that changed, forever, on 9/11."
—Hugh Hewitt, radio host and columnist for *The Weekly Standard*

Praise for Jim Geraghty and his blog, TKS

"I like TKS a lot, and am glad it's continued. You're a good writer!"
—Peggy Noonan, former Reagan speechwriter and
  contributing editor of *The Wall Street Journal*

"Must reading at the White House."
—Lee Bockhorn, White House speechwriter

"A good, credible conservative/Republican blogger who commands
attention and influences others."
—Marc Ambinder, ABC News

"Great work. Hope you keep the site going for a while."
—Lawrence F. Kaplan, *The New Republic*

"Great stuff. Kudos."
—Stephen F. Hayes, *The Weekly Standard*

VOTING
TO KILL

How 9/11 Launched the Era
of Republican Leadership

Jim Geraghty

A Touchstone Book
Published by Simon and Schuster
New York London Toronto Sydney

Touchstone
Rockefeller Center
1230 Avenue of the Americas
New York, NY 10020

Copyright © 2006 by Jim Geraghty
All rights reserved,
including the right of reproduction
in whole or in part in any form.

TOUCHSTONE and colophon are registered trademarks
of Simon & Schuster, Inc.

For information regarding special discounts for bulk purchases,
please contact Simon & Schuster Special Sales at
1-800-456-6798 or business@simonandschuster.com.

Designed by Elliott Beard

Manufactured in the United States of America

10   9   8   7   6   5   4   3   2   1

Library of Congress Cataloging-in-Publication data is available

ISBN-13: 978-0-7432-9042-5
ISBN-10:   0-7432-9042-9

TO MOM AND DAD

ACKNOWLEDGMENTS

Perhaps the two men most instrumental in bringing this book to fruition are my agent, Mel Berger, and my editor at Simon & Schuster, Brett Valley. Thanks to both.

Behind every good writer there is at least one good editor . . . telling him that his latest rewrite is almost there this time, it just needs to be tweaked a little, and to cut about half its current length. At *National Review,* I'm lucky to be edited by the light and helpful hands of Rich Lowry, Jay Nordlinger, Michael Potemra, and Kathryn Lopez. Writing a book seemed less intimidating after helpful talks with other *National Review* folks like Kate O'Beirne, John J. Miller, and Byron York.

Thanks to my interviewees whom I talked to in the course of writing this book, many of whom insisted on anonymity, lest they suffer the consequences of public association with the likes of me. If this book fools you into thinking I'm smart, it's the result of my conversations with a lot of smart people.

Then there are the folks who make up my sounding board, batting around politics or picking over the news of the day, bit by bit making sense of the world. Forget the cable talk shows; when you want to hear the straight dope on politics with a lot of insight and even more laughs, try to eavesdrop on Cam Edwards and Marshall Manson when we get together over Guinnesses at Union Street in Old Town Alexandria. Additional ideas and suggestions came from Shannon Lane, Brendan Conway, Mike Krempasky, Gerry Daly, and Jorgelina Pesce.

In the course of writing this book, I've had to run around four countries, seven cities, and meet up with a lot of folks. Thanks to Jim and Aileen Miller; Pete, Sue, and Katie Geraghty; and Len and Laura for their logistical assistance and emotional support.

This book was brought to you by the caffeine from the Starbucks on Arjentin Caddesi in Ankara, Turkey.

Finally, there is one person who has been a stable rock as my mood bounced between manic and depressive in the process of making this book. Here the previously anonymous "Mrs. KerrySpot," a.k.a. "Mrs. TKS," gets thanked the way she ought to: I would never have been able to do this without you, Allison.

CONTENTS

INTRODUCTION

"Aren't you completely wrong?"

It is a natural question to the ideas in this book. Today, the argument that 9/11 permanently changed American politics and the Republicans have a decisive advantage in this new era garners fewer nods of approval and more skeptical hoots and eye rolls.

Hasn't President Bush seen his poll numbers plummet? Didn't the Bush administration have a largely bumbling 2005 and a stumbling start to 2006? Haven't Democrats spent much of early 2006 confidently predicting they'll win back the House and Senate? Aren't Democrats nearly even with Republicans on the question of which party can better fight terrorism in recent polls? Don't other surveys show that only 6 percent of respondents say terrorism is the most important problem facing the United States? How can I possibly make this case?

The answer is "yes" to the first five questions. But here's the answer to the sixth: We can forget about the terrorists, but that doesn't mean they've forgotten about us.

It is wonderful, a near-miracle, that we have not seen another attack on our own soil as horrific as 9/11 for four years and counting. (I knock on wood as I write that sentence.) But the grim calculus of our age is that sooner or later, another strike will come, or at the very least be attempted. There are two ways we can truly return to the political world of September 10, or the halcyon façade of peace and prosperity of the 1990s: Either al-Qaeda will be completely defeated and consigned to the ash heap of history, or the public will experience mass amnesia.

It's safe to wonder if a growing segment of Americans are succumbing to the second option. As more and more days are put between September 11, 2001, and today, and as an embattled al-Qaeda shifts to hit lower-profile targets in Iraq, Egypt, and other far-off locales, terrorism subsides from our top concerns. Of course, our fear of hijackings, bombs, and other attacks will slowly recede as our minds and news headlines are dominated by this week's worry over prescription drug prices or high gas prices . . .

. . . until one day, it won't.

On July 6, 2005, the top issues of the day in London were the bid to host the Olympics, the G-8 summit in Gleneagles, Scotland, and Jack Straw addressing EU export subsidies. The *Observer* newspaper had recently showcased a poll demonstrating that the British electorate demanded radical action on climate change.

And then, the following morning, all of those concerns were swept from the ledger, at least temporarily, as everyone reacted to bombings on buses and the Underground and tried to figure out what was going on.

A political candidate or party who prepares to face the voters with a focus on the standard domestic concerns is likely to get caught flat-footed (again) sometime in the not-too-distant future.

Doesn't the souring public mood on Iraq show that Americans are tired of war, and have lost faith in the Republican Party's ability to protect us from terrorists?

Predicting the long-term political impact of Iraq is difficult in the best of circumstances; it's a fool's errand to try to do it in a book that will hopefully stand the test of time. But let's observe that recent difficulties in Iraq have provided too many Democrats a chance to vent their worst instincts.

To hear too many antiwar Democrats tell it, they never encounter a soldier proud of his or her work in Iraq. Rep. John Murtha, D-Pa., said he wouldn't join the military today. In a January 2005 town hall meeting, Murtha and another antiwar Democratic House member, Jim Moran, were confronted by former Army sergeant Mark Seavey, who recently returned from Afghanistan: "I keep hearing you say how you talk to the troops and the troops are demoralized and I really resent that characterization. The morale of the troops that I talk to is phenomenal." Seavey also noted that Moran failed to acknowledge, much less welcome, 200 of his constituents who had recently returned from Afghanistan.

Too many Democrats have embraced Cindy Sheehan, despite her less-publicized statements that the Iraq war was fought for Israel, her demand that U.S. troops immediately withdraw from *Afghanistan*, her labeling those attacking coalition troops in Iraq as "freedom fighters," and her comment that President Bush is "ten times the terrorist that Osama ever was."

The Democratic grass roots enthusiastically talk of President Bush's impeachment, as if the country is clamoring for a rerun of an unpleasant chapter of the Clinton years.

Both men on the 2004 Democratic ticket, John Kerry and John Edwards, have publicly renounced their votes in support of the Iraq war. Peter Beinart, former editor of *The New Republic*, regrets his advocacy of toppling Saddam and now contends that the leaky, unpopular sanctions regime on Iraq was sufficient.

Unfortunately, a voter can't quite be reassured by the about-face of prominent, once-hawkish Democrats. The argument of the born-again doves is that "we thought this was a good idea, and then we found out the circumstances had changed (no WMDs) and it got harder. We supported establishing a democracy in the heart of the Middle East until it got hard."

Perhaps the Democrats' widely disparate views on Iraq, Afghanistan, Iran, and the use of military force will someday congeal into a coherent set of policies that Americans will feel confident is up to the task of protecting them from a relentless, merciless, and blood-thirsty foe. Until that day, voters will have the choice of the Republican worldview, warts and all, or the incoherent option from the other side of the aisle.

We will see.

ONE

Post-9/11 America

The real human response to the horrors of life is to put them out of the mind—by focusing on the glories or the duties of life. For this reason terror campaigns provide their own antidote. They provide the people who are supposed to be terrorized with a powerful new duty—to save themselves, to destroy those who would destroy them. This is where we are headed now.

Michael Kelly, Atlantic, *November 2001*

Estimates vary a bit, but roughly 18 million to 20 million people live within a 50-mile radius of Ground Zero. It is safe to assume that the vast majority of those individuals witnessed the collapse of the towers and the sudden horrific deaths of thousands of human beings.

Within seven minutes of the first crash, almost the whole world, or at least those with access to television or radio, could vicariously experience the events at Ground Zero in New York City on September 11, 2001. Republican pollster David Winston estimates that 80 to 90 percent of Americans saw the second plane hit the tower as it happened. Even if that seems high, we can safely assume that a percentage in that neighborhood saw the collapse of the towers, live on their television set.

"There's a very big difference between watching an event on tape, on the news, and watching an event live," Winston says. "The moment the plane hit the tower, the audience was watching 500 people die in real time. It was a supremely unsettling experience, something a lot of people had to work through. It's not all that different from dealing with the death of a parent. You never forget it or get over it; you just have to learn how to live with it."

In an instant, the sense of safety that was so definitive that it could be taken for granted—a sense that seemed to define post–Cold War reality—was proven illusory. Fears that had seemed unimaginable or impossible were suddenly realities. Almost everything we thought we knew about the world was wrong. A part of us—the capacity to believe so thoroughly that concepts such as evil and barbarianism were irrelevant to modern life—died with the victims.

The details that came in the hours and days following 9/11 changed the scale of the event from soaring airliners and colossal office towers to the smaller but perhaps even more devastating impact on ordinary human lives. A mother tearfully told how her children had been asking to make a cell-phone call to their father in heaven.[1] A psychologist described a 3-year-old girl in his office who had been playing during a sibling's appointment, pushing little human figures off his desk. It took the therapist a moment to realize the child had caught a glimpse on television of people leaping to their deaths from the towers and was reenacting her nightmares. The altered skyline looked too alien, too wrong to spur the real pain in our guts. It was the smaller sights and details: seeing the toughest and strongest of men, working with callused hands, succumbing to grief as they dug through the wreckage at Ground Zero. Atlanta residents building a memorial of candles and flower petals on the front step of their neighbors who lost their son, a Cantor Fitzgerald employee, in the attacks.

The immediate victims' pain was so palpable and our empathy was so intense that many Americans felt the strange phenomenon of missing people they had never met. Weeks after the attacks, the satirical magazine the *Onion* would encapsulate ordinary Americans' supreme desire to help and their sense of helplessness with the article "Not Knowing What Else to Do, Woman Bakes American-Flag Cake."

There was shock, there was horror, there was fear. But there was also anger. "Find them and kill them," said David Gonzalez, a New York sidewalk vendor and Peruvian immigrant. "No court. No trial. Electrocute them."

Capital punishment opponents suddenly found themselves wishing for Osama bin Laden's head on a pike. Columnists joked that the front-page headline of the *Village Voice* ("The Bastards!") could have run in the *New York Post*.[2]

Today, five years later, the sounds and images of that day still pack an unequaled emotional punch. Watching the footage of two French documentarians, it is nearly impossible to have a dispassionate reaction to the drone of the first plane before it hits the tower and the instantaneous "holy s—t" from firefighters who were coincidentally responding to a routine gas-leak call. A short phrase, "Let's roll"—the galvanizing words of the passengers on United Flight 93—now has overwhelming emotional power.

So powerful are the images of that day that the sensitive souls who manage television news use this video footage minimally or not at all.[3] But its disappearance from our television screens has not dulled the vivid pictures imprinted on our mind's eye: The sight of people jumping to their deaths from 100 stories. The huge dust clouds of the exploding South Tower making well-dressed New Yorkers run for their lives. The Statue of Liberty standing in a hellish black cloud. The exodus of ash-covered New Yorkers over the Brooklyn Bridge. The snapshots taken by fleeing Trade Center employees of firemen ascending to danger while civilians fled from it. The cross that remained from the wreckage. The three firefighters raising a flag over Ground Zero.

But in addition to vicariously experiencing those events at the site, on that day Americans across the country had their own intensely emotional experiences reacting to the events in New York, Washington, D.C., and Pennsylvania. Winston describes a focus group convened in a northeastern city about six months after 9/11:

> One woman in this group had three or four kids. We were discussing the 9/11 attacks and how they affected us, and she went into this very short, very tense description of driving from school to school and picking up her children. All of us—myself, the other participants—were riveted. It was clear that while this story wasn't unique, something else was there. I was describing this woman's story to my wife, and her immediate reaction was, "Which child did she pick up first?" And with that, it was like the tumblers falling into place. That mother in that focus group and every mother who had children at more than one school had the moral equivalent of *Sophie's Choice*[4] on that day: Which child did she pick up first? All this mother wanted in a leader is to find someone who would make sure she never had to make that choice again.

The emotion has not dissipated with time.

Winston describes another focus group, this time in Ohio, during the presidential campaign:

We're again discussing the 9/11 attacks, and in all of the participants, but particularly these mothers, this remarkable detail is still there, this remarkable emotion still there, still front and center. It wasn't that they talk about it all the time, but the recall of the details of that day was very easy. They're describing this very personal situation, this fear of whether they will get to their children in time.

One woman described that she had just dropped her child off and was driving away when the radio is describing what is happening. And at first she is wondering whether she should turn around, but the message on the radio seems to be that everything's okay, and she decides not to pick up her child from school. Well, another mother sitting near her [in the focus group] turns around with this intense velocity and said, "I picked my kids up." It was an icy exchange, almost as if saying, "I was a good parent." They're discussing this three years later, and the emotion was like it was yesterday. What that told me was that the level of emotion and recall was still very much there.

President Bush actually referred to this agonizing choice parents faced in a campaign commercial in August 2004. Seated next to Laura Bush, the president spoke softly: "My most solemn duty is to lead our nation to protect ourselves. I can't imagine the great agony of a mom or a dad having to make the decision about which child to pick up first on September the 11th. We cannot hesitate, we cannot yield, we must do everything in our power to bring an enemy to justice before they hurt us again."

Some said this ad was emotionally manipulative, and Chad Clanton, one of John Kerry's campaign spokesmen, responded, "If you ever wanted proof that the Bush campaign has reached the point of desperation, now we have it." Kerry adviser Tad Devine said the ad was a sign that "the president and his campaign are floundering and in search of a strategy." *ABC News* political director Mark Halperin wrote, "Surely there will be for some a whiff of the desperate in using this [theme] now."

One wonders if they had seen the same focus groups that Winston did. Did the parents who watched the commercial see it as a desperate ploy? Or did they see it as their president articulating their deepest concern, demonstrating that he felt just the way they felt that day?

Undoubtedly, these kinds of thoughts went through Bush's mind that day—he learned of the attacks while at a school, looking into the faces of children. His first order upon returning to Air Force One was, "Be sure to get the first lady and my daughters protected." [5]

This great primal instinct of the lion and lioness protecting the cubs was ignited in every American with an intensity unrivaled in most citizen's lives. When adrenaline is released and the mind switches to the instinctive fight-or-flight mentality, all of the senses are sharpened, and the memory begins "recording" all of this sensory data, since the mind isn't sure what stimuli are important and are to be focused on. Almost everyone has very intense, vivid memories of the minute details of 9/11—the smells, the sounds, the sights.

Some Americans have had intense, traumatic experiences before. But this was the first nationwide near-death experience, when for one morning every American was suddenly seized by the thoughts of "What's happening? Where are my loved ones? How can I keep them safe?"

There is no doubt an event like 9/11 changes the way you look at the world; it also often changes a person's political beliefs. People whose top priorities were jobs and the economy or social issues suddenly find themselves confronting more immediate and personal issues: safety and protection from threats.

Ironically, media focus groups found this "protect my children first, all other issues second" phenomenon throughout the campaigns of 2002 and 2004. But somehow these public feelings didn't quite dominate the headlines or shape the campaign coverage.

"More than a year before the [presidential] election, we went to St. Louis to do focus groups with voters to talk about the economy," says Susan Page, political correspondent for *USA Today*. "Jim Norman, our polling director, and I went to St. Louis to do that, and we tried—we had these focus groups and tried to get people to talk about the economy. The economy was hurting in St. Louis. We had a woman whose husband had lost his job and she was concerned about health care coverage. We had a guy who'd had a skilled blue-collar job at the airport for 20 years. There'd been so many layoffs he was back to working the night shift, but we could not get them to continue focusing on the economy because they kept coming back to terrorism, on their own, and I remember one woman said, 'If you're dead, it doesn't matter how much money you're making.' "[6]

No event in this nation's history—indeed, world history—compared. In the space of just 102 minutes, more Americans were killed than were lost at Pearl Harbor. More Americans died on a single day during the battle at Gettysburg, but the 9/11 deaths were mostly civilians, not soldiers approaching a battlefield. The previous defining generational "where were you when you heard the news" moment, the assassination of President John F. Kennedy, was about the death of one high-profile figure.

These feelings may fade, but they don't disappear. We will move on, but the memories will always linger. We still, as political writer Peggy Noonan puts it, "get mugged by memories."

Some political observers see this emotional phenomenon and conclude that America is gripped by a paralyzing fear. One of those making this argument is University of Maryland political scientist Benjamin Barber, who advised Howard Dean's presidential campaign on foreign policy. In his international affairs tome *Fear's Empire: War, Terrorism, and Democracy,* Barber describes an America where "parents keep kids home or send them to school in a state of permanent anxiety,"[7] mothers buy gas masks for 2-year olds, and citizens engage in "quasi-hysterical behavior, including people wrapping their suburban homes in plastic sheeting."

Barber also contends Americans are "fearful of the otherness of the world, and oddly oblivious to the fact that they embody that otherness in their own diversity, they look to coerce hostile parts of the planet into submission with a strong-willed militancy." This seems hampered by excess intellectualism. Is it really an abstract otherness that Americans fear? Or is it slightly more specific concepts like airplanes leveling skyscrapers, anthrax in the mail, bombs in the subway, or a private plane targeting the nearest chemical plant?

Barber is right about the intense fear that terrorism can generate, but his picture of American life is more caricature than portrait. Today, a half-decade after 9/11, most U.S. citizens do not live in constant fear of terrorism. However, the issue is never far from their minds, and there are a thousand tiny reminders each day.

The events of any given day—Iraq, relations with Europe, developments in the Middle East—are big news, and Americans pay attention to them because of the memories of that day. Every time there is an accident at a chemical plant, a small plane crash, a train derailment, a power outage, the question hangs in the air, spoken or unspoken: Was it terrorism?

And, of course, there have been additional attacks. The anthrax mailings, attempted shoe bomber Richard Reid, Bali bombing, Madrid train bombings, bombing of the British consulate in Istanbul, Beslan school massacre, London Underground bombings. Sadly, by the time you read this, there will probably be more added to this list.

The nebulous and adaptable nature of the threat we face means that Americans rarely feel safe. Big cities are natural targets, but then again, so is the local post office. There's reason to worry if you live near a nuclear reactor or if you're in a rural part of the country with crop dusters. Perhaps the only location unlikely to be in a terrorist's crosshairs is, ironically, the Unabomber's shack in the middle of nowhere.

SECURITY MOMS

When it became acceptable to think about politics again in early 2002, pollsters and political taxonomists were classifying a new trendy voter subdemographic: security moms. These suburban mothers had formed a key part of Democratic victories in the presidential races of 1992 and 1996 and Gore's popular vote victory in 2000, but the attacks suddenly changed these voters' priorities dramatically. A constituency that had long supported gun control now wanted airline pilots to have guns and took up firearms lessons in dramatic numbers. Whereas once these women saw the Pentagon as a wasteful gobbler of funds that could be used in schools, now they wanted the troops to have every resource and advantage.

A gender gap that had been the bane of Republican campaign strategists evaporated. As one self-described security mom told *Time* magazine, "Since 9/11, all I want in a President is a person who is strong."[8] Far more women than men told pollsters that they were depressed, losing sleep and fearful after 9/11. Women's support for defense spending—even for expensive, untried concepts such as a missile defense system—shot up to levels roughly equal with men's.[9]

Broadly speaking, Dad had to worry if his office was going to be blown up, and how to react if he saw a suspicious guy taking pictures of the local power plant. Mom was the one picking the kids up from school that day and who bought the duct tape and the bottled water.

"National security had previously been seen as a guy thing. Now it was an issue that resonated with laptop mom, with diner mom, with soccer mom," says Alex Castellanos, the Bush campaign's top strategist for television advertising. "The challenge we faced was, how do we tell that this is an issue of personal safety? Terror is about you, your kids, and the shopping mall."

But the political world did not pick up on this phenomenon uniformly. Shortly before the 2004 election, several Democratic pollsters argued that the security mom demographic was a creation of media hype.[10]

Anna Greenberg, vice president of Greenberg Quinlan Rosner Research Inc., tried to debunk the idea that security moms represent a distinctive bloc of voters. By her analysis, the women most likely to be supporting Bush and the Republican Party are married and have young children—a group that she said makes up 26 percent of all female voters. "We know that married white women are conservative," she said. "The notion that this is a group that is moving around is false. It's a conservative group of voters—on security, social issues, and taxes."

Greenberg noted that when respondents were asked why they would vote for Bush, the war on terrorism was the second most important reason for men (30 percent) and the third most important reason for women (24 percent). In fact, even among white married women, the war on terrorism (24 percent) trailed behind a strong leader who does what he says (33 percent) and his faith and values (29 percent). When Greenberg asked women what they would like to see more of from Kerry, "a strong enough backbone to deal with terrorist threats" trailed plans for the economy and health care, plans for Iraq, honesty and convictions, and standing up to corporate interest for women, while it ranked second for men.[11] (The top answer for men was what Kerry would do differently on the economy and health care.)

And yet, on Election Day 2004, . . . the security moms showed up at the voting booth and pulled the lever for Bush.

Bush carried white women by 11 points (55–44)—a big improvement over the single point (49–48) by which he carried this group in 2000. Bush's margin among those who are married and have children expanded modestly, from 56–41 in 2000 to 59–40 in 2004.

A national *Los Angeles Times* poll released in late October found 64 percent of women with children said they planned to vote Republican and 28 percent Democratic because of concerns over domestic security. In New Mexico, a blue state in 2000, Kerry won 49 percent of the female vote, down 5 points from Gore's 54 percent. Analysts suggested Kerry would have won both Ohio and New Mexico had he maintained the level of support Gore had among women.

"We've gone from a country where the key vote is soccer moms to a country where the key vote is moms worried about lunatics from countries where the primary sport is soccer," comedian Dennis Miller joked.

Of course, one didn't have to be a mother to experience a dramatic change in political views on that Tuesday. Many conservatives were born on the morning of September 11, 2001.

WARBLOGGERS

On September 11, 2001, major news sites such as CNN, the *New York Times*, and the BBC were unavailable for much of the day due to high traffic. With the usual news sources down for the count, community Web sites, discussion groups, and mailing lists lit up with vast amounts of information about the attacks. Later in the day, when the telephone circuits began to jam, e-mail proved the only way to assure distant friends and relatives of someone's safety.

While the televised news coverage in the early days after the attack was heavily skewed toward talking heads, the Internet was rife with personal accounts from ordinary New Yorkers and Washingtonians. Web video of the attacks shot by amateurs offered raw, expletive-laden reactions to the events as they happened.

Blogs had been around a while, but they made their splash on the culture at large in days after the attacks. Many who went onto the Web looking to learn more about al-Qaeda and terrorism found an enormous amount of information: policy papers, timelines, interviews, research, firsthand accounts, and so forth. The attacks were a shock to many, but policy experts had been studying the growing threat for years, and the Internet was ready to reveal the face and the thinking of the enemy.

And with the ability to post one's own comments, chat boards became the national water cooler. At a time when Americans felt shocked, afraid, and angry, the Internet gave them an option to connect to many who felt the same way. It also allowed for expressions of anger or suspicion too raw for the sensibilities of television or newspapers. Sites such as Little Green Footballs kept a sharp eye on the reaction of the Arab press and offered a more blunt assessment on the role of Islam in the terrorists' motives.

There were thousands of blogs that grew in 2001. But if any philosophy dominated the most widely read blogs, it was probably that of the technophilic, comfortable if not wealthy, often-but-not-always male news junkie. On September 10, many were socially liberal and economically conservative libertarian types. But after 9/11, they described themselves as warbloggers—hawks who put fighting terrorism as their top issue, far above any other priority.

The pro-war libertarian style was typified by University of Tennessee law professor Glenn Reynolds, Colorado Springs–based writer Stephen Green, Los Angeles–based mystery novelist Roger Simon—guys who have little or no use for the Bush administration's stand on most social issues.

Reynolds summarized how the different style of the blogs refuted a lot of conventional wisdom in war coverage:

"Fact checking" journalistic reports was a major aspect of the warblogs' work, and the results were occasionally startling. Correspondent Jon Lee Anderson of the *New Yorker* reported from Baghdad that the American bombing campaign had left "a landscape of death and wanton devastation, all stamped 'Made in America.'" Warbloggers immediately noted that commercial satellite images of Baghdad, released by the private company SpaceImaging that same day, showed no such devastation, with the city remaining largely intact and traffic moving normally through the streets. This correction received a good deal of attention nationwide, and bloggers also noted on-the-ground reports from a blogger in Baghdad (the pseudonymous Salam Pax, now a columnist for the *Guardian* in London) that damage was less than Western media were claiming—and noting that Saddam's men had been filling trenches with oil and igniting them for several days.

Similarly, Australian journalist and blogger Tim Blair noted a report by Robert Fisk of the London-based *Independent* regarding an American missile that hit a marketplace in Baghdad. Blair reproduced the serial number reported by Fisk as proof that it was an American missile. But several knowledgeable readers weighed in to establish that while the missile was probably American, it was an antiradar missile. It likely struck the marketplace because the Iraqis had concealed a SAM battery there, perhaps in the hopes of drawing fire and causing civilian deaths that could be blamed on the Americans. So Fisk's reporting, which was expected to make the American effort look bad, thus wound up demonstrating that the Iraqi government was likely guilty of a war crime.[12]

How did the electorate go from 39 percent Democrats and 35 percent GOP in 2000 to a 37–37 split in 2004? Perhaps that 2 percent represents these 9/11 Republicans.

FROM THE ERA OF MICHAEL JACKSON
TO THE ERA OF ANDREW JACKSON

Hawkish political bloggers discovered a new term to describe themselves after 9/11: Jacksonians. Named after President Andrew Jackson, historian Walter Russell Meade described the philosophy:

> To understand how Crabgrass Jacksonianism is shaping and will continue to shape American foreign policy, we must begin with another unfashionable concept: honor. Although few Americans today use this anachronistic word, honor remains a core value for tens of millions of middle-class Americans, women as well as men.
>
> Jacksonian honor must be acknowledged by the outside world. One is entitled to, and demands, the appropriate respect: recognition of rights and just claims, acknowledgment of one's personal dignity. Many Americans will still fight, sometimes with weapons, when they feel they have not been treated with the proper respect. But even among the less violent, Americans stand on their dignity and rights.
>
> Courage is the crowning and indispensable part of the code. Jacksonians must be ready to defend their honor in great things and small. Americans ought to stick up for what they believe. In the nineteenth century, Jacksonian Americans fought duels long after aristocrats in Europe had given them up, and Americans today remain far more likely than

Europeans to settle personal quarrels with extreme and even deadly violence.

An honorable person is ready to kill or to die for family and flag.

Jacksonian America has clear ideas about how wars should be fought, how enemies should be treated, and what should happen when the wars are over. It recognizes two kinds of enemies and two kinds of fighting: honorable enemies fight a clean fight and are entitled to be opposed in the same way; dishonorable enemies fight dirty wars and in that case all rules are off.

An honorable enemy is one who declares war before beginning combat; fights according to recognized rules of war, honoring such traditions as the flag of truce; treats civilians in occupied territory with due consideration; and—a crucial point—refrains from the mistreatment of prisoners of war. Those who surrender should be treated with generosity. Adversaries who honor the code will benefit from its protections, while those who want a dirty fight will get one.

Probably as a result of frontier warfare, Jacksonian opinion came to believe that it was breaking the spirit of the enemy nation, rather than the fighting power of the enemy's armies, that was the chief object of warfare. It was not enough to defeat a tribe in battle; one had to "pacify" the tribe, to convince it utterly that resistance was and always would be futile and destructive. For this to happen, the war had to go to the enemy's home. The villages had to be burned, food supplies destroyed, civilians had to be killed. From the tiniest child to the most revered of the elderly sages, everyone in the enemy nation had to understand that further armed resistance to the will of the American people—whatever that might be—was simply not an option.

Jacksonians believe that there is an honor code in international life . . . and those who live by the code will be treated under it. But those who violate the code—who commit terrorist acts in peacetime, for example—forfeit its protection and deserve no consideration.[13]

A fascinating example of the Jacksonian spirit from an unlikely American source came at a November 2002 dinner at London's posh Charlotte Street Hotel. The scene: Hamish McAlpine, a British movie distributor, is dining with American movie director Larry Clark, creator of the gritty, sexually explicit, and controversial *Kids* and *Bully*. McAlpine is distributing Clark's upcoming film, *Ken Park*.

McAlpine gets revved about current events. According to Clark's account in the *LA Weekly*, a statement released by Clark's publicist, and a Londoner's account to Web-based Hollywood reporter Jeffrey Wells, the conversation went something like this:

MCALPINE: I would never live in America. I think September 11th was the best thing that ever happened to America. It will make Americans understand why the rest of the world hates them.

CLARK: Why?

MCALPINE: Israel and the American support of the Jews.

CLARK: Isn't it the fanatic Muslim fundamentalists who want to set the world back 1,000 years?

MCALPINE: No, it's f—ing Israel, and America supports and backs Israel. The Arabs want peace, and if Israel would go back to the borders before the 1967 war, there would be peace. The Arabs say that.

CLARK: Who says that?

MCALPINE: Yasser Arafat.

CLARK: Do you believe Yasser Arafat?

McALPINE: Hamas says it, too.

CLARK: Hamas sends in suicide bombers to kill innocent people and civilians. What about that?

McALPINE: They deserve to die.

CLARK: What!?

McALPINE: They f—ing deserve to die. What are you gonna do about it?

CLARK: What about the innocent little children and babies who get blown up?

McALPINE: They f—ing deserve to die.

McAlpine disputes Clark's account of the conversation, contending that the discussion was about "how to end the violence in the Middle East," that Clark used the words "sand niggers" to describe Arabs, and that 9/11 was never mentioned.[14] McAlpine subsequently commenced a libel action against Clark. But there is little disagreement about how the chat concluded: Clark, a New Yorker who witnessed the 9/11 attacks from his loft window, responded by punching McAlpine several times in the face—breaking his nose—and then overturning the dinner table on his debating partner.

"I was wrong," Clark said afterward to the *New York Post*. "I shouldn't have punched him. I shouldn't have lost it. But at the same time, I wouldn't have been able to look myself in the mirror the next morning if I hadn't done anything. I'm not gonna let this [bleeping] idiot talk about supporting terrorism and the killing of innocent people. I am an American!" Clark told the *Post* that the police who arrested him were sympathetic. "The cops were very nice and they seemed to feel like they would have done the same thing. They let me go with a ticket."[15]

Here we have a Hollywood director, whose fare before and after 9/11 is far from Frank Capra's *Why We Fight*, destroying his deal with his distributor and risking arrest and imprisonment simply to defend

American honor. The long-term effect of 9/11 is not just fear and a bare-knuckle intolerance for America-bashing, however.

"We as a country are sometimes taught to be cynical about each other, particularly before that day," Winston says. "What we watched on that day were average Americans just doing their jobs and being heroic. Suddenly this attitude of who we were became much more positive. Police, firemen, emergency responders—even the officials seemed to be rising to the moment. We had real American heroes again. It was the heroic nature of what this nation could be. Just average joes doing extraordinary things reestablished a faith in who we are."

Across the country, tens of thousands of Americans, eager to donate blood, lined up around the block from their hospitals, blood banks, and Red Cross centers.[16] Businesses were closed, normal life was on hold indefinitely, and waiting to donate helped people feel useful. Waiting with others, even complete strangers, was a chance to release the anger and to talk. After seeing the evil that humanity was capable of, it was reassuring to see strangers, ordinary folk, willing to wait as long as it would take and give a bit of what ran through their veins in the hope of alleviating the suffering of complete strangers.

Although fear reverberated and echoed through the nation, it was followed by an uncommon feeling in the day-to-day lives of Americans: courage, the absolute refusal to falter in the face of danger. The flag came out everywhere. For some, it was a defiant gesture. If being an American made one a target, many citizens weren't ashamed to wear the bull's-eye.

"Just as the terrorists know that we are watching them, we know that they are watching us," said Moses Davila, an unemployed teacher from Puerto Rico. "When they see us in the streets, wearing the flag, they know that we are not afraid of them, and that we will defeat them."[17]

The reaction to the attacks revealed that whatever their flaws in ordinary times, Americans pull together in a crisis. The vast majority of the nation's souls can harness deep reserves of determination, compassion, and strength in the face of adversity.

While the intensity of the post-9/11 emotions will fade to a certain extent, it is hard to dispute that something in the American consciousness changed permanently that day. Any given morning could bring an unexpected moment of danger, so Americans put a new precedence on preparedness.

"We are all soldiers now," Peggy Noonan wrote in the weeks after 9/11. "We have been drafted by history." [18]

Threats will never seem as theoretical or far-fetched. If evil was ever considered a theological artifact, a construct of an outmoded morality in a postmodern age, it was dispelled by the eyes in the mug shot of hijacking ringleader Muhammad Atta.

The argument that one man's terrorist is another man's freedom fighter sounds empty and naive in a time like this, repeated by those morally indifferent to what separates bomb victims and suicide bombers. What freedom were the hijackers fighting for that day?

Only a delusional political observer would predict that voters will stop thinking about terrorism when they go to the polls for the midterm elections of 2006, 2008, or even 2010. It is not merely the war on Islamist fundamentalist terrorism that will continue well into the next decade but candidates' emphasis of their ideas, resolve, and policy proposals on this issue.

Problems that seemed far away and irrelevant to American lives—"it's terrible what the Taliban did to those Buddha statues, but it's not really our problem"—suddenly seem to be an immediate concern with direct impact on the nation's future. The curriculum at Pakistani madrassas is suddenly almost as important as the curriculum at American grade schools.

The typical political issues of the day—the budget, what's on television—will always seem a bit more abstract and less compelling.

A 1984 Ronald Reagan reelection campaign commercial reminded voters that "there was a bear in the woods." (The large, menacing bear in the commercial clearly signified the Soviet Union, but the parallel may have been too metaphorical for some voters; there was some confusion over whether the president was touting his stand on foreign policy or hunting rights.) Beginning in 2001 and continuing through today, Americans face something scarier, the wolves of al-Qaeda, hungry for blood and unhesitant about attacking the most defenseless. The wolves metaphor was used in one of President Bush's 2004 campaign commercials.

"I don't think you'll ever see the public go fully back to the pre-9/11 mindset," says one Bush campaign insider. "I also think people want to look forward, and in the future, arguments about terrorism and 9/11 might not necessarily resonate as much as they did, but we're not going back to the days where the top issue is prescription drugs and school uniforms. This issue of who is going to keep Americans safe is going to at least always simmer beneath the surface as long as we are at war with al-Qaeda."

Only a few Democrats seem to grasp how the emotional intensity of this topic knocks all other political issues off the table. Senator Biden sounded like a Republican when he said, "Let me put it to you this way: The Lord Almighty, or Allah, whoever, if he came to every kitchen table in America and said, 'Look, I have a Faustian bargain for you, you choose. I will guarantee to you that I will end all terror threats against the United States within the year, but in return for that there will be no help for education, no help for Social Security, no help for health care.' What do you do? My answer is that seventy-five percent of the American people would buy that bargain." [19]

Biden has remained hawkish, but most Democrats are soft on the issue. The reelection of George W. Bush in 2004 proved that.

TWO

An Unpopular Position on Gay Marriage Is a Headache; An Unpopular Position on National Security Is the Ebola Virus

In this dramatically different world, candidates for public office face a new fundamental test: Can they keep the people safe?

This is the new criterion for political leadership, and since the attacks, this is the issue that has determined the winners and losers on Election Day. In a tribute to the psychological power of denial, those who have failed to convince the public that they can protect the country have begun insisting that our most recent elections were actually decided on other issues.

Almost immediately after Kerry's concession speech on November 3, 2004, Democrats set out to apportion the blame and organized their rhetorical firing squad in its traditional circular formation. The online magazine *Slate* ran a sometimes intentionally hilarious, sometimes not, series of articles by near-suicidal liberals attempting to explain "Why Americans Hate Democrats."

Perhaps the most vitriolic explanation came from novelist Jane Smiley, who wrote, "The election results reflect the decision of the right wing to cultivate and exploit ignorance in the citizenry. I suppose the good news is that 55 million Americans have evaded the ignorance-inducing machine. But 58 million have not. Ignorance and bloodlust have a long tradition in the United States, especially in the red states."

One can hardly wait to see the reaction to the campaign strategy that naturally emerges from this viewpoint. Picture a 2006 Democratic slogan in the red states: "Vote for Us, You Ignorant, Bloodthirsty Hicks."

Smiley's nuanced insight into red-state voter psychology was equaled only by Katha Pollitt, a columnist for the *Nation,* who wrote, "If a voter wants Christian Jihad, he may not be willing to desert the cause for health insurance."

ARE GAYS THE NEW RALPH NADER?

Shortly after the quadrennial recriminations began, a consensus emerged that Democrats' liberal views on social issues were a leading obstacle to their electoral success.

Steven Waldman, editor in chief of Beliefnet, a religion and spirituality Web site, pointed the finger at party members who were unable to say the word *God* without making air quotes. "On some level, the hardest thing that Democratic leaders, activists, and journalists have to do is honestly ask themselves this: Do you hold very religious people in contempt? If you do, religious people will sense it—and will vote against you. And there are more of them than there are of you," he advised.[1]

Hank Sheinkopf, a Democratic political consultant, chalked up his party's poor showing to cultural elitism. He told party leaders, "Dump the croissants and spend some time at a Veterans of Foreign Wars hall. Go to the local Wal-Mart, not to Starbucks. The Democrats might learn a lot more and then begin to understand the long road to winning this republic back."

Bruce Reed, president of the Democratic Leadership Council, concluded, "The number one issue on voters' minds Tuesday was something that we don't discuss in polite company in the blue states: moral values. The heartland—that great bastion of fiscal conservatism at home and restraint abroad—had good reasons to doubt Bush's values, but doubted ours instead."

In this discussion, gay marriage became the lightning rod and a leading scapegoat as the deciding factor in what many Democrats had declared to be a must-win election. Liberal bloggers snarked, "Gays are the new Ralph Nader."

California's Democratic senator Dianne Feinstein criticized San Francisco's mayor Gavin Newsom for his gay-marriage efforts. "I believe it did energize a very conservative vote. The whole issue has been too much, too fast, too soon."[2]

In some drastically underreported comments, former president Bill Clinton singled out the issue of gay marriage as the leading cause of John Kerry's defeat. In a quote omitted from wire service coverage of Clinton's speech to Utica, New York's Hamilton College, the former president said, "Gay marriage was an overwhelming factor in the defeat of John Kerry."[3]

His comments were covered only by the local newspaper. "With one decision of one [state] Supreme Court, all of a sudden we have a constitutional amendment designed, I think, to whip people up, to inflame them, make them stop thinking about other issues."

Clinton said the issue contributed to "an astonishing turnout among evangelical Christians who were voting on the basis of moral values."

Of course, the gay-marriage explanation was also being enthusiastically endorsed by social conservatives, eager to take credit for the president's win. "It was these value voters who ushered the president down the aisle for a second term," Tony Perkins, president of the Family Research Council, told the *San Francisco Chronicle*.

Same-sex marriage "was the great iceberg," said Robert Knight, director of the Culture & Family Institute, an affiliate of Concerned Women of America. "A lot of analysts saw the tip but didn't understand the power of the mass underneath. It galvanized millions of Christians to turn out and vote, and George Bush and the GOP got the lion's share of that vote."

Knight cited "massive efforts" by religious groups in Ohio "to rally pastors and to get Christians out of the pews and into the voting booths." Some gay leaders agreed. "I think it's pretty clear that [Bush political czar] Karl Rove's strategy of using gay and lesbian families as wedge issues in this election worked," said Christopher Barron, political director of the Log Cabin Republicans, who refused to endorse Bush. "It's hard to argue with results." [4]

No, actually, it's not.

THE SUPREMACY OF THE NATIONAL SECURITY ISSUE

Studies of voters didn't back the conclusion that gay marriage was the issue that put Bush over the top. Gay marriage isn't exactly sweeping the nation, and it may have helped energize some religious voters, but that wasn't what cost Kerry the election.

Among exit poll respondents who said top priority was:	Voted for Bush	Voted for Kerry
Moral Values (22 percent of respondents)	80 percent	18 percent
Economy/Jobs (20 percent)	18 percent	80 percent
Terrorism (19 percent)	86 percent	14 percent
Iraq (19 percent)	26 percent	73 percent
Health Care (8 percent)	23 percent	77 percent
Taxes (5 percent)	57 percent	43 percent
Education (4 percent)	26 percent	73 percent

Many Democratic analysts were struck by exit poll results indicating that 22 percent of respondents identified "moral values" as the most important issue—and that those voters sided with the president, 80 to 18. However, "terrorism" was named by 19 percent of the voters, and Bush did even better with this subgroup, winning 86 to 14.

Despite the widespread perception that moral values had exploded onto the scene in 2004, the number of voters who cited it as their top issue actually remained the same from 2000.

In a postelection roundtable with reporters, the Bush campaign architect Karl Rove said he thought gay marriage referendums in 11 states signaled the strength of the issue but didn't necessarily influence the presidential outcome. Appearing on *Meet the Press* the Sunday after the election, Rove said, "What essentially happened in this race was people became concerned about three issues—first, the war, then the economy, jobs, and taxes, and, third, moral values. And then everything else dropped off of the plate. And security grew the most in comparison to past races, but values grew second, the second most amount."

Put simply, Kerry lost because he was weak or was perceived to be less resolute and ruthless in fighting terrorism.

The final months of the campaign season were marked by several events that kept the terrorism issue front and center: the September 4 Beslan school massacre in Russia, a GOP convention that evoked 9/11 and the nation's response repeatedly, one-and-a-half debates focusing nearly exclusively on foreign policy issues, a continuing focus on the issue in Bush and Cheney's stump speeches and advertising, and on the Friday before the election, the appearance of Osama bin Laden on videotape.

"Seeing the awful images of carnage from the Russian school massacre locked in voters who were worried about protecting their children," says one GOP operative. "These voters knew it could happen here, and so they were willing to go with the guy who they had problems with elsewhere because they thought he would be more likely to prevent it from happening. It locked them in so much that George W. Bush could lose three presidential debates and still win by 3 points."

Other than pledges of multilateralism that didn't resonate outside the bluest states, Kerry brought little new or different to the discussion of how to most effectively fight terrorism. Throughout much of his campaign, Kerry's message on terrorism was "Bush has done X; I, as a new president, with a new cabinet, and with a Congress most likely controlled by the opposition party, will do X faster, spend more money on it, and do it better."

Kerry, and a good chunk of the Democratic Party, honestly and totally believed that the best way to prove that he had the best policies to fight the war on terror was to remind voters he fought in Vietnam. To many ears, that sounded like a non sequitur. Military service can be a plus in a presidential candidate, but Abraham Lincoln, Franklin Delano Roosevelt, and Ronald Reagan had little or no military experience, and they all did pretty well leading the United States during wars hot and cold.

Paul Freedman, associate professor of politics at the University of

Virginia, did serious number crunching and found that the political impact of the debate over gay marriage was overhyped.

> Why did states with gay-marriage ballot measures vote so heavily for Bush? Because such measures don't appear on state ballots randomly. Opponents of gay marriage concentrate their efforts in states that are most hospitable to a ban and are most likely to vote for Bush even without such a ballot measure. A state's history of voting for Bush is more likely to lead to an anti-gay-marriage measure on that state's ballot than the other way around.
>
> These differences hold up at the state level even when each state's past Bush vote is taken into account. When you control for that variable, a 10-point increase in the percentage of voters citing terrorism as the most important problem translates into a 3-point Bush gain. A 10-point increase in morality voters, however, has no effect. Nor does putting an anti-gay-marriage measure on the ballot. So, if you want to understand why Bush was reelected, stop obsessing about the morality gap and start looking at the terrorism gap.

Certain analysts did put values, gay marriage, and other social issues into perspective. Andrew Kohut of the Pew Research Center pointed out there was no disproportionate surge in the evangelical vote in 2004—evangelicals made up the same share of the electorate as they did in 2000.

USA Today's Susan Page stated in a postelection web chat, "I think the most fundamental factor to understanding the 2004 campaign is this: It was the first presidential election since the September 11 attacks. Many Americans felt President Bush had done a pretty good job in responding to that terrorist event—although many had concerns about the war in Iraq—and they weren't convinced that Senator Kerry would."

Page's comments came after her newspaper studied the counties across the nation that shifted parties from 2000 to 2004. The top reason, the paper concluded, was that "voters were drawn to Bush by memories of the 9/11 attacks and a reluctance to change leaders in the midst of war" and "Democrats were damaged by the perception that the party and its nominees are weak on national security." The "values" issues of abortion and gay marriage, as well as an effective GOP outreach to Hispanic voters, were also mentioned, but credited to a lesser degree.

As the postelection analysis continued, Democrats who were less invested in the social-values-trump-all argument started focusing on the national security issue. A postelection survey by Democratic pollster Stanley Greenberg and Democratic strategist James Carville found that Republicans scored a 28-point advantage over Democrats on "knowing what they stand for," a 27-point advantage on "strength" and a 25-point advantage on "protecting America against any threat."

Greenberg and Carville found that the Republicans' top "positive attribute" was their stand for "a strong military," with 44 percent of respondents naming it as one of the top phrases they associated with the Republican Party. "Religious faith" received 29 percent, and "defend the family" received 24 percent.

When asked for negative attributes, only 18 percent mentioned "too ready to use military force," and only 12 percent named "weaken civil liberties." The top three negatives for the GOP were "for the big corporations and most privileged" (34 percent), "spending overseas rather than attending to needs at home" (31 percent), and "big federal budget deficits" (29 percent).

Steve Rosenthal, of Americans Coming Together, architect of the Democrats' get-out-the-vote drive, discounted the notion that "values voters" put the GOP over the top. Instead, they put national security center stage:

- By 54 percent to 41 percent, voters decided that Americans are now safer from terrorist threats than four years ago, national exit polls said.
- By 55 percent to 42 percent, voters accepted Bush's view that Iraq is a part of the war on terrorism. By 51 percent to 45 percent, they still approved of the decision to go to war (though a majority expressed concerns about how the war is going).
- Just 40 percent said they trusted Kerry to do a good job handling the war on terrorism, compared with 58 percent who felt that way about the president.

"We lost 97 of the 100 fastest-growing counties across the United States in the last presidential election," said Tim Roemer, Democratic former member of Congress from Indiana and former member of the 9/11 Commission. "The suburbs outside Indianapolis. The suburbs outside Chicago. The suburbs outside Phoenix. The fastest-growing areas with families across this great nation. We didn't lose those 97 counties on cultural issues or on abortion. We primarily lost those because we did not have a compelling national security message. We needed to be able to convince soccer moms that we would make their children safer on the soccer field." [5]

There's another simple measuring stick. Policy on gay marriage, civil unions, and other values issues is set at the federal, state, and local levels. The response to terrorism and national security is mostly set at the federal level (although state governments may have some homeland security duties). If there's any area where Democrats haven't done quite as badly in recent years, it's in gubernatorial races and in statehouse races.

As John Kerry's advertising strategist Jim Margolis noted:

State House candidates aren't grappling with issues of terrorism and war, and that's where we're getting killed. At the end
of the day, the biggest structural problem for us as a party on
the federal level and Congress and with the presidential campaign is the public simply doesn't trust us to keep them safe.
. . . Kerry was dragged down by an enduring and, to a large
part, true set of negative stereotypes about the party. Until we
can fix that and convince Americans that we're not only the
party of Michael Moore, that we are a party determined and
willing and strong enough and brave enough to keep them
safe, we're going to keep getting these results on the national
level.[6]

What's more, 9/11 had a regional political effect that was not quite
enough to swing northeastern states, but it was enough to shift the
popular vote in the region and affect the nationwide total. Several of
those electoral vote–rich coastal Gore states are starting to turn a
paler shade of blue.

As veteran political reporter Robert David Sullivan noted, four of
the five counties with the biggest GOP gains in raw votes in the country were those that make up Long Island. Kings (Brooklyn), Queens,
Nassau, and Suffolk counties all went for Kerry, but his margin there
was more than 250,000 votes lower than Gore's in 2000. At the same
time, Staten Island flipped from 57 percent for Gore to a 50 percent
win for Bush, while New Jersey's Ocean County (which has a high re-
tiree population) went from a 49 percent plurality for Bush in 2000 to
a 60 percent landslide this time.[7]

In New York City, Bush's vote surged from 399,627 to
492,629. In Long Island and Westchester, it went from 607,224 to
720,719.

"Bush got a lot more votes in the five boroughs and in parts of New Jersey in 2004, and Kerry got a lower percentage than Gore did in a lot of places," says Ira Stoll, editor of the *New York Sun*. "If you look at districts where Bush did better, it's some of the places that lost a lot of people on 9/11. For example, I think a lot of Orthodox Jews may have voted for Gore-Lieberman in 2000 and may have voted Bush in 2004. Just anecdotally, I know people who were liberal Democrats before 9/11, and who are now still Democrats, but who voted for Bush and just think these terrorists are out to get us, and we've just got to do whatever it takes to defeat them before they get us again."

If you look at the eight New Jersey counties closest to Manhattan, where residents were most likely to have a view of the Twin Towers, Bush's number of votes and share of the vote increased by amounts ranging from the moderate to the dramatic.

Former Bush campaign staffer Patrick Ruffini examined Bush's vote at the municipal level in New Jersey, and found a stunning display of how Bush's share of the vote grew from 2000 to 2004. A smattering of municipalities saw Bush's share of the vote reduced from 2000—Harding Township, Mantoloking, Princeton. But large chunks of the state—just about everywhere south of Burlington and Monmouth, and almost all of the Bergen and Hudson county municipalities in the northeast, closest to New York City—saw dramatic gains in Bush's vote, from 4 percent to 14 percent higher than in 2000. The most dramatic turnaround came in Monmouth County, which lost 158 people on September 11, more than any other New Jersey county. Gore won Monmouth with 55 percent to Bush's 45 percent in 2000. In 2004, Bush beat Kerry 55 percent to 44 percent.

Overall, Bush's share of the vote in the Garden State increased by 6.2 percent from 2000. In New York, he increased his total by 5.3 percent, and in Connecticut, by 5.6 percent.

Ed Kilgore is vice president of the Democratic Leadership

Council, an organization dedicated to pulling his party to the center. He grasps—and fears—that a devastating gap has grown between the views of the Democratic base and the rest of the country on the issue of American military power:

> In the end, however, the folly of the administration's Iraq policy did little or nothing to undermine public faith in Bush's record on fighting terrorism generally, and that, not Iraq, was the ball game on national security. At a subrational level, many Americans who were disturbed by the course of events in Iraq—and retroactively, by the deceptions Bush used to get the war going—probably sized up Bush as follows: some Arabs killed a lot of Americans; Bush killed a lot of Arabs; and whatever else happened, there were no more attacks on the United States. Kerry's critique of Bush's record never adequately addressed those feelings, while reinforcing Republican claims that Kerry would be another Jimmy Carter, all talk and deliberation, but little or no action in difficult cases. . . .
>
> As University of Maryland professor and long-time DLC adviser (and, for the record, a vocal opponent of the decision to invade Iraq) Bill Galston has often pointed out, when asked if they believe U.S. military power is, on balance, a force for good or evil in the world, Americans endorse the positive view by a four-to-one margin. But the vast majority of the 20% who take what might be called the Michael Moore position are Democrats."[8]

Yet in some circles, the perception that gay rights and abortion represented electoral poison for the Democrats became so powerful that some wondered if the party could remain socially liberal.[9] Kevin Drum, the in-house blogger of the liberal *Washington Monthly*, rebuked his fellow Democrats for being all too willing to dump their principles on social issues while averting their eyes from the political costs on national security stances.

"Fighting terrorism is the major swing issue of the day, and perceived Democratic weakness toward terrorism is likely to remain our biggest electoral albatross for quite a while," Drum wrote. "It's remarkable, really, that an awful lot of commenters have seemed blithely willing to recommend that Democrats appease the Christian right on this, like abortion choice and gay rights, which are core issues for liberalism. At the same time, though, they're silent on the possibility of changing our tune on terrorism, which isn't."

THE FEEL-GOOD EXPLANATION

Of course, the "gay marriage brought out the yahoo vote" explanation is emotionally satisfying to Democrats. Those members of the party who buy into this conclusion can take solace in the idea that their losses in 2004 (and to a lesser extent, 2002) are a reflection of their sophistication and moral superiority. To use a metaphor that would outrage red staters, they believe Democratic candidates are bleeding at the ballot box like Christ on the cross, suffering for the sins of a homophobic electorate.

New York Times columnist Maureen Dowd wrote on the Thursday after the 2004 election: "The president got re-elected by dividing the country along fault lines of fear, intolerance, ignorance, and religious rule. He doesn't want to heal rifts; he wants to bring any riffraff who disagrees to heel. W. ran a Jihad in America."

Robert Borosage, codirector of the left-of-center Campaign for America's Future, declared, "[Bush] survived by waging the most negative and dishonest campaign that we have witnessed by an incumbent president, at least since Richard Nixon. He wrapped himself in the flag, he stoked the fears and passions of the evangelical right, he divided the country with gay-baiting." [10]

The overall message of these comments is essentially, "Don't worry, Democrats! Your defeat was just a sign that you're better people than the Republicans." How reassuring, how soothing, how much more comforting it makes the successive defeats feel. Why, when the leadership of the nation can be decided by the votes of mere plebes—a mass of fearful, emotional, hate-filled bumpkins—winning an election would almost feel like a moral compromise.

The explanation that weakness on terrorism has cost Democrats two straight elections provides no such consolation or sense of righteousness. In fact, it's perhaps the interpretation that is most disturbing, because it contends the party flunked one of the first tests of any political leader—can you keep the people safe?

THREE

Yes, It Is That Bad, Democrats

It is easy for a Democrat, looking for signs of optimism, to complete his autopsy of John Kerry's 2004 presidential campaign and conclude that the problem wasn't the message, it was the messenger. Kerry's aristocratic, Brahman style never resonated outside New England; in future races, a smoother, more charismatic candidate will carry the day with the same policies.

But behind Kerry's failed crusade lie dozens of other failed Democratic candidates: Tom Daschle, Max Cleland, Jeanne Carnahan, Jeanne Shaheen, Brad Carson, Erskine Bowles, Joseph Hoeffel, Betty Castor, Tony Knowles, Inez Tannenbaum. The high hopes of Democrat after Democrat, offed at the ballot box in 2002 and 2004.

The problems of the Democrats go way behind Kerry's flaws as a candidate. Unless you were alive during the time of Calvin Coolidge, you have never seen the Republican Party in a position of such political dominance.

After the 2004 elections, Democrats began debating what John Kerry did wrong and what the party should do now. Somewhat lost in the hubbub and ridicule of red-state voters was the fact that Democrats have been in a deep hole for more than a decade now. The Democrats not only lost control of the House of Representatives in 1994, but they have come up short in five consecutive elections. The only time the Democrats controlled the Senate was when liberal Republican Jim Jeffords left his party in mid-2001; the GOP then won it back against considerable historical odds in 2002.

Not only do Republicans control the governors' mansions of 28 states, but those governors' mansions are occupied by either multiterm veterans who bolstered their state parties (for example, Jeb Bush in Florida and Rick Perry in Texas) or rising stars with many potential incumbent races ahead of them (for example, Arnold Schwarzenegger in California, Tim Pawlenty in Minnesota, Sonny Perdue in Georgia, and Robert Ehrlich in Maryland). In 2004, Republicans held a majority of state legislators—a feat they initially achieved in 2002 after a half-century in the minority. The GOP also retained its advantage in control of legislatures. And as both parties know, control of state legislatures often means control of redistricting lines, creating districts for bulletproof incumbents.

Democrats can lament that they needed only 118,776 more votes to win Ohio,[1] but Republicans can look confidently at 31 red states. In addition, in 2004, New Hampshire was only 9,274 votes away from flipping to the Bush column, and Wisconsin was 11,384 votes away. If Democrats can aspire to find another 119,000 votes in the Buckeye State by 2008, Republicans can set goals for another 37,517 in Hawaii, 66,641 in Maine, 76,332 in Oregon, and 98,319 in Minnesota. The 2008 GOP candidate will gaze upon a panoply of low-hanging fruit, rich in electoral college votes.

The editors of the *New Republic* called the 2004 results "the most formidable challenge to American liberalism in our time." In fact, the voters' choices in that decisive year marked the end of the modern Democratic Party as we know it. After every previous defeat, the party denied reality and made excuses. Reagan was just a charming actor. The 1994 GOP takeover of Congress was a fluke. Gore was the real winner in 2000—Bush just stole the election. The entire 2002 results were a result of an attack ad on Max Cleland that compared the disabled Vietnam veteran to Osama bin Laden. Voters who keep throwing Democrats out of office are just simple-minded fools, swayed by Karl Rove's Jedi mind tricks.

In fact, even after 2004, some lefties tried to make the usual it-wasn't-so-bad-guys arguments. Jacob Hacker and Paul Pierson of the University of California, Berkeley, explained, "Tracking polls that looked at which congressional party voters preferred showed consistently that average voters favored the Democrats. In fact, this year Democrats led every one of the final 10 daily preelection tracking polls conducted by Rasmussen Reports by an average margin of between 2 and 3 points." These poll leads are all very nice, but the party didn't do nearly as well *among those who actually voted.*

Markos Moulitsas, the creator of the popular liberal Web site Daily Kos, pointed out, "More people voted against this president than any other in history. [The final count was about 59 million.] There's your mandate." Yes, but more than 62 million people voted *for* him.

On the "Donkey Rising" blog of Democratic pollster Ruy Teixeira, communications consultant John Belisarius wrote an essay entitled "The Democrats Didn't Lose in This Election, They Won." He contended that the 2004 campaign "made rank and file Democrats from every section of the party feel proud to be Democrats in a way they have not felt in decades."[2] Indeed, the Democrats' effort for that year marked a significant victory in the key objective of "feeling better about themselves."

For years, Democratic strategists have argued that if they could just increase turnout, their party would sweep into office with vast majorities. But, in the last presidential election, turnout did improve to the best level since 1968, and the Republicans still won. Not by a landslide but decisively. The only big races that went right for the Democrats were Ken Salazar's Senate campaign in Colorado and Barack Obama in Illinois. Obama had the advantage of having his original opponent brought down by revelations of a messy divorce with *Star Trek Voyager*'s Seven of Nine and having a new opponent who promptly bragged about his endorsement by Jesus and called Vice President Cheney's daughter a "selfish hedonist." Not exactly a withering gauntlet to overcome on the road to victory.

All of the Democratic Party's most powerful allies—Hollywood, trial lawyers, the unions, the *New York Times,* CBS, newly minted strident liberal talk radio, bombastic and inaccurate "documentaries," the 527s, African-American churches, other voter turnout professionals—brought their A-game, threw themselves into the fight, . . . and lost to the blogs, talk radio, alternative media, conservative religious groups, and a well-organized GOP ground game.

The old era, in which those tools were enough, are over. The party has to scrap its old playbook and start over, and that's why the postelection weeping and wailing was warranted.

The 2004 election was the first in which exit polls showed equal numbers of self-identified Republicans and Democrats—both at 37 percent. Democrats had enjoyed the advantage in voter identification for decades and had a 4 percent margin in 2000.

In addition to the House and Senate gains, Bush received more than 62 million votes, the highest raw vote total in American history (Kerry's total was second highest), and was the first presidential candidate to break the 50 percent barrier since 1988. On a percentage basis, he improved on his 2000 performance in 48 states. The long-held belief that high turnout favors the Democrats was refuted at both the national and state levels. Of the top 11 most improved states in turnout, every single one was a red state, including the decisive battlegrounds of Ohio and Florida.

The Democratic Party has not won a majority of white voters

since 1964. They have not won 50 percent of the national vote since 1976, suggesting that a Democratic presidential victory in the modern era requires either a presidential resignation and an unelected incumbent (1976) or a campaign by H. Ross Perot (1992, 1996). And in the last six congressional elections—starting with 1994—the Democrats have not cracked 48.5 percent of the national vote.

James Carville, architect of Clinton's 1992 win, understood the enormous opportunity that the Democrats faced against Bush in 2004. It was probably the best chance the Democrats would have for the foreseeable future.

Twelve days before the election, Carville opined in his trademark colorful language in a star-studded Beverly Hills living room: "If we can't win this damn election with a Democratic Party more unified than ever before, with us having raised as much money as the Republicans, with 55 percent of the country believing we're heading in the wrong direction, with our candidate having won all three debates, and with our side being more passionate about the outcome than theirs—if we can't win this one, then we can't win shit! And we need to completely rethink the Democratic Party."[3]

Also in 2004, the GOP demonstrated a new and stunningly effective get-out-the-vote system that Democrats were completely unprepared for. Under the radar screen of the opposition and much of the mainstream media, Republican strategists and Bush campaign staff tapped into a volunteer network using local party organizations, union rolls, gun clubs, and churches. Across the nation, the shift was stunning: 152 counties that voted Democratic for president in 1996 and 2000 chose Bush in 2004; only 11 chose Democrat John Kerry after voting Republican in 1996 and 2000.[4]

That year, says Democratic pollster Peter Hart, "a sense of Republicanism crept up the river. The president won Missouri, which was always a toss-up state, by more than 7 percent. Iowa flipped his direction, and in Minnesota and Wisconsin, we waited all night to find out that Kerry had just barely carried those states."[5] So the Upper Midwest is now trending Republican, following the South, Southwest, Great Plains, and Rocky Mountains.

The Republicans' improved get-out-the-vote efforts are not infallible, however. In 2005, the Republicans had a pretty lousy year, failing to pick up governors' seats in New Jersey and Virginia, and Governor Arnold Schwarzenegger saw all of his high-profile referenda defeated.

That year, the issue of national security was absent from the races—except perhaps the New York City mayor's race, where there was some grumbling about whether Mayor Mike Bloomberg, a liberal Republican, was overreacting to terror warnings about the subways. New Yorkers overwhelmingly decided they were happy with his leadership and that he was the right man to run the city that remains the preeminent target of al-Qaeda.

In New Jersey, GOP candidate Doug Forrester did periodically mention that Democratic lawmakers had awarded millions of state homeland security funds based on politics and ignored funding applications for towns with nuclear reactors, airports, and water treatment centers. However, Forrester didn't make that issue the centerpiece of his campaign. Instead, his last-ditch tactic was the over-the-top attack ad featuring Jon Corzine's ex-wife. He failed to exploit this ready-made message: "The state's Democrats are going to get you killed because they can't resist playing politics and their usual habits of cronyism." It's standard Garden State politics, and almost acceptable, to appoint your political friends to the board of the Museum of Science and Trucking, to use a fictional example from *The Sopranos.* But it's another thing entirely when the issue is protecting citizens from terrorism.

The elections of 2005 confirmed the lesson of post–September 11 elections: When the dominant issue in voters' minds is protecting their families from attacks and pursuing the terrorists, Republicans win. When it's a "mommy party" issue like education, health care, or reducing traffic, Democrats win.

A Democratic Party that had become very used to the levers of power since the days of FDR is now in the deepest hole since the 1920s. Worse, the 2004 debacle came under what could and should have been strong conditions for Democrats—a president defending a controversial war, a unified Democratic Party, a furiously energized grassroots effort, and with Democrats outspending Republicans on total campaign and party-building by $113.6 million.[6]

All of this came when the Democrats thought they had had an effective turnout effort. In fact, what ought to be most disturbing for the Democrats wasn't what went wrong in 2004—it was how they could get beaten so badly considering what went right.

For example, the premiere Democratic get-out-the-vote organization, Americans Coming Together, exceeded the goals it had set for the total Kerry vote in each of its target counties in Ohio. In Cuyahoga County, where ACT wanted to get about 350,000 votes for Kerry, he received 433,262. In Franklin County, where the goal was a little over 262,000 votes, Kerry had garnered 275,573. In fact, Kerry's 2.66 million votes were the most ever for a Democrat in Ohio. Kerry received a total of 4,862,000 more votes nationwide than Gore did, and, according to ACT's breakdown, 58 percent of that increase came in the 12 battleground states that ACT had targeted.[7]

"We had superb organization," said Mike McCurry, former press secretary for President Clinton who joined the Kerry campaign to help shape its strategy and message. "We had all the money in the world that you could possibly want. Reported today that, in fact, for the first time in anyone's memory here, the DNC raised more money than the RNC in this campaign, so we had plenty of resources. But we concentrated it on a strategy that was fundamentally flawed because we thought in the end of the day we would still have a majority the more people who voted." [8]

Terrifying as the thought may be for members of the party, Kerry's 2004 totals could indicate a high water mark for Democratic presidential candidates.

The GOP's revolutionary turnout system wasn't visible to Democrats partially because it was extensively deployed in small "exurban" communities. Urban-centric Democrats knew that these towns and suburbs were booming with potential voters, but they never imagined, much less predicted, that the GOP could pick up so many votes in them. The 10 Ohio counties with the highest turnout percentages all went for Bush, and all of them had a turnout rate of at least 75 percent. A *New York Times* writer described the scene as some kind of Democratic horror movie, "with conservative voters rising up out of the hills and condo communities in numbers the Kerry forces never knew existed."

Democratic prospects in certain red states have gone from uphill climbs to long shots to nonentities. Brad Carson, a well-regarded Democratic congressman who was defeated in the Oklahoma Senate race in 2004, dramatically illustrated the state of his party in a crimson-level red state:

> I had a Republican pollster come to me and he says, "I've got good news and bad news for you about how the campaign's going." He said the good news is that [Carson's Republican opponent] Tom Coburn is running 45 points behind George Bush in most of western Oklahoma, which was a swing area. . . . The bad news is that President Bush is at 90. So there's only so much you can overcome, and that proved in a lot of western Oklahoma counties, John Kerry—this is a U.S. senator, a decorated Vietnam veteran, a U.S. senator. He took 12

percent and 15 percent in many of the counties. . . . We've won races against people who were convicted, people who are not credible, and they take 25 percent. There are enough town contrarians who just want to register their disapproval, and you have a U.S. senator take 12 percent and 15 percent of the vote. That shows a systemic problem with the brand image."[9]

The Democrats are in the minority, lack strong leadership, and have a weak bench of future leaders, fed-up donors, disappointed, angry, dispirited grassroots.[10] Since the election, some Democrats have touted the fact that their members of Congress are unified. Indeed, but it is much easier to be unified when you're in the smallest minority in three generations. It's the big, boisterous, widespread majorities that tend to have lots of interparty squabbling and debates.

One blinking red dashboard light that should concern the Democrats is their slide among Jewish voters, traditionally one of the party's most rock-solid and loyal constituencies—the jump among Jewish voters from 16 percent for Bob Dole in 1996 to 25 percent for George W. Bush in the last election.

The Democratic share of the vote dropped significantly from 2000 to 2004 in four heavily Jewish counties in the New York City area—Kings, Queens, Nassau, and Suffolk, suggesting a 9/11 effect among the city's Jews. Seventeen congressional districts flipped from supporting Al Gore in 2000 to Bush in 2004; six of those were in the New York City metropolitan area. When a Republican presidential candidate gains ground in safely Democratic congressional districts like those of Democratic Reps. Jerry Nadler and Anthony Weiner, it may not necessarily put the state's electoral votes in play, but it does help the GOP candidate gain ground in the popular vote.

If the slide among Jews is a blinking dashboard light, the Democrats' share of the Hispanic vote is steam emerging from under the hood. The Republican Party's redoubled efforts to reach Hispanic voters paid off, as Bush garnered 44 percent of the vote among that demographic in 2004, doubling Bob Dole's 21 percent eight years earlier. Bush improved on his previous share of the Hispanic vote by 9 points. The Democrats have lost nearly a quarter of a core constituency in less than a decade—a constituency that just happens to be the fastest-growing in the country.

The preceding numbers are based on the national exit poll data, which was disputed by some pollsters, who contended that it oversampled Florida Cubans, usually the most pro-Republican Hispanics. A July 2005 report by the Pew Hispanic Center estimated that Bush's share of the Hispanic vote in 2004 was closer to 40 percent than to the 44 percent previously reported. However, that report concluded, "Bush also gained some ground among nearly all segments of the Hispanic vote." Their estimates put the number of Hispanics identifying as Democrats as dropping from the traditional two-thirds to about 55 percent.[11]

In 2004, Bush won two heavily Hispanic California congressional districts that Al Gore carried by wide margins four years earlier.[12]

There are major indications that 2004 election results do not mark the Republican apex but merely identify the moment that Republican electoral dominance accelerated. Marc Danziger, a Southern California–based UC-Berkeley graduate who blogs under the nickname "Armed Liberal," makes a comparison to the automotive world:

> If you looked at the product—at the cars they made—it was pretty clear who had a clue. GM tried everything; marketing, financial engineering, cost cutting—everything except making great cars efficiently. It wasn't hard, back in 1984, to guess what the long-term trend was going to be.
>
> Similarly, I don't have a hard time guessing what the long-

term trend is for the Democratic Party as it's being run today. The Democratic Party isn't only selling its soul to coke-addled Hollywood celebrities and telecom zillionaires by pandering to their corporate interests at the expense of—say—the working folks of the country. They are also mobilizing a base of activists and functionaries—really the bones of the party—who are consciously taking the party to a place where it will be unable to speak intelligently about defense for a generation.[13]

In the following chapters, we will see how that last line sums up the state of each party today. From the Carter presidency to the 1991 Gulf War, the Democratic Party had a reputation for being weak on defense. The relative calm of the 1990s let national security and foreign threats subside from voters' priorities—and Bill Clinton won two presidential elections, and Al Gore won the popular vote in 2000. But on September 11, 2001, the political preeminence of "lockboxes," prescription drugs, and school uniforms was destroyed along with the World Trade Center. In an era where terrorism and national security are the top issues, the Democrats have been caught flatfooted. At times, the party's elected officials such as John Kerry, John Edwards, and Tom Daschle have tried to establish credibility on national security issues only to be drowned out by loud, hyperbolic, and rabidly antiwar voices such as Michael Moore and Howard Dean.

The Republican Party knows that national security is its strongest issue, and it will not hesitate to campaign on this issue for the foreseeable future.

Bush's chief strategist Karl Rove has long been a student of William McKinley's presidential victory in 1896. While few Americans remember much about McKinley today, Rove reveres that year's election because it set off a political realignment of Republican dominance for a generation. Basking in the victory of 2004, Rove suggested that the most recent presidential decision could have a similar effect. "The victory in 1896 was similarly narrow, and I mean—not narrow, similarly structured. But it took—you know, we only knew that it was an election that realigned American politics years afterwards. And I think the same thing will be here." [14]

If there truly are 31 red states and 19 blue states as seen in the 2004 election, then the "natural" balance in the Senate would be a 62-seat Republican majority. Obviously, there are Republicans who can win in blue states (Rick Santorum, Norm Coleman, John Sununu, Judd Gregg) and Democrats who can win in red ones (Ken Salazar, Harry Reid, Tim Johnson). But unless current circumstances change to the Democrats' favor, in every six-year cycle GOP candidates will run with the wind at their backs in nearly two-thirds of the 100 Senate races.

And that is just a quick glimpse at the Senate. Democratic prospects in upcoming House races look worse. Bush won the popular vote in 255 congressional districts while John Kerry won 180. Of the 232 House Republicans, only 18 represent districts that were carried by Kerry. Out of 202 Democrats elected in November 2004, 41 won in districts that voted for Bush. The inevitable retirement of Bush district Democrats, such as Chet Edwards of Texas, Gene Taylor of Mississippi, Jim Matheson of Utah, Ike Skelton of Missouri, and Earl Pomeroy of North Dakota, suggests that the GOP has more low-hanging fruit to pluck in future election cycles. President Bush won at least 63 percent of the vote in their districts.

The nation's population is shifting to the south and west, away from the blue states and toward the red states (except California). In some circumstances, this may help Democrats, such as when the departure of urban liberals from Massachusetts turned New Hampshire into a blue state in 2004. But the phenomenon appears to be a net gain for the GOP. In 2002, the first election after redistricting from the 2000 census, the Republicans gained 1 seat in the states that lost seats and the Democrats lost 13. In the states that gained seats, the Democrats gained 4 seats and the Republicans gained 8.

There is nothing denoting that the American system of government must be dominated by two parties roughly at parity. From 1932 to 1968, Democrats dominated the executive and legislative branches and through nominations left a lasting mark on the judicial branch. With a few exceptions, the Republican Party of that era was marked by leaders and policies out of step with the majority of Americans and had only a peripheral impact on political debates.

In fact, never mind returning to control of Washington or remaining competitive; there is actually nothing guaranteeing that the Democratic Party will continue to have any influence in U.S. politics. A political observer in 1848 would tell you that the dominant political force in Washington was the Whig Party; by 1860, it had lost all political power and was well on the way to extinction.

By failing to adapt to the dramatically changed political terrain of the post-9/11 era, the Democrats are setting themselves up to be twenty-first-century Whigs.

The current Democratic hole may not be as deep as the two previous Republican holes in 1977 and 1993, but there are other factors that may mitigate the Democrats' climb back to a majority and the White House.

Political blogger Gerry Daly sees eight common traits in the Republican comeback years of 1980 and 1994:

1. The growth areas of the country (the South, the West) meshed perfectly with the ideology of the party's ascending faction—the conservatives.
2. Redistricting gains magnified this effect.
3. Both times, the Republicans found strong leaders to guide them (Reagan, Gingrich).

4. Both times, the mantra was the same: lower taxes, less government, stronger defense.
5. Both times, the appeal was toward the activist base of the party.
6. Both times, the GOP's leaders were selling not just specific policies but the overall philosophy—less government, more liberty, self-reliance, be strong in the face of threats.
7. Both times, they were aided by Democratic missteps.
8. Both times, they used the left flank of the Democrats as a pry against the center flank of the Democrats.

What do today's Democrats have in comparison, item by item?

1. The fastest-growing areas of the country pretty much reject the ideology of their coalition's ascending faction—the liberals. In places such as New Hampshire, population shifts may moderate a traditionally conservative area; but overall, the fastest-growing counties are turning Republican. When the red-versus-blue divide is broken down at the county level, we see that liberalism sells in cities and university towns, and that's about it.
2. Redistricting is working against Democrats; it is creating a cadre of entrenched liberals in deep blue districts while continuing to give conservatives favorable ground.
3. Democrats may have strong leaders, but their ability to appeal to a majority of voters nationwide is as of yet unproven (Hillary Clinton, Harry Reid, Nancy Pelosi, Howard Dean).
4. It is nearly impossible for the Democrats to unify around a simple mantra like "lower taxes, less government, stronger defense" at the national level. What a Democrat needs to win a race in Tennessee is completely different from what one needs to win in Vermont.
5. Dean is leading the appeal to the activist base. But Hillary

Clinton's rhetoric and votes have tacked to the center. Perhaps it can be finessed, but it is not the model the Republicans followed in their two ascents.

6. Neither Dean nor Hillary is selling the underpinning philosophy of where they are going—partially because unmitigated liberalism doesn't sell in red states. Dean speaks of "progressivism," without definition, but most of his rhetoric amounts to "Republicans are trying to destroy this country." Hillary arguably argues a philosophy, but it is not the one of her base, and her primary appeal is Clinton-style triangulation—a politics of picking one policy from column A and another from column B rather than a coherent, easily described philosophy of governance.

7. There have been plenty of Republican missteps, but Democrats have not often been able to translate them into electoral success. A terrific example is the August 2005 special House election in Ohio, where the Democrats nominated Paul Hackett, an Iraq war veteran, and took on Jean Schmidt, a Republican with close ties to the state's unpopular governor and terrible campaign skills. Hackett made the race close but ultimately fell short, garnering 48 percent of the vote. You have to wonder how much Hackett hurt his chances by shooting off his mouth, calling President Bush a "son of a bitch," and declaring Bush to be a greater threat to America's national security than Osama bin Laden.

8. The Dean strategy is to use the right flank of the Republicans as a pry against the center flank of the Republicans. In some areas—for example, the early 2005 controversy over Terry Schiavo—this worked effectively.

The current hole the Democrats have fallen into is not as deep as the ones the Republicans fell into in 1977 and 1991. However, demographic changes are working against them, and some of the proven methods the Republicans used to climb out either are not available to them or they have shown no inclination toward trying those methods. But perhaps the biggest reason the Democrats could be in serious long-term trouble is a chasm between their fervently antiwar base voters and their more hawkish policymakers and elites.

THE DIVIDE WITHIN THE DEMOCRATS

When Reagan lost, but then won, the leadership role in the party, he made sure to bring the other factions of the party along for the ride. The Gingrich revolution was similarly nonpurging; the conservatives ascended but did not openly drive out the moderates.

Today's Democratic Party has more bad blood between its liberals and moderates. On one side is the Establishment: Hillary Clinton, a lot of the Clinton administration veterans, Harry Reid, Joe Lieberman, red state Democrats, some editors of the *New Republic,* and the folks who read the Democratic Leadership Council's *Blueprint* magazine.

On the other side are the folks who proclaim themselves as representing "the Democratic wing of the Democratic Party." (The unspoken insinuation is that those who disagree are closet Republicans.) This group includes Howard Dean, Barbara Boxer, Ted Kennedy liberals, Michael Moore, MoveOn.org, the folks who post at Daily Kos, the Deaniacs, the Air America listeners, and most antiwar protesters.

The Dean wing looks at the party's fortunes and places the blame squarely on gutless Democrat-in-name-only sellouts who watered down the party's message. They see the Clinton years as a losing battle marked by a "triangulation" style that was all too willing to compromise on key principles for short-term boosts in poll numbers. They loved Gore's populism in 2000 and credit those stands for his popular vote majority. In 2004, they preferred Dean and settled for

Kerry; they genuinely feel a more stridently liberal and antiwar message would have delivered a majority. In 2008, these Democratic base voters may settle for Hillary Clinton as the party's nominee, but a surprising number of these folks see her candidacy as a rehash of more of the same Clinton-era triangulation and compromises. (Conservatives who see Hillary as Leftism Incarnate are utterly baffled by this.)

The Establishment sees the Deaniacs as borderline deranged, determined to drive the party off a cliff to a morally pure but politically disastrous McGovern-level electoral debacle. This wing's greatest fear about Hillary Clinton is that her baggage from the 1990s limits her ability to win over the red states.

The marriage between conservatives, libertarians, and moderate/liberal Republicans has been stormy and tempestuous—but the party's most prominent conservatives have rarely embraced purging their partners. In perhaps the most glaring example, President Bush, Vice President Cheney, rock-ribbed conservative Senator Rick Santorum, and the Republican National Committee rode to the rescue of Senator Arlen Specter (Pennsylvania) in his 2004 primary. Conservatives gnashed their teeth over the chance to replace the pro-choice, often-liberal Specter with the consistently conservative Pat Toomey. But the party's leadership preferred the security of the incumbent.

The Dean wing is unlikely to be able to prevent Hillary from winning the party's nomination in 2008. No doubt, Hillary Clinton would make a formidable candidate in the general election. If she wins, the party will unify behind her, and she will set the course for the party for the next four or eight years. The Dean wing will enjoy whatever perks a second Clinton administration gives it and will probably largely stay in line.

But . . . if the red states stay red and a Republican wins again on Election Night 2008, the intraparty détente will dissolve and the long-delayed bloodbath will begin. The Daily Kos–MoveOn.org wing will be unappeasable, and Clinton-style triangulation will be discredited as a relic of the 1990s. The Democratic Leadership Council, long regarded as apostate within the Dean wing, will be marginalized to irrelevance. The Deaniacs will insist one of their guys get the 2012 nomination . . .

. . . and then, barring a sudden sea change in American politics, the Democrats will get that long-feared McGovern-level debacle. This scenario would establish the first 16-year run for either political party since FDR and the first time the Republicans had held the White House that long since 1897–1913. It would also essentially guarantee a Supreme Court entirely selected by Republican presidents (perhaps Clinton appointee Stephen Breyer would hang on for a while).

Of course, even under this rosy scenario for Republicans, they would still have their problems; the tensions between social conservatives and libertarian wings are likely to be a constant irritant for years to come. But every GOP voter and strategist would gladly choose the headaches of managing a long-lasting majority over the soul-churning frustration of being powerless in the minority.

For the Democrats, the stakes are that high. They can either fix themselves on the issue of terrorism and protecting Americans or spend the better part of a generation in the political wilderness.

FOUR

It Takes Time and Effort to Build a Reputation as a Wimp

I'll be back. You can't keep the Democrats out of the White House forever. And when they get in, I'm back on the street! With all of my criminal buddies! Ba-ha-ha-ha-ha!

—*The criminally insane Sideshow Bob, the* Simpsons
episode "The Black Widower," first broadcast April 8,
1992

When did the Democrats—the party of FDR, Harry Truman, and John F. Kennedy—get a reputation as the guys who couldn't handle defense? When did the public start seeing the party as a bunch of wimps?

Many political scientists and historians have written about, analyzed, and debated these topics in books many times longer than the one you're reading. The aim of this tour from 1968 to 2001 is to paint a thumbnail sketch of how each party got the reputation it had when al-Qaeda attacked on 9/11.

Regularly over the past decades, American presidents have faced threats. Each commander in chief has faced multiple options in the face of those threats, but they basically have boiled down to two alternatives: be aggressive and go on the attack, or be reactive and go into a defensive crouch. Presidents chose between those courses and reaped the consequences. Recent history suggests that aggressive action sometimes works to deter or neutralize threats; sometimes it doesn't. Defensive crouches, however, have almost always invited further threats and attacks.

The legacy of FDR, Harry Truman, and John F. Kennedy began to erode when the movement that protested the Vietnam War took control of the party. "I think that the watershed moment was the 1968 Democratic National Convention," concludes Gerry Daly. "The battle between the hawks and doves in the Democratic Party was on stage for the entire world to see. It was violent and newsworthy, so everyone took notice—and began corresponding the antiwar/counterculture movement with the Democrats."

By early 1968, the Democratic Party was beginning to split over the Vietnam War. Senator Eugene McCarthy ran against President Lyndon Johnson for the Democratic nomination with an antiwar stance and finished a strong second in the New Hampshire primary. Senator Robert F. Kennedy entered the race as another antiwar candidate, and Johnson announced he would not seek reelection. Johnson's vice president, Hubert Humphrey, entered the race as the major pro-war candidate. Kennedy's candidacy picked up steam, and he had just won the California primary on June 5 when he was assassinated by Sirhan Sirhan.[1]

Pro-war Humphrey won the nomination of a party with largely antiwar grassroots, setting up the violent confrontations outside the convention in Chicago and antiwar protests throughout much of his campaign. The popular vote was close—43 percent for Nixon, 42 percent for Humphrey—but Nixon won the electoral college easily,

301 to 191. (George Wallace's pro-segregation American Independent Party won several states.) After Humphrey lost, the party lurched strongly to the left. The antiwar grassroots of the party were hungry for a "purer" candidate in 1972.[2] They got one in George McGovern.

On the heels of Presidents Truman, Eisenhower, Kennedy, and Johnson, McGovern was the first major presidential candidate who was not a dedicated Cold Warrior. McGovern said in 1972, "I don't like Communism, but I don't think we have any great obligation to save the world from it. That's a choice that other countries have to make."[3]

"I think the key moment was the Nixon-McGovern race," says one strategist close to the Bush White House. "Goldwater was certainly a daddy party kind of candidate, but at that moment the Democratic Party was still in large measure the party of JFK. Remember, Kennedy ran to Nixon's right on a lot of national security issues, talking about the 'missile gap.' When McGovern happened, it was, in some ways, a precursor to the Michael Moore phenomenon. He got young people involved, he energized the base, and there was an element of idealism to it, but the message was, 'Come home, America.' That phrase, and all that it signified, was a torpedo to the bow of the Democratic Party. It had an element of isolationism and moral equivalence, and the Democrats never really got away from it."

Peggy Noonan, a speechwriter for President Reagan and an adviser to the Bush-Cheney 2004 campaign, also points to the McGovern campaign as a pivotal moment in establishing the Democrats' image regarding national security:

I remember when Democrats were the burly party. It wasn't that long ago. A man who was a Democrat was a working man—tough, ethnic, masculine. Like the firemen of New York who dug us out of 9/11. When did this change, when did union members become Republicans, when did the guy at the VFW become a Republican? Two things, one of which followed the other. The first was the rise of McGovern and the capture of the party by his leftist followers and operatives. McGovern himself was not a big man in a historical sense, but his followers were big: they took over a party. In 1972, Americans looked at the Democratic platform and saw what it promised: high taxes, more government control of the arrangements of American life, radicalism on social issues, and an ambivalence about the purpose and uses of American power. This, I believe, set regular Democrats back on their heels. Jump ahead eight years, and you see the rise of Reagan and what he promised: lower taxes, less government, a non-radical approach to social issues, a confidence about expressions of power, and a desire to unflinchingly name and define the great disturber of peace in that moment, Soviet communism. McGovernism plus Reaganism left a generation of American Democrats watching, thinking, and finally saying, 'Guess I'm a Republican.' People talk about the sixties, but it all happened in the seventies."[4]

McGovern got shellacked by Nixon, gaining only 37 percent of the popular vote and 17 electoral votes. Over time, the antiwar movement became more influential and less coordinated, increasingly dominated by a counterculture that had arisen alongside it. A movement whose face had once been Eugene McCarthy was now associated with long-haired, drug-using, promiscuous hippies. The new leaders became increasingly strident, greeting returning soldiers with jeers and taunts, spitting on troops in airports and on public streets.[5]

As Vietnam progressed, antiwar Democrats began to speak as if they saw their country as a potentially powerful force for evil in the world. They talked about their fellow citizens and trusted—even beloved—military institutions as barely restrained monsters. Recall that during their time period, the proportion of Americans that had served in the military was much greater than today.

Ron Dellums, a California Democrat, said he feared America would adopt the tactics of Nazi Germany. "In the last year of the Second World War, after the Germans knew they were defeated, they went on an orgy of killing that exceeded the horrors of the earlier part of the war, haunting the conscience of mankind ever since," he said. "No longer able to impose our will on Southeast Asia, will our removal be in the same frenzied manner?"[6]

In a comment that would come back to haunt him decades later, we saw the young veteran and antiwar protester John Kerry comparing U.S. troops to Genghis Khan.

But the Democratic Party was not a monolithic block of antiwar voices, at least not yet. Senator Henry M. "Scoop" Jackson was perhaps the most prominent Democratic hawk, but there were a slew of others, many of whom would become so associated with the Reagan or Bush administration that a modern reader is surprised to learn they were Democrats: Jeane J. Kirkpatrick (Reagan's ambassador to the United Nations), Paul H. Nitze (Reagan's arms-control negotiator), Richard N. Perle (Bush administration Pentagon official), and Ben J. Wattenberg (influential journalist and writer).

But by and large, Democrats didn't want to send troops anywhere after Vietnam. They had seen enough war. Nor were they willing to send weapons to beleaguered allies facing a massacre.

As Khmer Rouge was advancing into Cambodia, Senator Chris Dodd, Connecticut Democrat, declared, "President Ford has tried to make this an issue of abandoning an ally. . . . The greatest gift our country can give to the Cambodian people is not guns but peace. And the best way to accomplish that goal is by ending military aid now."[7]

The peace of the grave, perhaps. In March 1975, the House Democratic Caucus voted overwhelmingly, 189–49, against any additional military assistance to Vietnam or Cambodia. Rep. Tom Downey (New York) said, "The administration has warned that if we leave there will be a bloodbath. But to warn of a new bloodbath is no justification for extending the current bloodbath."[8]

The U.S. State Department puts the total Khmer Rouge death toll between 1.2 million and 1.8 million; Math Ly, a member of the Cambodian politburo, put the number at 3.3 million.

THE THREAT: The Khmer Rouge.
THE LEADERS' POSITIONS: President Ford wanted arms exports. Most congressional Democrats were opposed.
THE DECISION: Ford didn't have the votes. No guns for the Cambodian government.
THE RESULT: Genocide.

THE CARTER PRESIDENCY—PIVOTAL, BUT IN A BAD WAY

After the devastating blow to public trust that was Watergate, and the widespread perception of bumbling incompetence on the part of Gerald Ford, America was ready to give the Democrats another shot.

The Democrats' first resurgence came with the party's celebrated congressional "class of 1974," whose 84 members proclaimed themselves to be the wave of the future. One of those 1974 freshmen, Gary Hart of Colorado, emphasized the new era by declaring in his first campaign, "We are not a bunch of little Hubert Humphreys."

While also a reference to the interest-group liberalism of Humphrey, Hart's declaration was a renunciation of the Cold War interventionism of the previous era's Democrats.[9]

By the time the 1976 election rolled around, in voters' minds the Republican advantage on protecting the country had solidified. Even while Carter was leading Ford at the polls, Ford beat him on questions like this in an August 1976 Harris survey: "Now, if you had to choose, who do you think could do a better job as president on . . . keeping the military defense of the country strong—Gerald Ford or Jimmy Carter?" Ford was named by 44 percent of respondents; 34 percent said Carter. Similarly, a September 1976 Gallup poll asked who would do a better job of "handling national defense." The results were 44 percent for Ford, 29 percent for Carter.

For a Republican to blow this kind of rock-solid support on this issue, he would have to commit a gaffe of historic proportions. Something so shocking, so unbelievable that a big chunk of the American public would stare slackjawed at a candidate's denial or ignorance.

Put simply, it takes something like Ford's declaration at the October 6 presidential debate: "There is no Soviet domination of Eastern Europe." The very next poll showed Carter leading him 41 percent to 39 percent on the handling of national defense.

America was ready for change, and Carter had proven himself at least "good enough" compared to the incumbent on the issue of national defense. Interestingly, Carter won with only 50 percent of the popular vote. His 1976 victory marks the last time a Democrat broke 50 percent.

THE THREAT: The Soviet Union.
THE LEADERS' POSITIONS: Little difference. The representative of the traditionally more hawkish party,

Ford, appeared to believe that Eastern Europe was not under Soviet domination. For a dove, Carter would appear to at least have his facts straight.

THE DECISION: With no difference between the GOP and Democrats, voters elected the first Democrat since 1964.

THE RESULT: President Jimmy Carter.

Once in the White House, Carter brought a drastically different approach to the Cold War. Among the statements and positions that would be almost unthinkable under a Cold War Republican, Secretary of State Cyrus Vance declared in 1978 that President Carter and General Secretary Leonid Brezhnev shared "similar dreams and aspirations" about the future of the world.[10] Carter nominated Paul Warnke, a former McGovern adviser, as chief negotiator on the 1979 SALT II (Strategic Arms Limitation Talks). Warnke had stated that he would be willing to make unilateral cuts to the American nuclear arsenal.[11]

Andrew Young, Carter's ambassador to the United Nations, declared, "We also have hundreds, if not thousands, of people in our jails that I would call political prisoners."[12]

The Soviets, meanwhile, had invaded Afghanistan. The Carter administration took decisive action against the military aggression by . . . not participating in the Olympics. President Carter also laid out the Carter Doctrine, which stated that the United States would use military force if necessary to defend its interests in the Persian Gulf region. The United States did not have significant military capabilities in the region when Carter made the announcement, so his administration began to build up the Rapid Deployment Force, which would eventually become CENTCOM (U.S. Central Command). However, whatever hawkish moves Carter made were overshadowed by a presidency-defining crisis.

The Iranian Hostage Crisis

Carter's last year in office was dominated by a foreign policy disaster that would hurt his party's image for years. On November 4, 1979, more than 3,000 militants raided the U.S. Embassy in Tehran, taking 66 hostages. The fate of the American diplomats and military personnel was in the hands of Ayatollah Khomeini's regime.

From the first days of the crisis, Carter rejected all military options despite the fact that the invasion of sovereign American soil, the illegal detainment of American citizens with diplomatic protections, and the humiliation of the hostages before television cameras all constituted acts of war. This decision at least partially reflects that the post-Vietnam military was incapable of projecting sufficient force in the region; some of this reflects Carter's fear that military action would result in the hostages' deaths.

Whatever the alchemy of the decision, Carter agreed to secretary of state Cyrus Vance's plan to use diplomatic pressure and patient negotiation. National security adviser Zbigniew Brzezinski and others urged him to take tougher action.

Carter continued to reject all military options as too risky. He responded, "The problem is that we could feel good for a few hours—until we found that they had killed our people." [13]

The immediate response of the Carter administration was to end oil imports from Iran on November 12. Two days later, Iranians in the United States were expelled, and around $8 billion of Iranian assets in the United States were frozen.

As the hostage crisis wore on, the frustration in the White House reached such intensity that First Lady Rosalynn Carter asked the president, "Why don't you do something?" The president asked her what she wanted him to do. She recommended mining Iranian harbors. His response was, "Okay, suppose I mine the harbors and they decide to take one hostage out every day and kill him. What am I going to do then?" [14]

For a long time, American policy was to refuse to negotiate with terrorists, reasoning that if a terrorist ever wins policy concessions, it will only encourage the practice. Carter was not willing to capitulate, but his administration was willing to look at thugs and barbarians who had committed an act of war and ask, "How can we work this out?"

On November 19 and 20, 13 of the hostages were released, but the remaining 52 continued to be held (an additional hostage was released because of illness on July 11, 1980).

The militants justified taking the hostages by claiming it was retaliation for the admission of Iran's deposed shah, Pahlavi, into the United States for cancer treatments back in October. However, the hostage-taking was less based around one specific event and was instead largely indicative of widespread anti-Americanism following the February 1979 revolution. Khomeini strongly advocated opposition to the United States in his rhetoric, labeling the country the "Great Satan" and its citizens as "infidels" and "enemies of Islam."

In his memoir, *Keeping Faith*, Carter called his approach "a cautious and prudent policy in order to protect their [the hostages'] lives during the preceding fourteen months."

Months of negotiations went nowhere. Eventually it became clear even to Carter that the Iranian government was not serious about releasing the hostages. The president finally approved a secret rescue mission, *Operation Eagle Claw*, a.k.a. Desert One. On the night of April 24–25, 1980, C-130 transport airplanes carrying the rescue team rendezvoused with U.S. helicopters at an airstrip in the Great Salt Desert of Iran. Two helicopters broke down in a sandstorm and a third was damaged on landing. The mission was aborted; as the aircraft took off again, one helicopter clipped a C-130 and crashed, killing eight U.S. servicemen and injuring four more. The retreating forces left behind enough equipment for the Iranians to later gleefully showcase to the world's media, another demonstration that America was a paper tiger.[15]

Former Navy Seal Richard Marcinko, working in intelligence for the chief of naval operations at the time, describes the mood in the Pentagon's Special Classified Intelligence Facility that evening:

> Fists clenched, numbed into horrified silence, some of us swallowing back tears, we could hear screams and chaos— the sounds of brave men burning to death. Then, finally, after what seemed like an eternity of shouting, confusion, explosions, and devastation, we listened as the remaining C-130s got off the ground, and what was left of Delta flew back to Masirah.
>
> To say that we all sat in that smoky, dead-air room stunned would be a gross understatement. This was the unthinkable. We'd just failed in an operation that had been almost half a year in the planning and billions in the funding. And there was no way of salvaging it. The black eye the United States was about to receive in world opinion would be a long, long time in healing.[16]

It was perhaps the single most psychologically devastating U.S. military failure in the Cold War. In military circles, Desert One became known as "the gold standard for how not to use force."[17]

Help for the hostages came from two unexpected developments. The shah died on July 27, removing a major symbol of American wrongdoing to the Iranians; then Saddam Hussein invaded Iran in September 1980. Suddenly the Iranians had more pressing problems than devising new ways to humiliate the suddenly impotent Great Satan.

It is hard to overstate the intense psychological impact of the hostage crisis on the American mood in 1980. Every night, Americans saw footage of angry mobs outside their defiled husk of an embassy, chanting "Death to America." Two bearded hostage takers used the Stars and Stripes to carry garbage out of the U.S. Embassy in Tehran, an image that presidential historian Edmund Morris wrote, "burned itself onto the retinas of every citizen who saw it." [18]

Election Day fell on the one-year anniversary of the seizure. Carter's rival, a cowboy out of the west named Ronald Reagan, had a reputation for being an aggressive, risk-taking hawk. On the campaign trail, he certainly didn't seem likely to be looking to negotiate. He not only called the Iranian militants "criminals and kidnappers," but he held the Iranian government responsible, labeling them "kidnappers" as well. He added that if the Iranians understood his rhetoric, "they shouldn't be waiting for me [to take office]."

Reagan and his aides adopted a threatening tone. "We'll just have to do something to bring [the hostages] home," the candidate warned. Edwin Meese III, his transition chief, spoke more explicitly: "The Iranians should be prepared that this country will take whatever action is appropriate" and they "ought to think over very carefully the fact that it would certainly be to their advantage to get the hostages back now." [19]

THE THREAT: Ayatollah Khomeni and his militant Islamist movement taking Americans hostage.

THE LEADERS' POSITIONS: Carter initially opposed military action; eventually approved a rescue mission, not punitive strikes on a nation that had committed acts of war. Although Reagan never actually faced the decision to use military force, he certainly did not sound hesitant.

THE DECISION: After humiliating Carter for a year, the Ayatollah realized the rules of the game would change under the new president.

THE RESULT: The hostages were released, although

the Iranian regime remained aggressively hostile to America and its interests.

Carter added to voters' concerns about his foreign policy acumen when a comment during a debate suggested that his 12-year-old daughter, Amy, was one of his advisers on nuclear arms.

Strikingly, Carter's reelection campaign ran ads suggesting that Ronald Reagan would make a dangerously hawkish president. One ad stated, "When you come right down to it, what kind of a person should occupy the Oval Office? Should it be a person who like Ronald Reagan has proposed 'occupation forces' to Rhodesia, and a destroyer to Ecuador to deal with a fishing controversy?" [20]

Having witnessed the current White House occupant appear more impotent than a Roman eunuch, the answer from the American people was: "Yeah, let's try that guy."

One national correspondent summarized Carter's presidency thusly: "Richard Nixon had grown fond of telling Americans that their country should never become a pitiful, helpless giant. In Jimmy Carter's last year, the crisis in Iran had made too many Americans feel that their country had become just that." [21] Reagan won decisively, 489 electoral votes to 49; 50.8 percent to 41 percent.

A defeated President Carter set about negotiating a release of the hostages. The back-and-forth with the Iranians intensified in the final night of his presidency. Carter agreed to exchange $8 billion to $9 billion in frozen Iranian assets for the prisoners' freedom. A bottle of champagne was popped in the Oval Office. [22]

One wonders whether this development truly was worth celebrating. By returning the assets, wasn't this agreement essentially a surrender to extortion?

Some of the hostages later concluded that the president had made a terrible error by first negotiating, then conceding to the captor's demands. Kevin Hermening at the time was a 20-year-old marine assigned to guard the Tehran Embassy. "I would further say that when President Carter agreed to return $9 billion of frozen Iranian assets to the terrorist government under the Ayatollah Khomeini, as Charles Scott said, Iran walked away with no cost in blood or treasure," he said in 2004. "In essence, the terrorist organizations, those who put a face on terrorism—al Qaeda, Hamas, and others—they get their support from governments. By not extracting a penalty, or anything punitive, I think it simply encouraged more acts against Americans."[23]

One cannot help but wonder how President George W. Bush would respond to an embassy takeover and hostage crisis, if, God forbid, one happened tomorrow. Is there any doubt that the response would be an ultimatum, followed by all-out war on the nation whose population had invaded sovereign American soil and detained American citizens? Does anyone imagine that the U.S. military response would be anything other than, to quote Gladiator, to "unleash hell"?

Just where did the Iranians get the idea that seizing the embassy in Tehran was "okay"? How did they come to the conclusion that those steps would not provoke a devastating military response?

THE REAGAN ERA

The hostages were released on Inauguration Day, January 20, 1981. It is hard to believe this was entirely coincidental with the new sheriff walking into town. It may have even been helpful to incoming President Ronald Reagan that he had long been demonized as an out-of-touch warmonger out of *Dr. Strangelove*. The Iranians now had someone to fear.

In his inaugural address, Reagan did not specifically mention the hostage crisis but simply stated, "When action is required to preserve our national security, we will act." It was the subtlest of stings at the outgoing president, a man beaten in all senses of the word.

Visiting Paris in June 1982, his first European trip as president, Reagan declared, "We . . . are moving forward to restore America's defensive strength after a decade of neglect. A strong America and a vital, unified alliance are indispensable to keeping the peace now and in the future, just as they have been in the past."

Throughout the 1980s, the Democrats opposed Reagan's proposed defense buildup. In 1982, Edward M. Kennedy and Republican senator Mark Hatfield of Oregon introduced legislation calling for a nuclear freeze.

In 1983, President Reagan asked for military aid to the government in El Salvador fighting communist guerrillas. Senator Christopher Dodd went on national TV with the Democratic response. He called the Reagan policy "folly, pure and simple," as it proposed "to wage a conflict which cannot be won."[24]

"In the early 1980s, with the impeccable timing of a maestro, Reagan galvanized the World War II generation into performing one last task: reminding a nation cynical after Vietnam and Watergate that America truly was the shining city on the hill," writes historian Douglas Brinkley. "What Reagan understood was that compared with the testimony of an Army Ranger who, climbing the Poine du Hoc cliffs, had been forced to watch a buddy drown in the turbulent English Channel or a young officer get his legs blown off by a Nazi mine, 1970s slogans like 'Acid, Amnesty and Abortion' were political throwaway lines of a decadent and largely self-indulgent recent past."[25]

Reagan won over the people. An array of polls in 1983 and 1984 showed more than 80 percent of Americans supported "counteracting Soviet and Cuban efforts" in Latin America. Majorities saw Nicaragua's regime as a threat to U.S. security. Forced to choose between "right-wing dictators" and Communists in Latin America, those polled split 47 to 5 percent, respectively (34 percent said neither). The liberal preference for the Sandinistas, found among Democratic policymakers and like-minded scribes, was shared by only 1 of every 20 Americans. By 75 to 20 percent, Americans agreed with Reagan that "most Communist countries are just puppets of the Soviet Union." By 73 to 23 percent, people said that "Communism threatens our religious and moral values."

Writing in the *New Republic* in 1984, columnist Morton Kondracke remarked, "The center and soul of the Democratic Party has gone very nearly pacifist." Alan Cranston's entire presidential campaign in 1984 was based on the nuclear freeze.

Reagan's first term presented several examples of a hawkish president confronting terrorism and threats—some not so flattering to the former president.

You Bomb Our Barracks, We Take an Island

On April 18, 1983, a suicide bomber detonated a truck full of explosives at the U.S. Embassy in Beirut, Lebanon. Sixty-three people were killed, including 17 Americans. The United States quickly tracked the bomber to Hezbollah, Lebanon-based Islamist terrorists with ties to the revolution in Iran. Hezbollah was supported by both Tehran and the Syrian regime of Hafez Assad. Retired marine lieutenant colonel Bill Cowan told PBS that a covert military team entered Beirut in order to gather intelligence in preparation for retaliatory strikes, but no military action was taken.[26]

More damaging to the American psyche was the October 23, 1983, bombing of the marine barracks in Beirut. Two hundred and forty-one U.S. Marines were killed and more than 100 others were wounded when a suicide bomber detonated a truck full of explosives at a barracks located at Beirut International Airport. The marines were in Lebanon as part of a multinational force to separate the warring Lebanese factions who were tearing the country apart.

Reagan's initial instinct was to fight, publicly declaring the United States would "resist those who seek to drive us out of that area." His national security team considered a military strike on a barracks in Lebanon where it was believed that Iranians were training Hezbollah, but Defense Secretary Caspar Weinberger scrapped the idea, fearing it would harm U.S. relations with other Arab nations. (He also contended, years later, that it was unclear which militant group was ultimately responsible for the attack.) Instead, the battleship USS *New Jersey* was stationed off the coast of Lebanon, within firing range of the hills near Beirut.[27]

The continued marine presence in Lebanon became very unpopular among the American public. Four months after the barracks bombing, they were ordered to pull out of Lebanon.

THE THREAT: A destroyed American Embassy and marine barracks.
THE LEADERS' POSITIONS: Reagan clearly wanted to hit back with military force, but he was willing to compromise in order to accomplish other priorities.
THE DECISION: No retaliation against Hezbollah.
THE RESULT: To this day, America's enemies cite the Marine barracks attack as evidence that U.S. forces will retreat if they suffer enough casualties.

However, very shortly thereafter, the Reagan administration demonstrated that the arsenal of democracy could still flex its military muscle on a very different battlefield: the tiny Carribbean island of Grenada. Two days after the barracks bombing and six days after Prime Minister Maurice Bishop was executed by Bernard Coard's Stalinist sect, the U.S. armed forces landed troops on Grenada's beaches.

The fight represented a psychologically uplifting miniwar against a Communist regime, even if the geopolitical strategic importance of Grenada was, uh, debatable. In 1984, Reagan often joked that the island had to be invaded because it was the world's largest producer of nutmeg, adding, "You can't make eggnog without nutmeg."

Well, okay, then.

THE THREAT: A Marxist takeover of Grenada suggested that the island's airstrip was being prepared to accommodate Soviet and Cuban transport craft as part of an effort to arm and aid Central American insurgents. In addition, the presence of 600 American medical students on the island spurred fears of another hostage crisis.

THE LEADER'S POSITIONS: Reagan supported a full invasion: Democrats mostly opposed it.

THE DECISION: "Attention, America's enemies: Do not poke an American president with an itchy trigger finger two days after our forces are attacked in the Middle East."

THE RESULT: 19 American soldiers dead, 116 wounded; 49 Grenadian soldiers dead, and 358 wounded; 29 Cuban soldiers dead and 100+ wounded. The Marxist regime was toppled and the medical students were freed. And America's strategic access to nutmeg remained secure.

Election 1984

The election year of 1984 saw the birth of a phrase that Republicans believe summarizes the Democratic foreign policy worldview in three words, and it is still commonly used today. Democrat Jeane Kirkpatrick's speech at that year's Republican National Convention is probably the only one that is remembered today. She summarized the perspective and instinct of her former colleagues among the Democrats simply and devastatingly: "Blame America First."

Kirkpatrick, at that point still a registered Democrat, began by praising the trinity of Democratic hawkish heritage—FDR, Truman, JFK:

> They were not afraid to be resolute nor ashamed to speak of America as a great nation. They didn't doubt that we must be strong enough to protect ourselves and to help others. They didn't imagine that America should depend for its very survival on the promises of its adversaries. They happily assumed the responsibilities of freedom.
>
> I am not alone in noticing that the San Francisco Democrats took a very different approach. When the San Francisco Democrats treat foreign affairs as an afterthought, as they did, they behaved less like a dove or a hawk than like an ostrich—like an ostrich convinced it could shut out the world by hiding its head in the sand.
>
> The Carter administration's motives were good, but their policies were inadequate, uninformed, and mistaken. They made things worse, not better. . . .
>
> Each step of the way, the same people who were responsible for America's decline have insisted that the president's policies would fail. . . . They said saving Grenada from terror and totalitarianism was the wrong thing to do—they didn't blame Cuba or the Communists for threatening American students and murdering Grenadians; they blamed the United States instead. But then, somehow, they always blame America first.

Kirkpatrick ripped Democrats for a "blame America first" attitude toward Lebanon, arms-control negotiations, and Marxist dictators in Central America.

In 1984, Reagan was reelected, carrying nearly one-quarter of all registered Democrats. Yet there was little sign that the landslide defeat had affected the Democrats' dovish instincts. In 1986, 76 Democrats voted for a resolution by Colorado Democrat Pat Schroeder to cut U.S. troops to NATO by 50 percent over five years. Ron Dellums of California targeted the B-1 bomber and Trident missiles on submarines; Ed Markey of Massachusetts sought to eliminate the MX missile.

The public consistently identified the GOP—by ratios of three to one in the 1984 and 1988 elections—as the party better able to contend with America's foes abroad.[28]

Undoubtedly, the Reagan presidency had foreign policy failures that would rival those of less stellar chief executives. If we cringe at Jimmy Carter giving in to extortion and trading $9 billion in frozen Iranian assets for the release of the hostages, then the arms-for-hostages deal at the heart of the Iran-Contra scandal must turn our stomachs for its outright willingness to negotiate with terrorists and their sponsors. Similarly, if President Clinton's decision to leave Somalia without punishing those who killed U.S. troops was an encouraging sign to terrorists around the world, then it was only a disturbing echo of U.S. troops leaving Lebanon after the marine barracks bombing in Beirut in 1983.

But Reagan always portrayed his presidency as focused on killing terrorists, not appeasing them. His use of military force against Libya may not have had the intensity or drama of either Gulf War, but it reflected the views of an increasingly confident American people tired of being victims. Instead of Americans fearing that their actions would provoke their foes, it was time for their foes to fear provoking America.

On December 27, 1985, Palestinian terrorists sprayed automatic weapons into crowds of passengers at the Rome and Vienna airports, killing 20 people, including an 11-year-old American girl and 4 other Americans. Colonel Muammar Qaddafi promptly called the suicide attack a "noble act." Authorities found a Tunisian passport on the corpse of one of the terrorists. Libyan officials had confiscated that passport from a Tunisian worker when he left Libya sometime earlier, making the passport a smoking gun covered in the fingerprints of Qaddafi's regime.

The U.S. severed all relations with Libya and deployed U.S. naval vessels close to Libyan waters. America's European allies were aghast. Admiral Sir James Eberle, then-director of the Royal Institute of International Affairs in London, wrote:

> Most Europeans do not understand why the President's executive order states that the actions and policies of Libya "constitute a threat to the national security and foreign policy of the United States" . . . To assert that [Qaddafi's] actions threaten the security of the United States, with its vast military and economic power, seems patently absurd. It is seen as further evidence of the propensity of the Reagan Administration to overreact and to see the use of military force as a solution to problems that it otherwise finds difficult to influence. . . . Public opinion in Europe has to a considerable extent become desensitized to the outrages of the terrorist—but not to the risk of war. The risks of terrorism have become an unpleasant but accepted part of the daily lives of people in Europe, just as Americans have grown used to a level of urban violence much higher than in any West European country. . . . People in Europe see the actions of these terrorist groups as being a challenge to society rather than to national security. They must be dealt with firmly, but within the due processes of the civil law.[29]

Nice to see so much has changed in 20 years. The Reagan administration took the unthinkable position that a Libyan-sponsored terrorist killing *one* American child was too many; never mind the four American adults also killed.

In March 1986, the Sixth Fleet deployed to the Gulf of Sidra, under orders to cross what Qaddafi called his "line of death," a boundary more than 100 miles off the coast of Libya, marking the dictator's territorial rights. (Those rights were deemed fanciful by naval law experts.)

Reagan wrote in his autobiography:

> I ordered that if Libya attacked our aircraft or ships, our forces were to reply in kind, but with a measured and limited response. Two days after the maneuvers began, Qaddafi's forces fired SAM missiles at several of our carrier-based planes (and missed) and sent several missile-firing boats within the vicinity of our fleet—an act of aggression in international waters. We responded by sinking the Libyan vessels and knocking out the radar installation that had guided the Libyan missiles.[30]

Newsweek found that about 75 percent of Americans believed the U.S. military action was justified.

THE THREAT: Libyan-sponsored terrorist attacks on Americans in Europe.
THE LEADERS' POSITIONS: Reagan began with sanctions and progressed to military action. Democrats were largely quiet, although Democratic senator Howard Metzenbaum advocated assassinating Qaddafi. European allies thought military force was outlandish, provocative, and unthinkable.

THE DECISION: Deliberately provoking Qaddafi into a military clash with U.S. Naval Forces.

THE RESULT: While the American public supported hitting back at Qaddafi and forcibly retiring some of the Libyan Navy's fleet, the Libyan dictator was not yet deterred.

On April 5, 1986, a bomb exploded in the La Belle disco in West Berlin. Two people were killed (including an American soldier) and hundreds were wounded, including dozens of Americans. In the hours before and after the bombing, the NSA intercepted several messages between the Libyan government in Tripoli and its embassy in East Berlin indicating their responsibility for the attack.[31]

Reagan and his administration treated Libya's actions as an act of war. Many European allies feared the American response would be too provocative. The United States ignored the hand-wringing and bombed Tripoli. On April 14, 1986, U.S. jets from British bases and carriers in the Mediterranean dropped bombs on five targets. For American pilots based in Britain, the operation lasted more than 14 hours from takeoff to touchdown, making it the longest fighter mission in U.S. history.[32]

The Libyans reported many casualties, including Qaddafi's 18-month-old adopted daughter, Hana. An F-111 was destroyed by a Libyan SAM (surface-to-air missile); pilot Captain Fernando Ribas-Dominicci and weapons system officer Captain Paul Lorence were killed.

Reagan's pitch-perfect response:

Today we have done what we had to do. If necessary, we shall do it again. It gives me no pleasure to say that, and I wish it were otherwise.

Long before I came into this office, Colonel Qadhafi

[Qaddafi] had engaged in acts of international terror, acts that put him outside the company of civilized men. For years, however, he suffered no economic or political or military sanction; and the atrocities mounted in number, as did the innocent dead and wounded. And for us to ignore by inaction the slaughter of American civilians and American soldiers, whether in nightclubs or airline terminals, is simply not in the American tradition. When our citizens are abused or attacked anywhere in the world on the direct orders of a hostile regime, we will respond so long as I'm in this Oval Office. Self-defense is not only our right, it is our duty.

We believe that this preemptive action against his terrorist installations will not only diminish Colonel Qadhafi's capacity to export terror, it will provide him with incentives and reasons to alter his criminal behavior. I have no illusion that tonight's action will ring down the curtain on Qadhafi's reign of terror. But this mission, violent though it was, can bring closer a safer and more secure world for decent men and women. We will persevere. This afternoon we consulted with the leaders of Congress regarding what we were about to do and why. Tonight I salute the skill and professionalism of the men and women of our Armed Forces who carried out this mission. It's an honor to be your Commander in Chief.

We Americans are slow to anger. We always seek peaceful avenues before resorting to the use of force—and we did. We tried quiet diplomacy, public condemnation, economic sanctions, and demonstrations of military force. None succeeded. Despite our repeated warnings, Qadhafi continued his reckless policy of intimidation, his relentless pursuit of terror. He counted on America to be passive. He counted wrong. I warned that there should be no place on Earth where terrorists can rest and train and practice their deadly skills. I meant it. I said that we would act with others, if possible, and alone if necessary to ensure that terrorists have no sanctuary anywhere. Tonight, we have.[33]

The following day, Reagan made some prescient remarks:

Let us be clear: Yesterday the United States won but a single engagement in the long battle against terrorism. We will not end that struggle until the free and decent people of this planet unite to eradicate the scourge of terror from the modern world. Terrorism is the preferred weapon of weak and evil men. And as Edmund Burke reminded us: In order for evil to succeed, it's only necessary that good men do nothing. Yesterday we demonstrated once again that doing nothing is not America's policy; it's not America's way. America's policy has been and remains to use force only as a last result—or resort, I should say. We would prefer not to have to repeat the events of last night. What is required is for Libya to end its pursuit of terror for political goals. The choice is theirs.

During the first 24 hours, the White House received 126,000 phone calls in response to the attack; in the following 24 hours, there were 160,000 calls. They were more than 70 percent favorable.

Some Democrats, including John Kerry, argued that the airstrikes that nearly killed Qaddafi were not "proportional." "While I stated that my initial inclination was to support the President," Kerry wrote, "I pointed out that two essential tests had to be met in determining whether or not the U.S. action was appropriate. First, the United States had to have irrefutable evidence directly linking the Qaddafi regime to a terrorist act and, second, our response should be proportional to that act."

Though Kerry admitted that the evidence tying Tripoli to the disco bombing was "irrefutable," the United States had failed the proportionality test, he insisted. "It is obvious that our response was not proportional to the disco bombing and even violated the Administration's own guidelines to hit clearly defined terrorist targets, thereby minimizing the risk to innocent civilians."

Kerry said it was a "mistake" for Reagan to have targeted the "head of state of another country—no matter how repugnant we find the leader. . . . We are not going to solve the problem of terrorism with this kind of retaliation. . . . There are numerous other actions we can take, in concert with our allies, to bring significant pressure to bear on countries supporting or harboring terrorists."[34]

THE THREAT: Additional terrorist attacks from Qaddafi.

THE LEADERS' POSITIONS: Reagan approved military strikes on the Libyan military and the leader himself; some Democrats on Capitol Hill saw the response as disproportional.

THE DECISION: Attack.

THE RESULT: Two lost U.S. pilots, an unknown number of Libyan military casualties, the death of Qaddafi's adopted daughter, and injuries to two of his sons. Libya's Soviet-built air defense system was proven to be junk; Qaddafi's military forces panicked. While Qaddafi did not completely renounce terrorism after the attack, his military was humiliated, he faced internal dissent, he was weakened as a national and regional leader, and he became a B-list sponsor of terrorism.

"As tragic as the loss of life was, I don't think they were lives lost in vain: After the attack on Tripoli, we didn't hear much more from Qaddafi's terrorists," Reagan wrote in his autobiography. Reagan is not entirely correct. While Libya became a much less prominent state sponsor of terrorism in the following years, there were two awful exceptions: the bombings of Pan Am flight 103 over Lockerbie, Scotland, in 1988, and UTA Flight 772 over Niger in 1989.

However, Reagan is not remembered by most Americans as an ineffectual hawk who negotiated with terrorists and sold arms to Iran. In circles far beyond die-hard Republicans, Reagan is simply "the man who won the Cold War." Those on the left who argue against this have to persuade the American public that it is just a giant coincidence that the Soviet Union decayed from a position of strength on January 20, 1981, to the verge of collapse when George H. W. Bush took office eight years later.

THE PERSIAN GULF WAR

With the end of the Cold War, it appeared that national security and foreign policy would recede from the top of the political agenda. But the presidency of George H. W. Bush would be recalled for one decisive clash that would affect the Middle East for years to come.

In 1991, Democrats overwhelmingly opposed the Gulf War. Of the party's 54 senators, 45 opposed authorization for war against Iraq in January 1991.

Perhaps more ominously for Democrats, many of their leading figures made predictions of doom before the conflict that didn't pan out. In fact, the result was a stunning victory for America and its allies that demonstrated all that high-tech weaponry stockpiled during the Cold War came in handy.

New York governor Mario Cuomo suggested that the Iraqis might be induced to leave Kuwait if only Americans agreed to let them keep part of Kuwait's territory. Congressman Dick Gephardt said that Congress could always cut the funding for the war midway if it was unhappy with President Bush's handling of it.[35] The newly elected Paul Wellstone of Minnesota argued that "President Bush appears to be on the verge of making a terrible mistake that will have tragic consequences for the whole world."[36] In his first speech as a U.S. senator, Wellstone predicted a war with Iraq would cost thousands of American lives, deeply divide the American public, fracture the U.S. economy, leave the Middle East in flames, and possibly prompt an invasion of Israel.

Barbara Boxer, then a congresswoman from Marin County, California, said that 3,000 to 4,000 dead American soldiers was "the best-case scenario."[37]

Former president Jimmy Carter: "The devastating consequences will be [felt] . . . for decades to come, in economic and political destabilization of the Middle East region."

Senator John Kerry: "I do not believe our nation is prepared for war. If we do go to war, for years people will ask why Congress gave in. They will ask why there was such a rush to so much death and destruction when it did not have to happen."

Former national security adviser Zbigniew Brzezinski: "The United States is likely to become estranged from many of its European allies."

Senator Edward M. Kennedy: "It'll be brutal and ugly. The 45,000 body bags the Pentagon has sent to the region are all the evidence we need of the high price in lives and blood that we will have to [bear]."[38]

In the end, fewer than 150 Americans lost their lives in combat. Iraq was ejected from Kuwait. Third-world regimes around the globe kicked their T-72 Soviet tanks in frustration, realizing that

American-made precision bombers, night vision, stealth technology, Patriot missile batteries, GPS satellites, and other advances had made their arsenals largely obsolete.

THE THREAT: Saddam Hussein's invasion of Kuwait and potential attack on Saudi Arabia.

THE LEADERS' POSITIONS: After initial fears by Maggie Thatcher that he would "go wobbly," President Bush declared "naked aggression will not stand." Democrats mostly opposed the use of military force, preferring sanctions.

THE DECISION: First, Desert Shield, the deployment of U.S. and coalition troops to keep the Iraqis out of Saudi Arabia; then Desert Storm, military force designed to forcibly eject Iraq out of Kuwait.

THE RESULT: Iraq ejected from Kuwait and the reestablishment of Kuwaiti sovereignty. There were 147 U.S. battle-related deaths, 325 non-battle-related deaths; 65 total coalition deaths; an estimated 10,000 to 12,000 Iraqi combat deaths in the air campaign and as many as 10,000 casualties in the ground war.

For a political party, bad predictions are not the end of the world. And clearly, by 1992, a troubled economy and lackluster Bush campaign set the stage for one of the defining figures of the twentieth century to assume the presidency: Bill Clinton. Still, it is worth noting that Bill Clinton didn't win the presidency because he had neutralized the Democrats' vulnerability on national security issues; it was because the end of the Cold War meant those issues were no longer preeminent in voters' minds.

Even in July 1992, when Clinton had stormed to a 56–34 lead

over Bush in the Gallup survey, Gallup was finding that the public felt, by a 57–28 margin, that Bush would better handle national defense.

In early January 1993, right after Clinton had a comfortable electoral college win (and before the gays-in-the-military flap), Greenberg/Lake and the Tarrance Group (today's Battleground survey), by a 56–32 percent margin, Americans had more confidence in Republicans in Congress than in President Clinton on "maintaining a strong national defense." Even when the Democrats won, they were viewed as weaker than Republicans on this issue.

During the eight-year holiday from history that constituted much of the 1990s, the Democrats didn't win by getting stronger on defense and national security; those issues just decreased as a priority among most voters.

THE CLINTON ERA: STRENGTHENING THE DEMOCRATS' IMAGE—EXCEPT IN NATIONAL SECURITY

In Bill Clinton, the nation had a Democratic commander in chief for the first time since Desert One. It was a golden opportunity to refute some stereotypes and widely held beliefs about Democrats, national security, and the use of military force.

But if Clinton challenged the stereotype that Democrats refused to use force, he didn't quite project an image of mastery. Even his staunchest defenders would admit his use of military force was uneven at best. While Clinton remains revered by many Americans for a strong economy, welfare reform, NAFTA (North American Free Trade Agreement), and tireless efforts to create lasting peace in Ireland and the Middle East, Clinton's legacy is damaged by the perception of defeat in Somalia, a bizarrely disproportionate focus on

Haiti, and a Kosovo operation that resembled chaos. More damning were his lack of a decisive response to al-Qaeda attacks and sporadic, half-measured bombing of Saddam Hussein in Iraq when he refused to cooperate with United Nations weapons inspectors.

Somalia

A great deal of blame for America's problems in the Somali intervention can be laid at the feet of the outgoing president George H. W. Bush, who deployed U.S. troops in what was initially designed as a humanitarian relief mission but quickly evolved into the kind of "nation-building" mission that many Republicans would spend the following decade or so mocking. In the final weeks of the first Bush presidency, 25,000 U.S. troops were deployed to Somalia.

Unfair or not, when Clinton took office, Somalia had become a major commitment of U.S. Armed Forces in a hostile land. What began as a heavily armed relief operation became, in the words of Madeleine Albright, an "unprecedented enterprise aimed at nothing less than the restoration of an entire country."

There is no doubt that helping starving, impoverished, fearful Somali civilians was the morally right thing to do. But it was light-years away from any foreign policy priority of Clinton's 1992 campaign (in which he had famously promised to "focus like a laser beam on the economy") and it was not really a pressing priority of the American people, either.

In May 1993, Operation Somalia-2 began in an effort to create conditions to enable the Somalis to rebuild the country. The United States cut its troops in Somalia to some 4,000 and then added 400 Army Rangers in August 1993. At that time, confronting criticism at home that the United States was getting more deeply involved in the factional violence in Somalia without a clear rationale, Defense Secretary Les Aspin explained that U.S. troops would remain until order had been restored in Mogadishu, Somalia's capital; progress had been made in disarming rival clans; and effective police forces were operating in the country's major cities. At the same time, the United States increased its military efforts against a leading Somali warlord, Mohamed Farrah Aidid.[39]

In September, General Colin Powell, then chairman of the joint chiefs of staff, asked Aspin to approve the request of the U.S. commander in Somalia for tanks and armored vehicles for his forces. Aspin turned down the request. Shortly thereafter, Aidid's forces in Mogadishu killed 18 U.S. soldiers and wounded more than 75 in fighting that also resulted in the shooting down of three U.S. helicopters and the capture of one pilot.[40] In the face of severe congressional criticism, Aspin admitted that in view of what had happened he had made a mistake, but he stated that the request for armored equipment had been made within the context of delivering humanitarian aid to Somalia rather than protecting troops.

Years later, the best-selling book and dramatic film *Black Hawk Down* spurred continued public discussion of just what went wrong in Somalia. A consensus built that an inexperienced commander in chief, who had found himself in an ugly and high-profile fight with the Pentagon over gays in the military, saw the carnage and decided to quit the fight.

Somalia was and is remembered as a U.S. defeat. Aidid died in his home in southern Mogadishu in August 1996, shot by rival warlords. Osama bin Laden was free to interpret the events as a sign of American cowardice.

"It cleared from Muslim minds the myth of superpowers," Osama bin Laden said of Somalia in his interview with *ABC News* journalist John Miller in May 1998. "The youth were surprised at the low morale of the American soldiers and realized more than before that the American soldiers was a paper tiger and after a few blows ran in defeat."

"The great tragedy of Somalia is that it was, given what those

Rangers did, one of the great feats of arms in American military history," said retired general Kenneth Allard, MSNBC military analyst and author of the 1995 review "Somalia Operations: Lessons Learned."[41] "Two congressional medals of honor that were given out as a result of that—guys that gave their lives, laid down their lives willingly; 82 more that were wounded. That is a classic definition of American courage. It is a classic example of what the American fighting man is capable of doing. Because we withdrew those troops under pressure, the lesson that was given to the rest of the world was that the United States can be had. All you need to do is to shed their blood. And if you do that, they'll cut and run."

Despite the ineffectiveness of the United Nations in handling Somalia, few Democrats had their faith in international institutions shaken.

Senator Richard Lugar, an Indiana Republican, is far from a fire-breathing archconservative. But his assessment of Clinton's handling of Somalia is scathing:

> The Clinton administration gave virtually no attention publicly to Somalia. Privately some members of the administration must have worried about this predicament but hoped that it would not intrude upon the domestic agenda that was before the country. The president had widely celebrated statements—"it's the economy, stupid"– [that] meant that in other words [what was important was] the domestic agenda, the rearrangement of the budget, the tax questions.

THE THREAT: Um . . . initially, the sad sight of starving Somalis on CNN; eventually, Aidid's attacks on Somalis and coalition troops.
THE LEADERS' POSITIONS: GOP congressional leaders

had mixed feelings on continuing the Somalia intervention; their Democratic counterparts were no more unified. There is debate as to just what course President Clinton preferred and when.

THE DECISION: Eventually to cut losses and end U.S. military presence in Somalia.

THE RESULT: To this day, America's enemies cite Somalia as a sign that America is a paper tiger, even more than the 1983 Marine barracks bombing.

If the Somalia intervention could be excused by Clinton's defenders as a rookie mistake due to an ugly mess left by the first Bush administration, his bizarre semi-intervention in Haiti is harder to explain.

Haiti

On September 30, 1991, the Haitian army deposed Jean-Bertrand Aristide and his democratically elected government. Aristide fled into exile, first to Venezuela and then to the United States. The U.S. and concerned neighboring countries pushed for the restoration of the elected civilian government in Haiti.[42]

On October 11, 1993, in preparation for implementing a new accord, the United States sent a contingent of 193 United States and 25 Canadian troops, engineers, and trainers to Haiti aboard the USS *Harlan County.* The group was the first wave of a 1,267-man U.N. police and military mission to train the Haitian police and army and rebuild the Haitian infrastructure, as agreed to under a recent accord. Arriving in Port-au-Prince a week after 18 U.S. soldiers had been killed by tribal guerrilla forces in Somalia, the *Harlan County* was greeted by angry, chanting crowds and denied entry to the dock.[43]

According to the *New York Times,* "The demonstrators, who were allowed into the port area by police officers rerouting traffic to clear the way, beat on the cars of diplomats and kicked reporters waiting at the gates of the port, screaming, 'We are going to turn this into another Somalia!' "[44] Not wishing another bloody intervention with no exit strategy and limited benefit, President Clinton ordered the *Harlan County* to retreat.

For many in the military, this decision was the straw that broke the camel's back, and it hardened their worst suspicions about Clinton. The U.S. military had seen some bad days since the end of Vietnam—Desert One, the bombing of the Lebanon barracks, Somalia. But to the fraction of the American public paying attention, this was intolerable. The greatest military power in the world, the arsenal of democracy, the institution that stormed Omaha Beach does not turn around when confronted by an angry, chanting crowd.

For another year, Aristide, the Haitian military, the United Nations, and the Clinton administration made additional efforts to find a diplomatic solution. Finally, in September 1994, the military government of Raoul Cedras surrendered power when facing an imminent invasion by the United States. While the armed forces were ready for an invasion, Congress and the American public were not. Furthermore, they were even less prepared to get involved in an ongoing peacekeeping effort, which Clinton had committed the United States to whether or not there was an invasion. In a *Newsweek* poll, only 34 percent of those surveyed favored U.S. participation in a multinational intervention. There was a general feeling that no vital U.S. interest was at stake in Haiti. There was also suspicion that Clinton's main reason for invading would be to avoid looking weak in the face of his repeated threats just weeks before a congressional election.[45]

Shortly before the military not-quite-invasion, Mark Helprin, a right-of-center journalist and former member of the Israeli infantry and air force, lambasted Clinton's incomprehensible sense of priorities:

Mr. President, in trumpeting this gnatfest at a hundred times the volume of the Normandy invasion, you have invited challenges from all who would take comfort at the spectacle of the United States in full fluster over an object so diminutive as to be a source of wonder.

Anyone considering a serious challenge to the United States has been reassured that we have no perspective in international affairs, that we act not in regard to our basic interests but in reaction to sentiment and ideology, that we can be distracted by the smallest matter and paralyzed by the contemplation of force, that we have become timid, weak, and slow. This is what happens when the leaders of the world's most powerful nation take a year to agonize over Haiti. This is what happens when the elephant ignores the jackals and gravely battles a fly. . . .

Why Haiti? Because, like the father in Joyce's story, "Counterparts," who bullies his son because he cannot bully his boss, what you do in Haiti says less about Haiti than about North Korea, Europe and the Middle East, where the real challenges lie, and where you cannot act because you do not have a lamp to go by and you have forced your own military to its knees.[46]

Once again, it can easily be argued that restoring a democratically elected Haitian president is the right thing to do. Making the case that it represented a U.S. foreign policy priority at that time is well nigh impossible.

THE THREAT: Honestly, How about "additional waves of Haitian immigrants straining resources of the state of Florida"?

THE LEADERS' POSITIONS: Clinton, after great deliberation, authorized the use of military force in what could be described as a unilateral preemptive regime change. He managed to pick what is arguably the one country that Republicans had no interest in invading.

THE DECISION: A reasonably peaceful invasion, followed by a sporadically violent occupation.

THE RESULT: Before the U.S. intervention, Haiti was an economic and political basket case; after the intervention, Haiti was . . . still an economic and political basket case. In early 2004, Jean-Bertrand Aristide, who the United States had fought to restore, had become enough of a corrupt dictator to spur another rebellion against him. This time, the United States called for his ouster; Aristide claimed there was a CIA plot against him. (Because the CIA did not have anything else on its plate from September 2001 to that time.) In the early morning of February 29, 2004, after being harshly condemned by the American and French governments, Aristide left Haiti on a U.S.-dispatched airplane to the Central African Republic. He later claimed that America had kidnapped him.

But the centerpiece of Clinton administration's record in military intervention is the bombing campaign against Serbian dictator Slobodon Milosevic in Kosovo in response to ethnic cleansing.

Kosovo

At a NATO (North Atlantic Treaty Organization) ministers' conference in Toronto a few months after the war, one defense minister began his remarks on the lessons learned during "Operation Allied

Force" by suggesting that the most fundamental lesson was "we never want to do that again."[47]

Like the interventions in Somalia and Haiti, it is easy to make the case that military intervention was the morally right thing to do. Unfortunately, the execution of the operation was not as sterling as the motives of the Clinton White House. A military operation that once again began with the best of intentions resulted in a nightmare of unintended consequences. History has shown that anything and everything can go wrong in the fog of war; but in Kosovo, what went wrong was severe enough to question the purpose of the entire operation.

Clinton claimed in his March 24, 1999, national address that one purpose of bombing Serbia was "to deter an even bloodier offensive against innocent civilians in Kosovo and, if necessary, to seriously damage the Serbian military's capacity to harm the people of Kosovo."

But before the bombing began, the CIA and other skeptics inside and outside the administration argued that bombing could spur the Serbian army to greatly accelerate its efforts to expel ethnic Albanians. Once the bombs started falling, that is exactly what happened. In fact, many of the horrors the operation aimed to deter simply got worse: savage ethnic cleansing, executions of Kosovar Albanian leaders, the forced expulsion of more than 130,000 Kosovars in the first week alone.[48] A large part of Podujevo—just north of Pristina, Kosovo's provincial capital—was reportedly burned to the ground.

Confronted with what appeared to be a terrible but honest miscalculation, the supreme allied commander of NATO, General Wesley Clark, contradicted the president and asserted that from the beginning "we never thought that through air power we could stop these killings on the ground."[49]

As Fareed Zakaria calculated, a regional military conflict that had killed 2,500 people in a year, mostly soldiers and partisans, had escalated to an 11-week war that killed at least 10,000 people, mostly Albanian civilians. The number of displaced shifted from around 230,000 Kosovars before the war to 1.4 million Albanians afterward.[50]

Most of the Albanians would eventually return, but the war would also result in more than 150,000 Serbs fleeing the province. Kosovo was physically laid to waste; without international aid, mass starvation would soon set in. The European Union estimated that Yugoslavia had been bombed back 50 years and that it would take decades and more than $50 billion to rebuild the civilian infrastructure of the country.[51] Recall, again, this was all the result of a war waged with humanitarian intentions.

In any war with aerial bombing, missiles will go off course and the wrong targets will be hit. But an insistence on low-risk, high-altitude flight paths, coupled with the inherent difficulties of finding targets on the mountainous, often heavily forested, hidden-among-civilians terrain in bad weather, meant that the Kosovo war had a dispiriting number of errant bombs.

On April 6, 1999, two bombs presumably aimed at a military barracks missed by half a mile and hit apartment blocks, killing 4 civilians, injuring 30, and destroying a medical clinic.

On April 12, a NATO air strike on a bridge near the village of Grdelica accidentally hit a passenger train, killing 10 and wounding 16.

On April 14, NATO bombs accidentally hit two convoys of ethnic Albanian refugees being escorted by Serb police near Djakovica, Kosovo. Yugoslav officials put the death toll from the incident at between 60 and 85.

On April 23, NATO approved a strike on Serbian television and radio designed to eliminate Milosevic's ability to spread propaganda. Sixteen employees were killed. The term *war crimes* is thrown around with reckless abandon by antiwar protesters, eager to smear all of

America's men and women in uniform as barbarians, "reminiscent of Genghis Kahn," as John Kerry crassly put it. But it is hard for an American to look at this bombing run and not shudder at the moral compromises it represented. Clearly Milosevic's propaganda efforts were an impediment to winning the war. In addition to housing Belgrade's main television and radio studios, NATO said the building "also housed a large multipurpose communications satellite antenna dish" and charged that the facilities "are being used as radio relay stations and transmitters to support the activities of the FRY [Federal Republic of Yugoslavia] military and special police forces, and therefore they represented legitimate military targets."

Maybe the deed was necessary, but it burns at the conscience. The building was occupied by at least 120 working technicians and other production staff at the time of the bombing—mostly civilian cameramen, technicians, and a 26-year-old makeup artist, Jelica Munitlak. Clark later said that he called the CNN reporter working in the building to warn them. They left, but Milosevic's goons forced the Serbian civilian employees to stay. None of the station's senior officials or key journalists were on the premises. Witnesses say the editor in chief left an hour before the attack. The suspicion is that those who remained in the building had been deliberately left to die for propaganda purposes.[52]

On April 27, a 2,000-pound laser-guided bomb launched by an F-15 fighter missed its target—an army barracks—by 500 yards. The bomb hit a residential district and killed 16 civilians, including 11 children, according to the Serbians. NATO officials said the bomb went astray when smoke from a previous strike diffused the F-15's laser and muddled its guidance system.

On April 29, NATO accomplished a new feat by managing to bomb the wrong country. One of the alliance's jet fighters launched the missile in self-defense in response to the threat from a surface-to-air missile after Yugoslav ground radar locked onto the plane. The missile strayed from its target and unintentionally landed in Sofia, Bulgaria's Goma Banja district, about 30 miles east of the Yugoslav border. Thankfully, there were no injuries.

On May 1, NATO officials released a statement confirming that an air strike designed to destroy a bridge hit a bus near Luzane north of Pristina, killing at least 34 people, including 15 children, and injuring 5.

On May 7, 3 Chinese journalists were killed and 20 other Chinese were injured when NATO accidentally bombed the Chinese Embassy in Belgrade. NATO attributed the mistake to outdated maps, claiming that NATO's maps identify the building as the headquarters of the Federal Directorate of Supply and Procurement. Massive protests erupted in Beijing, trapping American ambassador James Sasser in the U.S. Embassy for more than 48 hours.

Also on May 7, a NATO cluster bomb did extensive damage to several streets near the vegetable market in the southern town of Nis. The toll of that bomb was 15 dead and 60 injured.

On May 13, more than 80 ethnic Albanians were killed and at least 100 were injured, by Yugoslav count, when NATO bombed a village believed to have been a Serb military post. NATO claimed the victims were being used by Serb troops as human shields.

On May 14, a civilian convoy was hit by bombs in Korisa, killing 87 and wounding at least 58 people. Serbia blamed NATO planes; NATO contended the deaths were the result of Serbian shelling. There were also reports that civilians were being used as human shields on Serbian military convoys.

On May 21, NATO again hit an unintended target—a Kosovar Liberation Army stronghold. One member of the rebel group was killed and at least 15 were injured.

On May 31, three NATO missiles hit a bridge in the town of Krusevac, killing 11 and injuring 40.

All in all, one wonders if it would have been worth it to risk more coalition forces on the ground in order to provide more accurate intelligence for air strikes.

Tales of erroneous missiles are easier to take when you know that the vast majority of the munitions are hitting and eliminating their intended targets. Unfortunately, that was not the case. A confidential postwar U.S. military investigation concluded that the damage claims of NATO commanders during the war had been exaggerated nearly 10-fold. In reality, only 14 tanks, 18 armored personnel carriers, and 20 artillery pieces were taken out, despite the claimed dropping of more than 20,000 bombs on the Serbian military.

During the final days of the campaign, General Wesley Clark was bothered by a CNN headline that stated, "Despite the Negotiations, NATO Continues to Bomb." In his autobiography, Clark wrote that he himself "called the network to explain that the story reflected a misunderstanding: it was the bombing that was responsible for causing the negotiations."[53] Thus, the supreme commander of Allied Forces who had such trouble bringing Milosevic to his knees was at least able to get faster results with Wolf Blitzer.

Though it would not come to light until years later, Clark claimed that the White House pressured him to end the conflict to avoid repercussions in Al Gore's upcoming presidential campaign. "There were those in the White House who said, 'Hey, look, you gotta finish the bombing before the Fourth of July weekend. That's the start of the next presidential campaign season, so stop it. It doesn't matter what you do, just turn it off. You don't have to win this thing, let it lie,' " Clark said in a January 2000 interview with NATO's official historian, four months before leaving the post of supreme allied commander Europe (SACEUR).

When the *Washington Post* reported these comments in February 2004, Clark said Clinton was "totally committed" to the Kosovo war, and described his statement to the historian as "a stream-of-conscious dictation . . . [about] a complex period of time."

Kosovo never caught the public's attention and popular consciousness the way the Gulf War had earlier in the decade. When the war began, few Americans understood it; while it occurred, few Americans followed it closely; after it ended, few Americans remembered it, making it a virtual victory.[54] Clark has lamented that Kosovo became a forgotten war, that its ending occasioned no victory parades, no new rush of patriotism. When he came home, he was struck by the fact that many people didn't seem to even know that there had been a war, much less what it had been fought over or who had won. When Clark began looking for a publisher for his memoir, the major houses said they weren't interested in the story of the war in Kosovo.[55]

As with the previous Clinton-era military operations, it is easy to see the good intentions and moral correctness behind the decision to use force. But once again, the execution was execrable.

The most devastating criticism of Clark's Kosovo war management comes from the RAND research institute report, "NATO's Air War for Kosovo: A Strategic and Operational Assessment." The review paints Clark as a leader in nearly constant conflict with the officers directly under him, the micromanaging boss from hell.

Clark's system of having himself, an army general, managing the air campaign broke dramatically from the American system in other previous conflicts. In the Bosnia campaign in 1995, then-SACEUR army general George Joulwan left the day-to-day responsibilities for the air campaign to navy admiral Leighton Smith in order to focus on diplomatic duties. General H. Norman Schwarzkopf, on the eve of Desert Storm, put his faith in the air campaign strategy drawn up by the air force's then–lieutenant general Charles Horner.

After weeks of seemingly fruitless bombing, the Clark strategy of focusing on Serbian forces in the field ("tank-plinking") was dropped and the campaign focused on targets in Belgrade that were important to Milosevic. The RAND report concluded, "The majority of the combat sorties that SACEUR [Clark] insisted be devoted to finding and attacking enemy forces in the [Kosovo Engagement Zone] arguably entailed a waste of munitions and other valuable assets."

Clark was hobbled by furious infighting by Hugh Shelton and Secretary of Defense William Cohen. But one has to wonder how Kosovo would have turned out had Clark's superiors signed off on his strategic recommendations. As the war progressed, Clark was increasingly convinced that a land invasion would be necessary.

Clark continued to focus on preparations for a ground war, and the plan he ultimately proposed was greeted in Washington with astonishment. "Gallipoli springs to mind," one defense expert, who made a study of Clark's plan, says. Clark advocated an invasion of Kosovo with a force of two hundred thousand troops, mostly American. The force would move into Kosovo through Albania, because Macedonia had declared that it would not allow its territory to be used for launching an attack. Aside from the most obvious difficulty with Clark's plan—that a major American-led ground invasion in the Balkans could not win the support of Congress, the Pentagon, the White House, or NATO—there was a real problem regarding Albania. The country was already in chaos, and had almost no infrastructure. There was only one major road, and it was only partly paved, and there were few bridges that could support the mammoth tanks and fighting vehicles of the American Army. If an invasion were to occur on Clark's time line, which was early autumn, the infrastructure would have to be put in place during the summer.[56]

(Recall that Clark's strongest point as a presidential candidate in 2004 [and 2008?]—perhaps his sole qualification—was the perception that he is a strong leader who knows how to manage a war.)

In fact, the conclusion of the defense minister who declared "we never want to do that again" was taken to heart by Pentagon officials in the Bush administration. Kosovo's complicated system of requiring all NATO members to sign off on bombing targets became exhibit A of what not to do when fighting a war. In a 2003 article in the *Washington Monthly*, Clark recalled how he visited the Pentagon soon after the 9/11 terrorist attacks, offering suggestions on the war against terrorists. "We read your book," on Kosovo, Clark wrote that he was told. "And no one is going to tell us where we can or can't bomb."[57]

THE THREAT: "Ethnic cleansing" by Milosevic and further destabilization of the Balkans.

THE LEADERS' POSITIONS: After prodding by Prime Minister Tony Blair, Clinton supported military force; most Democratic lawmakers agreed. Some congressional Republicans such as John McCain supported military force; others did not.

THE DECISION: A long, slow, clumsy, and hobbled but ultimately effective air campaign.

THE RESULT: After nearly a decade of horrific ethnic genocide that rivaled the worst images of World War II, international peacekeepers are forcing Balkan ethnicities to coexist in a tense peace. While the ethnic groups still hate each other, the populations seem exhausted enough from the fighting to resist the urge for war.

Clinton on al-Qaeda

From the Iranian hostage crisis to the hostage-taking in Lebanon in the 1980s and the plane hijackings during the Reagan era, terrorism became the asymmetrical warfare option of choice for America's enemies. Unfortunately, just as America had elected a president who had pledged to "focus like a laser beam on the economy," terrorists around the world were ready to step up their game.

Five days after Clinton took office, Mir Aimal Kasi shot two Central Intelligence Agency employees in their cars while waiting in the morning traffic outside CIA headquarters in Langley, Virginia. The attack left three other people wounded. Kasi was captured by the FBI in Pakistan in 1997. (He spent much of his time on the run in Afghanistan.) He was executed in Virginia in 2002.

Clinton had been in office just 38 days when terrorists bombed the World Trade Center, killing 6 people and injuring more than 1,000. The immediate perpetrators were arrested and prosecuted, but to this day law enforcement and intelligence sources debate ties to other terrorists and perhaps a state sponsor. In April 1995, for example, terrorism expert Steven Emerson told the House International Relations Committee that there was information that "strongly suggests a Sudanese role in the World Trade Center bombing. There are also leads pointing to the involvement of Osama bin Laden, the ex-Afghan Saudi mujahideen supporter now taking refuge in Sudan."[58]

If al-Qaeda's plot to crash a plane into the White House on September 11 sounded vaguely familiar, it may be because it already happened. On September 11, 1994, Frank Eugene Corder stole a single-engine Cessna plane from an airport north of Baltimore, then flew it south to Washington. He came in low over the White House South Lawn, skidded across the South Lawn, and crashed into a wall two stories below the presidential bedroom. Federal officials said they did not believe the crash was politically motivated.

A joke at the time reflected how much the Clinton administration was focused on terrorist threats at that moment. R. James Woolsey, President Bill Clinton's first director of Central Intelligence, reportedly had great difficulties getting Clinton to meet with him face-to-face to discuss national security matters. When word of the White House crash broke, wise guys at Langley joked that the pilot had in fact been Woolsey, making one last desperate attempt to see Clinton.

It seems odd that so many of these attacks never registered in the American consciousness, but a review of official records reveals that Islamist terrorist groups attacked Americans again and again overseas, rarely bringing any serious response and never any military response.

On March 8, 1994, two unidentified gunmen killed two U.S. diplomats and wounded a third in Karachi, Pakistan. On November 13, 1995, a bomb was set off in a van parked in front of an American-run military training center in the Saudi Arabian capital of Riyadh, killing five Americans and two Indians. Saudi Arabian authorities arrested four Saudi nationals whom they claim confessed to the bombings, but U.S. officials were denied permission to see or question the suspects before they were convicted and beheaded in May 1996.

On February 23, 1997, Ali Abu Kamal, a Palestinian gunman, opened fire on tourists at an observation deck atop the Empire State Building in New York City, killing a Danish national and wounding visitors from the United States, Argentina, Switzerland, and France before turning the gun on himself. A handwritten note carried by the gunman claimed this was a punishment attack against the "enemies of Palestine."

On November 12, 1997, two unidentified gunmen shot to death four U.S. auditors from Union Texas Petroleum Corporation and their Pakistani driver after they drove away from the Sheraton Hotel in Karachi. The Islami Inqilabi Council, or Islamic Revolutionary Council, claimed responsibility in a call to the U.S. Consulate in Karachi. In a letter to Pakistani newspapers, the Aimal Khufia Action Committee also claimed responsibility.

On December 28, 1998, Yemeni militants kidnapped a group of western tourists, including 12 Britons, 2 Americans, and 2 Australians, on the main road to Aden. Four victims were killed during a rescue attempt the next day.

These were the small attacks during the Clinton years. During these years, al-Qaeda inaugurated the era of mass-casually attacks—superterrorism.

Khobar Towers

On June 25, 1996, a bombing killed 19 U.S. military personnel at Khobar Towers, a barracks in Saudi Arabia, wounding about 300 others. One of the definitive accounts is given by Elsa Walsh in the May 2001 issue of the *New Yorker*.

With FBI help, the Saudis were able to identify the truck chassis used in the bombing and trace it to the purchaser, who acknowledged being part of a cell trained by members of the Iranian Revolutionary Guard.

On several occasions, FBI director Louis Freeh urged the White House to pressure the Saudis for more cooperation. More than once, Walsh reports, Freeh was frustrated to learn that the president barely mentioned the case in meetings with Saudi leaders.[59]

Walsh reported that in September 1998, Freeh, angry and losing hope, took the extraordinary step of secretly asking former president George H. W. Bush to intercede with the Saudi royal family. Acting without Clinton's knowledge, Bush made the request, and the Saudis began to provide new information, which indeed pointed to Iran.

On November 9, 1998, FBI agents watched and listened as Saudi law enforcement interrogated eight suspects. The suspects confessed to their roles in the bombing and described how the Iranians had ordered, supported, and financed their actions.

In late 1998, Walsh reports, Freeh went to national security adviser Sandy Berger to tell him that it appeared the FBI had enough evidence to indict several suspects:

> Almost before Freeh could finish, Berger demanded, "Who else knows about this?" Did the press know? This was the last question that Freeh expected from a national-security adviser. Not many people knew, Freeh replied. The information was very closely held. Berger also questioned some of the statements linking the bombing to the Iranian government.
>
> "That's just hearsay," Berger said.
>
> "No, Sandy," Freeh replied. "It's testimony of a co-conspirator in furtherance of a conspiracy." Berger, Freeh later thought, was not a national-security adviser; he was a public-relations hack, interested in how something would play in the press. After more than two years, Freeh had concluded that the Administration did not really want to resolve the Khobar bombing.

The 9/11 Commission reported that the Clinton administration struck back by unmasking Iranian intelligence officers around the world. Undisclosed until 2004, Operation Sapphire took place in 1997. Though the bombers who struck the Khobar Towers barracks were mostly Saudis, U.S. investigators determined that Iranian intelligence officials had trained and organized the plotters. A former U.S. official claimed Iran was intimidated enough by the U.S. counterspy operation that it stopped targeting Americans after the bombing.[60]

Thus the Clinton doctrine: If you train Saudis to kill 19 American servicemen, we will force you to take early retirement.

But the Khobar Towers attack seemed small in comparison to al-Qaeda's coming-out party in Africa. On August 7, 1998, bombs exploded at U.S. Embassies in Nairobi, Kenya, and Dar es Salaam, Tanzania. More than 200 people were killed, including 12 Americans.

On August 20, Clinton ordered cruise-missile strikes on a bin Laden camp in Afghanistan and a pharmaceutical plant in Sudan. But the strikes were at best ineffectual. Sudan angrily denied that the factory produced chemical weapons, and the administration's evidence was hotly contested. In Afghanistan, the cruise missiles missed bin Laden and had little or no impact on al-Qaeda activities. Coming amidst the Monica Lewinsky scandal, many Clinton administration critics dismissed the airstrikes as a cynical wag-the-dog distraction.[61]

THE THREAT: Osama bin Laden and the al-Qaeda declaring open season on American civilians.

THE LEADERS' POSITIONS: Clinton wanted a military option; a lack of resources in Afghanistan and no cooperation from Pakistan meant that cruise missiles were the only option that had minimal risk of U.S. casualties. Republicans certainly supported military attacks against terrorists, but many saw the decision as a wag-the-dog distraction, designed to deter a decline in Clinton's approval rating, not more attacks.

THE DECISION: The cruise missile strikes in Afghanistan and Sudan.

THE RESULT: Counterproductive. There is no evidence that the strikes hindered al-Qaeda in any significant way; casualty-averse America had not looked so impotent since Desert One. Had these attacks been just the first step in a continuing military campaign, perhaps they would be remembered differently; but in

retrospect, they resemble an expensive, ineffective, halfhearted swat at a fly.

On October 31, 1999, EgyptAir Flight 990, a giant twin-engine Boeing 767 on the way from New York to Cairo, crashed with 217 people aboard. It had taken off from Kennedy Airport in the middle of the night, climbed to 33,000 feet, and flown normally for half an hour before mysteriously plummeting into the Atlantic Ocean 60 miles south of Nantucket.

The subsequent investigation was marked by a lengthy fight between the Egyptian government and the National Transportation Safety Board. The NTSB's final report, issued March 21, 2002, stated:

> In summary, the evidence establishes that the nose-down elevator movements were not the result of a failure in the elevator control system or any other airplane system but were the result of the relief first officer's manipulation of the airplane controls. The evidence further indicates that the subsequent climb and elevator split were not the result of a mechanical failure but were the result of pilot inputs, including opposing pilot inputs where the relief first officer was commanding nose-down and the captain was commanding nose-up movement. The Safety Board considered possible reasons for the relief first officer's actions; however, the Board did not reach a conclusion regarding the intent of or motivation for his actions. The National Transportation Safety Board determines that the probable cause of the EgyptAir Flight 990 accident is the airplane's departure from normal cruise flight and subsequent impact with the Atlantic Ocean as a result of the relief first officer's flight control inputs. The reason for the relief first officer's actions was not determined.

William Langewiesche wrote the comprehensive analysis, "The Crash of EgyptAir 990," in the *Atlantic Monthly*, November 2001. In a separate interview in the magazine, he concluded:

> Some people within the NTSB wanted to draw a line in the sand by wrapping up the investigation in the first six months and moving on to the things that they considered more important. But the much larger and more powerful political system in Washington did not allow that to happen—and that may have been appropriate. There are things more important than aviation safety, that's for sure. They were dealing with a very important ally in a very unstable part of the world. There was a level of concern out there about not pissing off Mubarak. Mubarak's a guy who's easily pissed off. He's an autocrat. He's used to having temper tantrums. Everybody knew that. So there was no way the NTSB could really fight back against these manipulations of the system. They were told, in no uncertain terms, "You will not offend the Egyptians. If the Egyptians bring up objections and want you to continue the investigation, you will continue the investigation." They were never told, "You will alter the truth." But they were told. "You will not just wrap it up and move on, you will not just be technocrats, you will have to respond to the political realities of our time." [62]

The FBI and U.S. authorities never established any direct ties between the relief crew pilot who was believed to have brought down the plane, Gamil el-Batouty, and terrorist groups. But after the suicide hijackings of 9/11, you cannot help but wonder if the jihadi philosophy of suicide attacks influenced the pilot. There are a lot of ways to commit suicide; intentionally taking down an airliner takes 216 other men, women, and children with you. One doesn't need to go through a training camp in Afghanistan to be a terrorist; for all we know, some jihad-minded extremist could have had tea with el-Batouty and inspired the idea. The mysterious crash of Flight 990 is one of those events that just looks and feels different after 9/11.

The final major terrorist attack of the Clinton presidency was on October 12, 2000, when bin Laden operatives bombed the USS *Cole* in Aden, Yemen. One of the most sophisticated U.S. warships was nearly sunk, 17 American sailors were killed, and 39 were wounded.[63]

During this time, getting bin Laden had become a U.S. government priority, or so officials of that time claim. But if the will was there, action was rare. Intelligence reports showed that bin Laden and his key lieutenants kept their families with their entourage, and Clinton opposed any operation that might kill women and children.[64] Pro-U.S. Afghanis were told by the CIA that an ambush on bin Laden's convoy would "violate U.S. law."

CIA director George Tenet said he felt "bound by the dovish attitude of Clinton and his advisers."

After the 9/11 attacks, there were also revelations that the State Department under the Clinton administration had been, at times, unbelievably naive about the Taliban:

> Some U.S. diplomats described the Taliban as almost quaintly amicable. "You get to know them and you find they really have a great sense of humor," one State Department staffer told journalist Richard Mackenzie a few months before the Taliban entered Kabul. Others even managed to find in the Taliban a streak of cosmopolitanism: In one December 1996 briefing, Assistant Secretary of State for South Asian Affairs Robin Raphel made sure to mention that the Taliban were composed of "intelligentsia" and "former civil servants," among other seemingly reformed elements.[65]

As for their primary military opponents, the Clinton administration had opposed arming the Northern Alliance because of concerns that among their ranks there were serial human rights abusers, drug dealers, and some had ties to Russians and Iranians.[66] Some members of the Northern Alliance were guilty as charged, but the U.S. rarely gets perfect allies to work with in far-off corners of the world. If the U.S. could work with Stalin to defeat Hitler, it could work with the Northern Alliance to fight al-Qaeda and the Taliban.

To the extent that the Clinton administration celebrated their foreign policy accomplishments, they discussed growing U.S. trade, efforts at Mideast peace, and successful Northern Ireland peace accords. But throughout the 2000 presidential campaign, George W. Bush contended Clinton left the American military underfunded.

"He had almost an allergy to using people in uniform," explains former Clinton adviser Dick Morris. "He was terrified of incurring casualties; the lessons of Vietnam were ingrained far too deeply in him. He lacked a faith that it would work, and I think he was constantly fearful of reprisals. . . . On another level, I just don't think it was his thing. You could talk to him about income redistribution and he would talk to you for hours and hours. Talk to him about terrorism, and all you'd get was a series of grunts."[67]

"The Clinton administration was not comfortable with the use of military power," concluded the ordinarily soft-spoken Indiana Republican senator Richard Lugar. "They simply hoped it wouldn't have to be used, or if it did, then it would be shared in responsibility with others, and that there might be some overall legitimacy through the United Nations or some international command. . . . The Clinton administration didn't want to spend money on military affairs; it wanted to downsize its military budget as a major way of trying to bring along economic planning that it felt was important. They were uncomfortable, I suspect, with some individual persons and plans that were left over, and wanted to put an imprint on the military."[68]

Much of the conservative criticism of Clinton's record can come across as overbearing. While it seems likely that the American public would have supported policies aimed at killing terrorists, it wasn't demanding them. The post-Somalia Pentagon was uneager to go to war under a commander in chief whom it didn't trust to finish the job. The wag-the-dog arguments criticized Clinton even when he did take action against terrorists. Pre-9/11 Pakistan was a long way from being a U.S. ally against the Taliban and al-Qaeda. And President Clinton thought he was defusing a key motivator of Islamist extremists by seeking a peace deal between Israelis and Palestinians.

But in the end, these are excuses. The job wasn't done; al-Qaeda grew from a minor threat to a major threat between January 20, 1993, and January 20, 2001. Reagan's flaws are forgotten by history, because the year after he left office, the Berlin Wall came down and the Soviet Union collapsed. Clinton's flaws in this area will never be forgotten, because less than one year after he left office, Americans saw the worst terrorist attack in their history. The American public knows that the 9/11 plot was in the works long before George W. Bush put his hand on the Bible and took the pledge.

By 1999, only 2 to 3 percent of Americans identified defense and foreign policy as the most pressing issues of the day.[69] In the 2000 election, defense and national security were largely marginal issues, generating only a bit of discussion after the Cole bombing.

The new Bush administration was slow to address the threat of al-Qaeda. The opening months of the new president's term were dominated by a conflict with the Chinese over a downed surveillance plane, missile defense, the collapse of the Middle East peace process, and continued attacks on U.S. pilots enforcing the no-fly zone in Iraq. A meeting of the deputy administration officials took place on

April 30, 2001, where it was agreed to explore policy options on Afghanistan, "including the possibility of regime change." [70]

The first Principals Committee meeting on al-Qaeda occurred on September 4, 2001. The use of an armed predator to kill al-Qaeda leadership, including bin Laden, in the training camps was expected to be ready by spring 2002.

On September 10, 2001, deputy national security adviser Stephen Hadley gathered the deputies to finalize a three-year plan to pressure and perhaps ultimately topple the Taliban. Also that day, Senate Foreign Relations Committee chairman Joe Biden made a serious speech objecting to missile defense.

On that Monday, few if any Republicans gave much thought to their record on national security in the preceding 40 years; it appeared that in the post–Cold War era, protecting the country was destined to be a second-tier issue. Compassionate conservatism, not hawkish conservatism, was the new mantra. Clearly, Democratic lawmakers weren't too worried about their political record since Vietnam; their Clintonian instincts seemed perfectly attuned to the era of the soccer mom. The country didn't need to be focused outwardly on foreign threats; it needed to be focused inwardly on domestic concerns, spending on social programs, and catering to the domestic comforts of suburban voters—school uniforms, car seats, no-smoking zones, a hike in the minimum wage, help paying for grandma's prescription drugs.

The following day, the world changed forever.

FIVE

How Did Each Party React to 9/11?

> You know, people are looking to buy a way of life
> here, and [DNC chair Terry] McAuliffe looks like
> he's trying to sell them a used Z28. I think you're
> talking about 7 out of 10 people are thinking what
> I'm thinking. They want to be protected. It's fine to
> talk about health care, but I think most people are
> thinking they don't want to have to use their health
> care to get stitched up after they're blown up in a
> bomb blast by a nut case. They want the nut case
> killed before that happens. So, in that case, it be-
> comes preemptive health care. As I get older, it
> seems unsafe to me to be anything but a conserva-
> tive.
> —*Dennis Miller, comedian*

Think back to the emotional state of Americans on September 11 and the days immediately afterward. Every man and woman, and every child old enough to understand, endured a traumatic experience; for most, witnessing the instant deaths of thousands live or on television was the most traumatic experience of their lives.

The crisis has triggered Americans' primeval instincts and adrenaline, and they perceive their surroundings with a sharper, clearer eye. This covers not just their immediate surroundings but beyond—stimuli from within the national borders and beyond are being assessed for threats or opportunities for safety.

In London, the queen had the American National Anthem played during the changing of the guard at Buckingham Palace—a musical declaration "at a moment when you are a target and victim, we stand with you." (On July 7, 2005, when al-Qaeda set off bombs on a London bus and Underground trains, the U.S. State Department raised the British flag, the first time a foreign flag has been raised at the State Department.)

From the Middle East, we saw different images, no less memorable. A blogger writing under the name of the Anchoress described the instant rage provoked just by the memory:

> Do you remember the dancing woman in the black hijab? On 9/11, we saw pictures from the West Bank, of people dancing in the street, shooting off guns in that insane celebratory fashion they so love, children eating candy . . . and one woman, wearing a black hijab, missing a few teeth because the society in which she lives doesn't offer much by way of dentistry. She shoved her face into the camera and whooped it up in that primitive and shrill style that is part of a woman's limited freedom of expression in her culture: she teased the roof of her mouth with her tongue, flicking it back and forth while keening loudly. This woman in the black hijab rejoiced in the slaughter of 3,000 American civilians and probably went home to make dinner wishing the number had been 300,000.
>
> I remember seeing that woman. I watched her over and over—on 9/11, on 9/12 and for weeks afterward. And every

time I saw her, I thought to myself, quite uncharacteristically: Give me five minutes alone with her. Just five minutes.

In this moment, Americans are hugging their kids, wondering where they will go if they suddenly have to flee a poison gas cloud, radiation, or anthrax from a crop duster. After the airliners began flying again, many citizens still watched them as they crossed the sky, wondering if they would make it to their destination or suddenly veer off course. They are also angry—they want their foes to come out in the open so that they can fight them directly. They are looking for leadership.

For all of his stumbles in the first hours of the crisis, by the time the week was over, George W. Bush was a very different man than the caretaker president elected with a minority of the popular vote. By and large, the response from the Right half of the political spectrum, from elected Republican officials to columnists to talking heads to the average amateur pundit on a bar stool, was uniform and simple: Kill 'em, Kill 'em good.

Bush and the team around him were speaking differently—at least differently than Americans were used to from their leaders. Blunt, plainer, more direct. Bush had said, "When I take action, I'm not going to fire a $2 million missile at a $10 empty tent and hit a camel in the butt. It's going to be decisive," as reported in the September 24, 2001, issue of *Newsweek*.

For a president often dismissed as a cowboy, Bush's first comments regarding the perpetrators of the attacks cemented the John Wayne image in listeners' heads, both here and abroad. "I want justice," Bush said. "And there's an old poster out West . . . I recall, that said, 'Wanted, Dead or Alive.' . . . We're going to find those evildoers, those barbaric people who attacked our country, and we're going to hold them accountable. We're going to hold the people who house them accountable. The people who think they can provide them safe havens will be held accountable. The people who feed them will be held accountable. And the Taliban must take my statement seriously."

This was not a moment to reach for the thesaurus or to aspire to the eloquence of, say, Tony Blair. At a time of crisis, demanding clarity and directness, the phrase "smoke 'em out" was just what the American people wanted to hear—or at least most; the liberal magazine the *Nation* called the phrase "inappropriate, unpresidential." Perhaps they wanted a metaphor with less risk of encouraging teen tobacco use.

The afternoon of the attacks, the secretary of defense, Donald Rumsfeld, addressed reporters while the building was still burning: "I should add that the briefing here is taking place in the Pentagon. The Pentagon is functioning. It will be in business tomorrow." Moments later, the chairman of the Joint Chiefs of Staff, Hugh Shelton, said, "I will tell you up front, I have no intentions of discussing today what comes next, but make no mistake about it, your armed forces are ready."

Vice President Cheney appeared on *Meet the Press* on NBC the Sunday after the attacks, the first time a television program broadcast from Camp David. He echoed other senior officials in declaring that any nations harboring terrorists like bin Laden would face "the full wrath of the United States."[1]

Cheney said he saw nothing to prevent the United States from killing bin Laden if he could be found. Asked by interviewer Tim Russert if he would like bin Laden's "head on a platter," Cheney replied, "I would take it today."

When asked by Russert whether the policy of the administration regarding any future hijacked flights was to "take the plane down," Cheney answered, "Yes. The president made the decision, on my recommendation as well, wholeheartedly concurred in the decision he made, that if the plane would not divert, if they wouldn't pay any attention to instructions to move away from the city, as a last resort, our pilots were authorized to take them out. Now, people say, you know, that's a horrendous decision to make. Well, it is."

Americans suddenly saw a different side of their leaders. There was no longer the time or inclination to make things "pretty."

There was a remarkable broadness to Cheney's first comments:

> It's also important for people to understand that this is a long-term proposition. It's not like, well, even Desert Storm, where we had a buildup for a few months, four days of combat, and it was over with. This is going to be the kind of work that will probably take years because the focus has to be not just on any one individual, the problem here is terrorism. . . . The groups that are terrorist organizations, people that oftentimes move around them, sometimes share common ideologies that operate on a worldwide basis. And what we have to do is take down those networks of terrorist organizations, and as say I think this is going to be a struggle that the United States is going to be involved in for the foreseeable future. There's not going to be an end date that we say, "There, it's all over with." It's going to require constant vigilance on our part to avoid problems in the future, but it's also going to require a major effort and, obviously, quite possibly use of military force.

After the attacks, many commentators observed that Americans were now experiencing what many other nations had suffered for years—mass casualty terrorism on their home soil. Britain had suffered the Irish Republican Army, the Spaniards were attacked by Basque separatists, and the Germans feared the Red Brigades and the Baader-Meinhoff gang. In many countries, terrorism was and is a part of life.

Americans did not accept that, and it is impossible to imagine they ever will. They will take drastic, extreme measures before they resign themselves to accepting terrorist attacks as part of life.

Football fans will understand the metaphor of the "prevent defense," a laid-back approach that focuses solely on stopping the big score and often lets an offense make big gains. Very few football fans like seeing their team use the prevent defense; the common joke is that what it actually "prevents" is you from winning the game. Football fans want to see their team blitz. They want to attack, they want to go on offense, and they want to be feared, not fearful.

The situation is binary—either we are killing them or they are killing us. There is no détente, no stasis, no peaceful coexistence. Any policy that indicates a letup in aggression is opening the door to more mass murder of loved ones.

The Bush administration was lucky—their preferred policy options of ultimatums and military force were exactly what an angry American public demanded.

THE LEFT'S REACTION TO 9/11

On September 12, 2001, neither Noam Chomsky nor Michael Moore was considered the face of the Democratic Party. Chomsky, a professor at the Massachusetts Institute of Technology, describes himself as a libertarian anarchist. Nonetheless, he is definitely considered a member of the Left and is an inspirational figure to many liberals. Moore had established himself as an up-and-coming documentarian and filmmaker with a liberal bent, taking on corporate irresponsibility in *Roger and Me,* American militarism in the satire *Canadian Bacon,* and muckraking journalism in his populist television series *The Awful Truth.* (His critics believed the title was only half right.)

Both men were kind enough to post their initial reaction to the 9/11 attacks on the Internet.

Chomsky, writing on September 12, 2001:

The September 11 attacks were major atrocities. In terms of number of victims they do not reach the level of many others, for example, Clinton's bombing of the Sudan with no credible pretext, destroying half its pharmaceutical supplies and probably killing tens of thousands of people (no one knows, because the US blocked an inquiry at the UN and no one cares to pursue it). . . . It is likely to prove to be a crushing blow to Palestinians and other poor and oppressed people. . . .

In short, the crime is a gift to the hard jingoist right, those who hope to use force to control their domains.

Moore, writing on September 12, 2001:

We fund a lot of oppressive regimes that have killed a lot of innocent people, and we never let the human suffering THAT causes to interrupt our day one single bit.

We have orphaned so many children, tens of thousands around the world, with our taxpayer-funded terrorism (in Chile, in Vietnam, in Gaza, in Salvador) that I suppose we shouldn't be too surprised when those orphans grow up and are a little whacked in the head from the horror we have helped cause. . . .

In just 8 months, Bush gets the whole world back to hating us again. He withdraws from the Kyoto agreement, walks us out of the Durban conference on racism, insists on restarting the arms race—you name it, and Baby Bush has blown it all. . . .

Many families have been devastated tonight. This just is not right. They did not deserve to die. If someone did this to get back at Bush, then they did so by killing thousands of people who DID NOT VOTE for him! Boston, New York, DC, and the planes' destination of California—these were places that voted AGAINST Bush!"

(Moore quickly removed that passage from his Web site and its archives, but outraged bloggers had already cached the page.)

There are a few other reactions of note on that Wednesday. Senator Robert Torricelli (Democrat from New Jersey) spoke on the Senate floor, like many of his colleagues. Some of his remarks hit just the right note. "At the outset, it must be made clear this is not a law enforcement matter," Torricelli said. "It does not matter who rented the cars or even who flew the airplanes. They are agents of others. I will find no satisfaction in their indictment, whether they are alive or deceased. It is those who wrote the plan, harbored the conspirators, gave them sanctuary within their borders."

But Torricelli appeared to be one of the first to argue that some portion of the American people's anger ought to be focused on their own government for failing to protect them:

I cannot return to the people of New Jersey who have lost hundreds or, tragically, even thousands of citizens without explaining the role of the U.S. Government in their defense. The scale of what occurred in the last 48 hours may have been unpredictable, but the source and the means and the targets were not. The American people have trusted this Government through our intelligence communities to defend our Nation and its people and our varied interests. This has not occurred. It is my belief that the President of the United States should form a board of general inquiry to review the actions of the U.S. intelligence community and the failures which led to this massive loss of life and compromise of national security.

It was ironic that this New Jersey senator would be the first to point the finger at the intelligence community, when he was the architect of the Torricelli Rule, a policy change that required a top CIA official—not a field officer—to approve the hiring of an informant with ties to human rights violations. The policy arose in the mid-1990s after Torricelli harshly criticized the agency's hiring of an informant with links to the murders of two American citizens. The resulting "scrub" of agents removed about 1,000 clandestine sources from the CIA's roster, about one-third of the total.[2]

Many intelligence officials and right-of-center national security analysts argued Torricelli's rule had a chilling effect on the recruitment of informants inside terror cells, and after the 9/11 attacks, Congress quickly repealed the policy. But Torricelli insisted that there was no evidence that the policy had impeded U.S. intelligence-gathering.

When President Bush met with congressional leaders on September 12, Senator Tom Daschle cautioned Bush about his rhetoric, saying that "war is a powerful word" (and therefore perhaps should not be used), and Senator Robert Byrd warned Bush that he should not expect a Tonkin Gulf–style "blank check" to conduct war. Fascinatingly, about 24 hours after the passengers of Flight 93 prevented the likely destruction of the U.S. Capitol Building, Byrd found time to worry that Bush would exceed his constitutional authority.[3]

The following day, Byrd won Senate approval for a new $2 million West Virginia University computer network serving the Robert C. Byrd Regional Training Institute, then under construction at the National Guard's Camp Dawson post in Kingwood in his home state. Byrd made the case that the spending was necessary to help the war on terror, arguing that the computer network would link emergency workers with national specialists who could get help to people nearby. He openly discussed his aim to turn the National Guard camp into a national antiterrorism center, despite the fact that Fort McClellan in Alabama already performed a similar function.

If the worst mistakes that Democrats made on the issue of terrorism were excessive caution in rhetoric, a knee-jerk protection of their constitutional authorities in war, using the crisis as an excuse for additional pork, and finger-pointing at the intelligence community, then they would be small sins. Republicans such as Ted Stevens of Alaska had been nearly as enthusiastic about justifying spending in their home states in the name of national security, and Richard Shelby's (Alabama) review of the intelligence community was marked by a strong, some said personal, animosity toward CIA director George Tenet.

But if most Democratic officeholders were only making excusable mistakes in their immediate response to the crisis, the thinkers, writers, and activists who were popular voices within the party were not nearly as careful.

The vast majority of Democrats directed their outrage at the hijackers, their al-Qaeda support network, terrorist mastermind Osama bin Laden, and the Taliban regime that sheltered and aided them. Not quite everyone, however, was rolling up their sleeves to take the fight to al-Qaeda. A gleeful "America had it coming" mold began to sprout on the farthest left branches of the Democratic Party, overlapping a bit with some Green Party members, and those so far to the extreme that no major political party represented their views.

Peter Beinart, editor of the left-of-center but often hawkish *New Republic* magazine, noted a disturbing reaction among some members of the antiglobalism protester crowd:

"World Trade Centre . . . anti capitalism . . . anti globalisation . . . was it one of us?" So read a Tuesday posting on www.urban75.com, a site popular with antiglobalization activists from around the world.

"Can we draw one tiny element of goodness from this, in that it will maybe make America think again about its apparent invincibility in the modern age, or will this only serve to make them worse?" From someone called "twisted nerve": "Maybe this is what was needed to make a change for the better??? It was only a matter of time." Another correspondent joked, "looting anyone?"

Perhaps the initial comments of Chomsky and Moore could be dismissed as impertinent and shocked reactions to stunning events. And perhaps the Web postings noticed by Beinart were the tasteless snarky bile of nose-ringed teenagers still working out their Freudian issues. But neither additional years nor the passage of weeks seemed to temper the reaction of those farthest to the left. In fact, as the grim work of excavating the bodies began in earnest, the denunciations of America picked up steam as well.

Katha Pollitt, *Nation* magazine columnist, wrote on September 20, 2001:

My daughter, who goes to Stuyvesant High School only blocks from the World Trade Center, thinks we should fly an American flag out our window. Definitely not, I say: The flag stands for jingoism and vengeance and war. . . . Bombing Afghanistan to "fight terrorism" is to punish not the Taliban but the victims of the Taliban, the people we should be supporting. At the same time, war would reinforce the worst elements in our own society—the flag-wavers and bigots and militarists.

Also on September 20, *San Francisco Chronicle* columnist Debra Saunders reported the tasteless politicization of a Day of Remembrance for victims of the 9/11 attacks. Paul Holm, attended to remember his former partner, Mark Bingham, who was on United Airlines flight 93. Saunders wrote:

> Nice idea, except that former San Francisco Supervisor Amos Brown actually used the event to attack America—stoking some residents' sense of superiority on foreign policy issues.
>
> Said Brown: "America, America, what did you do—either intentionally or unintentionally—in the world order, in Central America, in Africa where bombs are still blasting?"
>
> And: "America, what did you do in the global warming conference when you did not embrace the smaller nations? America, what did you do two weeks ago when I stood at the world conference on racism, when you wouldn't show up?"
>
> The crowd cheered.
>
> Holm walked out.
>
> "I thought this was a day of remembrance and not a political event," Holm explained yesterday. "These were innocent people, a number of whom gave their lives for the country and to save other innocent people."

Some Democrats, who knew they would face voters the following November, took a more responsible tone. Saunders noted that Representative Nancy Pelosi (Democrat from San Francisco) publicly chided Brown. She noted, "The act of terrorism on September 11 put those people outside the order of civilized behavior, and we will not take responsibility for that."

But—in a sign that certain Democrats lacked the spine to clash publicly with the "America had it coming" crowd—Ross also went up to Senator Barbara Boxer and Governor Gray Davis at the Day of Remembrance ceremony and told them Brown's comments were a disgrace. But neither objected publicly like Pelosi.

These were key moments for the Left and the Democratic Party. It was hard to make the traditional isolationist argument—the war itself had come to America's cities. Traditional nonmilitary options such as trade sanctions or diplomatic isolation would have little effect on the Taliban.

Many antiwar protesters focused on the inevitable Afghan civilian casualties that would result from almost any military action against the Taliban. This pacifist position concluded that war—any war, no matter how carefully executed—required too much of a moral compromise. Of course, neither al-Qaeda nor the Taliban gave a moment's thought to the moral compromises of flying hijacked airplanes into buildings.

Many on the right began referring to George Orwell's essay, "Pacifism and the War":

Pacifism is objectively pro-Fascist. This is elementary common sense. If you hamper the war effort of one side you automatically help that of the other. Nor is there any real way of remaining outside such a war as the present one. In practice, "he that is not with me is against me." The idea that you can somehow remain aloof from and superior to the struggle, while living on food which British sailors have to risk their lives to bring you, is a bourgeois illusion bred of money and security. Mr. Savage remarks that "according to this type of reasoning, a German or Japanese pacifist would be 'objectively pro-British.' " But of course he would be! That is why pacifist activities are not permitted in those countries (in both of them the penalty is, or can be, beheading) while both the

Germans and the Japanese do all they can to encourage the spread of pacifism in British and American territories. The Germans even run a spurious "freedom" station which serves out pacifist propaganda indistinguishable from that of the P.P.U. They would stimulate pacifism in Russia as well if they could, but in that case they have tougher babies to deal with. In so far as it takes effect at all, pacifist propaganda can only be effective against those countries where a certain amount of freedom of speech is still permitted; in other words it is helpful to totalitarianism.[4]

There was, and is, no pacifist wing of al-Qaeda.

With no serious or immediate proposals to stop further attacks, the message from these voices of the antiwar Left was clear: "I value my moral purity more than your life."

Many Democrats didn't agree with that, of course. Some disagreed publicly and passionately. Others, like Boxer and Davis, held their tongues. Perhaps the quiet Democrats found the antiwar voices to be fellow travelers who had proven too helpful and passionate to rebuke publicly. Trashing them in public would sound too much like giving aid and comfort to the Bush administration, and the last thing one wanted to do was encourage the right-wingers. Best to keep it in the family. The honor of men like Mark Bingham and Tom Burnett was small potatoes compared to the more pressing priority of maintaining a political coalition.

A clear split emerged between liberals who faced reelection in 2002 and those who sat secure in tenured faculty lounges or Hollywood throwing darts at the pro-war majority in newspaper and magazine columns.

"It may have seemed meaningless at the time, but now we know why 7,000 people sacrificed their lives: So that we'd all forget how Bush stole a presidential election," wrote cartoonist Ted Rall in the

September 27 Philadelphia *City Paper.* (Rall would later gain notoriety for a cartoon that mocked 9/11 widows as publicity-seeking gold diggers.)

Filmmaker Oliver Stone started defending the hijackers, as quoted by Jeffrey Wells on Reel.com, October 10:

> Six men [the heads of Viacom, Fox News Corp., Disney, Vivendi, Sony, and Time Warner–AOL] are deciding what you're seeing in film, and they own all the small companies. . . . Now, within reason, they let [filmmakers] do certain things, and that is far better obviously than, say, the Arabs where they don't let you do anything, and I agree it's relative. But we are in a dilemma. We have too much order. . . . And I think the revolt on September 11 was about order. It was about f—k you, f—k your order. . . . And is it time perhaps to reconsider the world order? Is it time to wonder why the banks have joined the movie companies and all the corporations, and where this is all going?

"Does anybody make a connection between the 2000 election and the events of September 11th?" Stone asked, adding, "Look for the thirteenth month!" He went on to say that the Palestinians who danced at the news of the attack were reacting just as people had responded after the revolutions in France and Russia.[5]

Hollywood, for better or for worse, has long been associated with the Democratic Party. The party loves celebrities' glamour, star power, and fund-raising abilities but could do without their wackier recommendations for American national security strategies. For example, Richard Gere, in an interview with ABC News Radio, October 10, 2001, said, "In a situation like this, of course you identify with everyone who's suffering. [But we must also think about] the terrorists who are creating such horrible future lives for themselves because of the negativity of this karma. It's all of our jobs to keep our minds as expansive as possible. If you can see [the terrorists] as a relative who's dangerously sick and we have to give them medicine, and the medicine is love and compassion. There's nothing better."

While Hollywood was calling for strikes of love and compassion, most Americans preferred the use of daisy-cutter bombs and special forces. Congress was nearly entirely united in support of military force. But there was opposition from a few Democrats representing the safest of seats. Dennis Kucinich of Ohio told the Cleveland *Plain Dealer,* "Afghanistan may be an incubator of terrorism, but it doesn't follow that we bomb Afghanistan."[6]

His colleague from Hawaii, Neal Abercrombie, endorsed Kucinich's longtime suggestion to establish a "Department of Peace." "Only now are we trying to figure out what is Islam," Abercrombie said. "Maybe if there was a Department of Peace, they would be able to say, 'Uh-oh, we've got some problems with these people. . . . I truly believe that if we had a Department of Peace, we would have seen [9/11] coming."[7]

On October 1, 2001, the *Nation* established itself as the leading publication for the "Don't Hit the Taliban" coalition: "This is not really the war of democracy versus terror that the world will be asked to believe in the coming days," wrote Robert Fisk. "It is also about US missiles smashing into Palestinian homes and US helicopters firing missiles into a Lebanese ambulance in 1996 and American shells crashing into a village called Qana and about a Lebanese militia— paid and uniformed by America's Israeli ally—hacking and raping and murdering their way through refugee camps."

On October 3, the *Village Voice* asked prominent New York intellectuals how they would respond to the 9/11 attacks:

Howard Zinn, author of ***The People's History of the United States:*** Treat this as if a criminal is taking refuge in a neighborhood of poor, desperate people who will not give him away. Try to apprehend the evil one. Don't bomb the neighborhood, but clean it up with food, jobs, good housing, and health care, in order to get at the root of terrorism and eliminate the pool of desperation from which terrorists are recruited.

Gloria Steinem, founder, *Ms*. magazine: Many of the Afghan women who have been warning us about the Taliban for years say that bombing would be the surest way to unite most Afghanis around them. We need an act as positive as the terrorists were negative. For example, a massive airlift of food and medicine into Afghanistan. Instead of dividing the world into Islam and the West, we need to make clear that we are part of the same world.

Alice Walker, novelist: In a war on Afghanistan, Osama bin Laden will either be left alive, while thousands of impoverished, frightened people are bombed into oblivion around him, or he will be killed in a bombing attack for which he seems quite prepared. But what would happen to his cool armor if he could be reminded of all the good, nonviolent things he has done? Further, what would happen to him if he could be brought to understand the preciousness of the lives he has destroyed? I firmly believe the only punishment that works is love.

The smoke was still burning where two skyscrapers had once stood, and Americans were still mourning the murder of more than 3,000 of their countrymen. To declare "love" the appropriate response to the situation is to merrily vault beyond the crudest "kumbayah" parody.

Obviously, these intellectuals, thinkers, writers, and columnists were not elected members of the Democratic Party. And only a few stray House members were echoing their arguments. Many elected Democratic officials who began their political career protesting the Vietnam War, including John Kerry, Barbara Boxer, and Representative Jerrold Nadler of New York, were among those vocally backing military action.

But those pro-war comments were not what stuck in the minds of many conservatives and more than a few independents. They remembered the intellectuals' and celebrities' outrageous comments of veiled support for al-Qaeda. The best news for the DNC taken from these ill-considered comments was merely that the public perception was that "liberals are wimps on terror" instead of "all Democrats are wimps on terror."

As the party would soon learn, once the former conclusion took hold, it wasn't hard for the latter to set in as well. This perception took root among many voters beyond Bush's usual loyal constituency of conservatives. A lot of people who hadn't paid attention to politics, the news, or current events were shaken awake by the events of that Tuesday. And in the following weeks and months when they started paying attention, a segment of the Left was proudly shouting, "Don't hit back."

This issue was light-years away from the typical political dispute over taxes, education, or the environment. It was a gut-level need for justice, coupled with a palpable fear of what al-Qaeda still had up its sleeve.

Liberals who argued against the fight at that moment—preferring to accept the risk to American lives rather than make moral compromises—made enemies in those days. The newly awakened pro-war independents would not forget those leftists' words, which they characterized as naïveté, cowardice, or outright sympathy with the terrorists.

While antiwar voices made themselves heard on campuses and newspaper pages, there was only one war opponent in the Congress. The only member to vote against a resolution authorizing military action against the Taliban was Representative Barbara Lee (Democrat from California). This was her statement delivered on September 14, 2001:

> Mr. Speaker, I rise today with a heavy heart, one that is filled with sorrow for the families and loved ones who were killed and injured in New York, Virginia, and Pennsylvania. Only the most foolish or the most callous would not understand the grief that has gripped the American people and millions across the world. This unspeakable attack on the United States has forced me to rely on my moral compass, my conscience, and my God for direction.
>
> September 11 changed the world. Our deepest fears now haunt us. Yet I am convinced that military action will not prevent further acts of international terrorism against the United States.
>
> I know that this use-of-force resolution will pass although we all know that the President can wage a war even without this resolution. However difficult this vote may be, some of us must urge the use of restraint. There must be some of us who say, let's step back for a moment and think through the implications of our actions today—let us more fully understand its consequences.
>
> We are not dealing with a conventional war. We cannot respond in a conventional manner. I do not want to see this spiral out of control. This crisis involves issues of national security, foreign policy, public safety, intelligence gathering, economics, and murder. Our response must be equally multi-faceted.

We must not rush to judgment. Far too many innocent people have already died. Our country is in mourning. If we rush to launch a counter-attack, we run too great a risk that women, children, and other non-combatants will be caught in the crossfire. Nor can we let our justified anger over these outrageous acts by vicious murderers inflame prejudice against all Arab Americans, Muslims, Southeast Asians, or any other people because of their race, religion, or ethnicity. Finally, we must be careful not to embark on an open-ended war with neither an exit strategy nor a focused target. We cannot repeat past mistakes.

In 1964, Congress gave President Lyndon Johnson the power to "take all necessary measures" to repel attacks and prevent further aggression. In so doing, this House abandoned its own constitutional responsibilities and launched our country into years of undeclared war in Vietnam. At that time, Senator Wayne Morse, one of two lonely votes against the Tonkin Gulf Resolution, declared, "I believe that history will record that we have made a grave mistake in subverting and circumventing the Constitution of the United States. . . . I believe that within the next century, future generations will look with dismay and great disappointment upon a Congress which is now about to make such a historic mistake."

Senator Morse was correct, and I fear we make the same mistake today. And I fear the consequences. I have agonized over this vote. But I came to grips with it in the very painful yet beautiful memorial service today at the National Cathedral. As a member of the clergy so eloquently said, "As we act, let us not become the evil that we deplore." [8]

Lee's arguments, no matter how well-meaning, were nonsensical. They also were more than a little insulting to the vast majority of

Americans who supported hitting back at the Taliban as soon as possible.

One cannot say, "Let's step back for a moment and think through the implications of our actions today—let us more fully understand its consequences," without inferring that those who did support the resolution—420 out of 431 members of the House—didn't think through the implications or fully understand its consequences. It takes either extraordinary confidence or extraordinary arrogance to stand alone and declare, "I am correct; every last one of my peers is wrong."

Either way, history has proven that Lee made a spectacularly wrong prediction when she suggested that bombing the Taliban would "spiral out of control." She lamented the "rush to judgment." Just how much colder did she want the trail to bin Laden to become?

She said, "We run too great a risk that women, children, and other non-combatants will be caught in the crossfire"—this is unfortunately the nature of all wars. To refuse to strike at enemies for fear of hitting noncombatants in the crossfire is to refuse to ever take military action at all.

Notice also the non sequitur that somehow taking military action against the Taliban will "inflame prejudice against all Arab Americans, Muslims, Southeast Asians." There were, unfortunately, some cases of anti-Muslim and anti-Arab hatred after 9/11. The Council on Foreign Relations stated that in the six months after the attacks, the FBI had initiated some 325 investigations of possible September 11–related hate crimes involving Arab, Muslim, or Sikh victims. The Justice Department listed nine murders as possible hate crimes.

However, some perspective is in order. Imagine a 9/11-style attack in Moscow, and imagine how the famously tolerant Russian society would treat Chechens, Tartars, Jews, or any other foreign presence in its midst. Or how the Chinese would handle a threat from ethnic Tibetans. Or how the French would treat Algerians after a devastating attack that killed thousands. Or the Turkish Republic's delicate and gentle touch when dealing with Kurdish separatists and responding to terrorist attacks of the PKK (Kurdistan Workers Party).

The concept of many different cultures, races, and religions living together in harmony is a fairly new concept in human history—and that social cohesion is put to the test after any traumatic experience. For a society to overwhelmingly resist the eons-old temptations of paranoia, tribalism, scapegoating, and mob justice is a giant step in humanity's violent history.

We would all prefer to live in a world where no one reacted to a massive terrorist attack with ethnic-based hatred. But as long as there are humans, there will be a small minority who hate. For a nation of 280 million traumatized citizens to only experience several hundred instances of hate crime is actually a significant accomplishment.

Note that Lee urges the need for an "exit strategy." At a time when everyone in America was focused on the mission—eliminating the threat posed by al-Qaeda and its Taliban protectors—Lee focused on how quickly the mission could be finished and U.S. forces could return home. At that moment, what mattered were objectives, not deadlines.

But no objection to any modern war from the Left is complete without a comparison to Vietnam. No matter whom the United States is fighting, no matter how different the terrain, nations in the combat zone, the combatants' culture, language, history, military training and skills, allies, opponents, technology, tactics, supply lines, infrastructure, or belief system, too many American liberals see "Vietnam all over again."

While fires were still burning at Ground Zero, a Democrat stood on the House floor and argued for a pacifist course of action. It was a key portentous sign of the problems her party would face in the coming years.

Yes, Barbara Lee is only one member of Congress. But when the vote is 420 to 1, people notice that one. And no voter mistook her arguments, logic, or viewpoint for that of the Republican Party.

Her vote also stuck in the craw of the pro-war majority—or at least in the craw of many conservatives. How could anyone oppose hitting back at the Taliban when they refused to hand over bin Laden? And, they wondered, did Barbara Lee symbolize the Democratic antiwar id, barely repressed during a time of crisis?

Her notorious vote would come back to haunt Texas Democrat Ron Kirk, who ran for his state's open Senate seat in 2002. His opponent, John Cornyn, scored points by spotlighting Kirk's appearance at a California fund-raiser with Lee. "I don't know how my opponent can talk strong on national defense, and then cavort happily in San Francisco with the very people trying to subvert his agenda," Cornyn said.[9]

Of course, Lee was not the only Democrat to make a comment that looked foolish in hindsight. Nicholas Lemann of the *New Yorker* interviewed Senator Hillary Rodham Clinton on September 25. "We talked about possible responses to the attack," Lemann writes, "and then I asked her how she thought people would react to knowing that they are on the receiving end of a murderous anger." "Oh, I am well aware that it is out there," Senator Clinton responded. She continued:

> One of the most difficult experiences that I personally had in the White House was during the health-care debate, being the object of extraordinary rage. I remember being in Seattle. I was there to make a speech about health care. This was probably August of '94. Radio talk-show hosts had urged their listeners to come out and yell and scream and carry on and prevent people from hearing me speak. There were threats that were coming in, and certain people didn't want me to speak, and they started taking weapons off people, and

arresting people. I've had firsthand looks at this unreasoning anger and hatred that is focused on an individual you don't know, a cause that you despise—whatever motivates people.

Comparing her experiences with angry protesters to the 9/11 attacks was clumsy at best and shockingly narcissistic. (Almost alone among Democrats, Senator Clinton has sounded like a resolute hawk since the attacks, making this gaffe an early misstep she has largely avoided since.)

On October 9, Representative Jim McDermott criticized the U.S.-led attacks on military targets in Afghanistan, questioning whether President Bush had "thought this action out completely or fully examined America's cause."

"The destruction of the infrastructure did not work in Iraq a decade ago," McDermott said in the statement. "This sounds an awful lot like Iraq. Saddam Hussein is still in power! It is Iraq's citizenry, not Saddam, which continues to suffer the consequences of those air and missile strikes during the Gulf War and the sanctions we subsequently imposed against that nation. . . . I miss the point of needing to strike now. He has not made that clear to anybody, either in his public statements or anything I've heard in the Congress."

In his written statement, McDermott also took issue with what he perceived as a rush to war: "I am not so sure that we have fully developed a comprehensive strategic plan. It has been less than a month since the terrorist attacks against our country. A scant four weeks to plan and implement an operation like this doesn't seem like a very long time to me."

McDermott did not address the differences between the extensive air defense system and the large number of troops that defended Iraq during the Gulf War and the Taliban's limited military infrastructure. His statement came the day an *ABC News–Washington Post* poll revealed that 94 percent of Americans supported the strikes against Taliban targets in Afghanistan.

Around this time, New York's mayor Rudolph Giuliani turned down a $10 million donation from a Saudi prince, Alwaleed bin Talal, because it was accompanied by a statement from Alwaleed demanding that America "re-examine its policies in the Middle East and adopt a more balanced stance toward the Palestinian cause."

Shortly after the news of this rejection broke, Representative Cynthia McKinney (Democrat from Georgia) wrote a public "letter of apology" to Alwaleed. The letter began by agreeing with the Saudi's anti-Israel views, then went on to describe America's social problems and offered to help steer the donation to charities she felt were deserving:

> Although your offer was not accepted by Mayor Giuliani, I would like to ask you to consider assisting Americans who are in dire need right now. I believe we can guide your generosity to help improve the state of Black America and build better lives. My office can provide you with a list of charities who labor under the most difficult circumstances to try and improve the lives of the people they serve. I hope you will consider reaching out to our charities and to our people who are in need. Please do not hesitate to contact me with any questions you may have.

Again, these were the moments when the American people were paying the closest attention to their leaders. Craven opportunism and sucking up to a hateful oil baron who wanted to use his charity-with-strings as a chance to lecture Americans about the sinfulness of their policies confirmed everyone's worst suspicions of what politicians are made of. With $10 million on the line, and a Saudi prince on one side and the American people on another, McKinney made it clear whom she stood with.

At a time when the Democrats needed to look serious, thoughtful, and determined, their most prominent foreign policy voice in the Senate was behaving . . . *oddly*. Michael Crowley reported in the *New Republic* on October 22:

Joe Biden is bounding up the steps of the Russell Senate Office Building, wearing his trademark grin. As he makes for the door, he is met by a group of airline pilots and flight attendants looking vaguely heroic in their navy-blue uniforms and wing-shaped pins. A blandly handsome man in a pilot's cap steps forward and asks Biden to help pass emergency benefits for laid-off airline workers. Biden nods as the men and women cluster around him with fawning smiles. Then he speaks. "I hope you will support my work on Amtrak as much as I have supported you," he begins. (Biden rides Amtrak to work every day and is obsessed with the railroad.) "If not, I will *screw you badly.*"

A dozen faces fall in unison as Biden lectures on. "You've not been good to me. You're also damn selfish. You better listen to me. . . ." It goes on like this for a couple of minutes. Strangely, Biden keeps grinning—even fraternally slapping the stunned man's shoulder a couple of times. . . .

At the Tuesday-morning meeting with committee staffers, Biden launches into a stream-of-consciousness monologue about what his [Senate Foreign Relations] committee should be doing, before he finally admits the obvious: "I'm groping here." Then he hits on an idea: America needs to show the Arab world that we're not bent on its destruction. "Seems to me this would be a good time to send, no strings attached, a check for $200 million to Iran," Biden declares. He surveys the table with raised eyebrows, a *How do ya like that?* look on his face.

The staffers sit in silence. Finally somebody ventures a response: "I think they'd send it back." Then another aide speaks up delicately: "The thing I would worry about is that it would almost look like a publicity stunt." Still another reminds Biden that an Iranian delegation is in Moscow that very day to discuss a $300 million arms deal with Vladimir Putin that the United States has strongly condemned.

It is conceivable that "I will *screw you badly*" and "You're also damn selfish" are not quite the pitch-perfect responses to employees of an industry that had recently heard of their colleagues having their throats slashed and who at that moment faced unprecedented financial and security crises. And sending a $200 million check to the world's top sponsors of terrorism seems, perhaps in retrospect, a wee bit counterintuitive in a war on terrorism.

On October 24, Representative David Bonior (Michigan), perhaps angling for Arab-American votes in the 2002 governor's race, attacked the FBI over a Michigan State Police report on alleged terrorist activity in the Wolverine State. The report alleged "almost every major terrorist organization has operatives in Michigan," which has one of the biggest concentrations of Arabs outside the Middle East. "The Detroit/Dearborn area is a major financial support center for many Mideast terrorist groups," the report stated. "Southeast Michigan is known as a lucrative recruiting area and potential support base for international terrorist groups. It is also conceivable that 'sleeper cells' may be located in that area of the state."

Bonior declared that he did not share the bureau's suspicions.

"I'm often skeptical of the FBI pointing fingers," he said. "They have a history of doing this and not being correct. This insinuation, this kind of character assassination of a community, is the kind of thing that went on during the McCarthy era."

On November 7, 2001, Bill Clinton spoke at Georgetown University. He found himself in hot water for these comments:

> First of all, terror, the killing of noncombatants for economic, political or religious reasons, has a very long history as long as organized combat itself, and yet, it has never succeeded as a military strategy standing on its own, but it has been around a long time. Those of us who come from various European lineages are not blameless. Indeed, in the first Crusade, when the Christian soldiers took Jerusalem, they first burned a synagogue with 300 Jews in it, and proceeded to kill every woman and child who was Muslim on the Temple Mount. The contemporaneous descriptions of the event describe soldiers walking on the Temple Mount, a holy place to Christians, with blood running up to their knees. I can tell you that the story is still being told today in the Middle East and we are still paying for it. Here in the United States, we were founded as a nation that practiced slavery, and slaves were, quite frequently, killed even though they were innocent. This country once looked the other way when significant numbers of Native Americans were dispossessed and killed to get their land or their mineral rights or because they were thought of as less than fully human, and we are still paying the price today. Even in the 20th century in America, people were terrorized or killed because of their race. And even today, though we have continued to walk, sometimes to stumble, in the right direction, we still have the occasional hate crime rooted in race, religion, or sexual orientation. So terror has a long history.[10]

Clinton's comments were factually true, but "those of us who come from various European lineages are not blameless" were just the wrong words at the wrong time. As University of Tennessee law professor Glenn Reynolds put it, "At another time, Clinton's remarks might have sounded different—but context is everything, as politicians are supposed to know. A war, and the aftermath of an attack in which thousands of Americans were killed, is just not the right time to be giving a speech that talks about America's historical shortcomings. Sorry, but it's just not."

The pacifism of Barbara Lee, the I'm-a-victim-too solipsism of Hillary Clinton, the incoherence of Joe Biden, the it-will-never-work pessimism of Jim McDermott, the opportunism of Cynthia McKinney, the knee-jerk cries of McCarthyism from David Bonior, and Bill Clinton's clumsy "we're not blameless" rhetoric all painted a portrait of a Democratic Party caught flatfooted, unprepared, and unready to fight a war on terror. The Democrats who were singing from the hawkish songbook faded into the time's overwhelming patriotism, but these discordant notes stood out as completely out of tune with public sentiment.

One hundred two days after the 9/11 attacks, the Taliban had been removed from power. After the Taliban fell and Americans saw Afghanis celebrating their defeat, it would have been a terrific time for the Left to reconsider its views. Instead, James Carroll, a liberal columnist for the *Boston Globe*, found reason for gloom: "The celebrated results have so far followed from the American war —collapse of the Taliban, liberation of women —are welcome indeed, but they are relatively peripheral outcomes, unrelated to the stated American war aim of defeating terrorism. And these outcomes pale in significance when the conflict is seen in the context of a larger question: Does this intervention break, or at least impede, the cycle of violence in which terrorism is only the latest turn? . . . The more this war is deemed 'just,' the more it seems wrong." [11]

THE MISSTEPS ON THE RIGHT

Some Republicans and conservative leaders also made comments after 9/11 that look foolish, obnoxious, or hateful now. Ann Coulter wrote in her syndicated column on September 13, "We should invade their countries, kill their leaders and convert them to Christianity. We weren't punctilious about locating and punishing only Hitler and his top officers. We carpet-bombed German cities; we killed civilians. That's war. And this is war."

Then there was the infamous exchange between Jerry Falwell and Pat Robertson on the *700 Club* on September 13, 2001. Falwell said, "I really believe that the pagans, and the abortionists, and the feminists, and the gays and lesbians who are actively trying to make that an alternative lifestyle, the ACLU, People for the American Way—all of them who have tried to secularize America—I point the finger in their face and say, 'You helped this happen.' " Robertson replied, "Well, I totally concur, and the problem is we have adopted their agenda at the highest levels of our government."

And on September 17, Representative John Cooksey (Republican from Louisiana) said, "If I see someone come in that's got a diaper on his head and a fan belt [wrapped] around [it], that guy needs to be pulled over and checked."

But unlike many on the Left, all of these voices on the Right suffered consequences from their ideological brethren. *National Review Online* dropped Coulter's column. Falwell apologized after being widely criticized by conservative columnists. And White House press secretary Ari Fleischer's infamous "watch what they say" remarks were in reference to Cooksey's remarks, not Bill Maher's.

At the September 26, 2001, press conference, Fleischer said, "And that's why—there was an earlier question about has the president said anything to people *in his own party*—they're reminders to all

Americans that they need to watch what they say, watch what they do. This is not a time for remarks like that; there never is."

Think back to Michael Moore's first public words the day after the attacks. Now read *Time* magazine essayist Lance Morrow:

> Anyone who does not loathe the people who did these things, and the people who cheer them on, is too philosophical for decent company.
>
> It's a practical matter, anyway. In war, enemies are enemies. You find them and put them out of business, on the sound principle that that's what they are trying to do to you. If what happened on Tuesday does not give Americans the political will needed to exterminate men like Osama bin Laden and those who conspire with them in evil mischief, then nothing ever will and we are in for a procession of black Tuesdays. . . .
>
> This is the moment of clarity. Let the civilized toughen up, and let the uncivilized take their chances in the game they started.[12]

Morrow's words nailed the national consciousness much more accurately than Moore's. Glenn Reynolds observed, as the sign on a local sporting goods shop put it, less grandly but no less eloquently: "You Sorry Bastards Are F—ed."

It's easy to forget just how intense the public anger was in those first weeks. *Newsday* reported that a poll conducted from September 12 to September 19 found that one-third of New Yorkers supported internment camps for people who are "sympathetic to terrorist causes."

Nearly 90 percent of those surveyed in an NBC/*Wall Street Journal* poll conducted in early October said that taking up arms against the terrorists is worth it even if it risks further attacks on America. Of course, a particular branch of conservative thought—the infamous "neocons"—have come up with a more detailed plan: kill the terrorists, kill the dictators, and let the Muslim world share the fruits of democracy and capitalism. They've taken the Pearl Harbor comparisons to heart and concluded this is a sequel to World War II's noble cause—except this time it is the Middle East that must be liberated from merciless and expansionist regimes.

Behind the scenes, the talk in Bush's White House was even more pugnacious. Informed on the evening of 9/11 that al-Qaeda was a "60-country problem," Bush replied, "Let's pick them off one at a time." A week later, he declared, "We're going to rain holy hell on them. . . . I want to have them quaking in their boots."

Cofer Black, a CIA counterterrorism chief, said in official meetings, "When we're through with them, they will have flies walking across their eyeballs. . . . We're going to kill them. We're going to put their heads on sticks. We're going to rock their world." [13]

Surely some Democrats talk like this. But it's almost unimaginable that one would use these words in public rhetoric.

THE 2002 CAMPAIGNS

Republicans entered 2002 knowing that the political landscape had been changed forever. While bin Laden had escaped from Tora Bora, many al-Qaeda trainees and some leaders were killed and captured. The Taliban had been driven from power; the rulers of Afghanistan were reduced to hiding in caves in the mountains.

The White House knew that President Bush and his party had a strong record on what was now the preeminent issue in American politics. On January 19, 2002, Bush's top political adviser, Karl Rove, told a high-level gathering at the Republican National Committee,

"We can go to the country on this issue, because they trust the Republican Party to do a better job of protecting and strengthening America's military might and thereby protecting America."

Democrats were outraged that Rove said that. However, they didn't act as if it were true and that it could cost them in the upcoming elections.

Democratic pollster Mark Mellman repeatedly argued that voters in post-9/11 America wouldn't be all that different from the ones in the previous era. He insisted health care, education, and prescription drugs were as potent voter concerns as terror threats, making the case in an essay in the trade publication *Campaigns and Elections*, citing his own polls, as well as interviews with *USA Today* and *The Hill*. With the 2002 elections fast approaching, he declared that health care was "the dominant issue of the next decade." [14]

While the pollsters were telling the Democrats that the strategy from the year 2000 would still work, some members of the party were finding new ways to look paranoid or arrogant. Representative Cynthia McKinney—writer of the infamous letter to the Saudi prince—called for an investigation into whether President Bush and other government officials had advance notice of terrorist attacks on September 11 but did nothing to prevent them. She stated, "persons close to this administration are poised to make huge profits off America's new war." In an interview with a Berkeley, California, radio station, McKinney said, "We know there were numerous warnings of the events to come on September 11th. . . . What did this administration know and when did it know it, about the events of September 11th? Who else knew, and why did they not warn the innocent people of New York who were needlessly murdered? . . . What do they have to hide?" [15]

In May 2002, the nation's political leaders concluded that enough time and emotional distance from the attacks had passed to wonder about the performance of the FBI, CIA, and executive branch. (Aside from Torricelli, who began questioning these agencies less than 24 hours after the attacks.)

If there is any Democrat who understands the consequences of the war on terror, it is Tom Daschle. In the fall of 2001, his office was attacked by anthrax in the mail from an assailant unknown at this time. By every account, Daschle handled the crisis about as well as humanly possible.

But even he couldn't avoid hitting the wrong tone. During the debate about whether to establish an independent commission to investigate the attacks, Daschle appeared to indicate that the terrorists' success was attributable to Bush ignoring warnings—and that some other figure would have known how to react to the not terribly specific chatter about hijackings. "I'm gravely concerned about the information provided us just yesterday that the president received a warning in August about the threat of hijackers by Osama bin Laden," Daschle said on May 16, 2002.

It's not often that an alternative-weekly comic strip gets cited on *Meet the Press*, but Tim Russert asked the Senate majority leader for his reaction to Ruben Bolling's "Tom the Dancing Bug," which poked fun at Daschle's insinuation that he could have connected the dots and prevented the attacks. "Sometimes cartoons have a way of cutting through these issues," Russert said.

The comic strip is titled "What if Tom Daschle were president in August 2001?" After being told by a staffer about "increased noise about an al-Qaeda hijacking plot," President Daschle leaps to his feet and immediately orders, "OK, alert the media, and send a mailing to every American. Close down the Empire State Building . . . and the World Trade Center! Federalize airport security immediately, and change the policy for all weapons checks! I want every passenger checked not just for bombs and guns, but also knives . . . even box cutters! And for God's sake—check their shoes!" The scene then changes to a Portland, Maine, hotel, where two men say they're ready to check out. The bald desk clerk thinks to himself, "Hmm. Staying one night. Paying cash. Suspicious." The desk clerk suddenly rips off a *Mission Impossible* style mask—and the terrorists exclaim in shock, "President Daschle!" As he punches out the would-be hijackers, Daschle explains, "It was just a hunch, evil-doer, but it paid off!"

The 9/11 Commission was ultimately formed, because Americans did deserve answers. But the enormity of the events and the intensity of the emotions surrounding them meant a large chunk of the American public had little patience for the usual political Monday morning quarterbacking.

Heading into the fall of 2002, the race for control of Congress pitted the strategies of Tom Daschle and Dick Gephardt on one side, and Karl Rove and the Bush White House on the other. Daschle and company set out to campaign on prescription drugs. The president asked the country to give him a Republican Senate in order to pass a bill establishing a Department of Homeland Security. Democrats wanted to preserve civil service protections for government employees whose agencies would now be under the new DHS. Republicans felt that DHS employees should have the more limited rights of employees of agencies like the FBI, where staff can be reassigned at will to deal with crises. A similar point of contention was language giving the president the authority to waive union agreements when national security is at stake.

The prospect of war with Iraq hung in the background. Republicans unified behind giving the president the authority to do whatever was necessary to deal with Saddam Hussein; Democrats were divided on whether military action against Iraq was warranted.

Bush's campaign message was simple and direct: His administration had al-Qaeda on the run. Securing the country from more attacks required a new Homeland Security Department, but that change was being held up by Democrats who were playing games over labor protections. He hammered how he needed like-minded lawmakers, particularly in the Senate, to protect the country. The president sounded like a broken record on the campaign trail that fall.

Bush, speaking at a fund-raiser for Representative Anne Northrup of Kentucky, September 5, 2002: "I am not going to accept a bill where the Senate micromanages, where the Senate shows they're more interested in special interests in Washington and not interested in the security of the American people."

Bush, speaking at an event for congressional candidate Chris Chocola in South Bend, Indiana, September 5, 2002: "Listen, there are senators up there who are more concerned about special interests in Washington, and not enough concerned about the security of the American people."

Bush, speaking on behalf of Mitt Romney in Massachusetts, October 4, 2002: "They want these work rules to make it difficult for the secretary and the president, and future secretaries and presidents, to be able to move people to the right place at the right time in order to respond to an enemy. For example, if you're working for Customs, we thought it was a wise idea to have people wear radiation-detection devices in order to be able to determine whether somebody is trying to smuggle weapons of mass destruction into America. The union wanted to take that to collective bargaining. It would have taken over a year to determine whether or not people could carry detection devices. That doesn't make any sense for me. . . . I'm all for public employees being able to bargain collectively if that's what they choose to do. But I'm also for making sure the president, in the name of national security, has the capacity to put people at the right place at the right time to protect America."

Bush, speaking on behalf of Norm Coleman in Minnesota, October 18, 2002: "In the name of national security, the president has got to be able to respond quickly. The Senate wants to take away that authority. . . . This is a big issue in this campaign. There's no question where Norm Coleman will stand. He will stand with this president and future presidents."

Bush, speaking on behalf of Jim Talent in Missouri, October 18, 2002: "The Senate wants to say, you can have that authority, Mr. President, to suspend workers' rights or workers' rules, in the case of a national emergency, in the Agriculture Department, but not for the homeland security. And that's not right. Jim Talent understands what I'm talking about. You put him in the Senate, we'll get us a good homeland security bill, which will make it easier for presidents to protect America. . . . You can express yourselves, right in the ballot box. That's the way you can send a message loud and clear about the importance of having a homeland security department that will work today, that will work tomorrow, and will work for decades to come, because this threat, folks, is real for a while."

Bush, speaking on behalf of Saxby Chambliss in downtown Atlanta on October 18, 2002: "Senate Democrats want to tie the hands of this department and determine who we can hire and who we can fire and whether or not people can be moved. Any president must have the capacity to put the right people at the right time at the right place, in order to respond to threats to our homeland. . . . There's no question in my mind, if Saxby Chambliss were in the Senate, I would not have to worry about his leadership or his vote on this important matter."

Bush speaking on October 24, 2002, in Charlotte, North Carolina, campaigning for Elizabeth Dole: "The Senate is stuck. They're more interested in some special interests up there. And I'm not going to stand for it. It's not right for America. I need to be able to put the right people at the right place at the right time to protect America, and Elizabeth Dole will be a strong ally."

The message was clear: When the nation was in a life-or-death struggle, the opposition party had found the time to play partisan politics—and to put the priorities of a preferred special interest group above the needs of the country. If the Democrats couldn't be trusted on homeland security, Bush asked implicitly, how could they be trusted on any other issue?[16]

Other Republicans found their own angles in the national security debate. In New Hampshire, Sununu attacked Shaheen for accepting contributions from the Council for a Livable World—a group critical of the administration's missile defense plans.

The Democratic effort to convince voters that they weren't a bunch of doves got dented on September 29, 2002, when Representatives David Bonior and Jim McDermott appeared live from Baghdad on ABC's *This Week*. Host George Stephanopoulos asked McDermott about his recent comment that "the president of the United States will lie to the American people in order to get us into this war."

McDermott stood his ground: "I believe that sometimes they give out misinformation. . . . It would not surprise me if they came out with some information that is not provable, and they, they shift it. First they said it was al-Qaeda, then they said it was weapons of mass destruction. Now they're going back to saying it's al-Qaeda again."

When Stephanopoulos pressed McDermott about whether he had any evidence that Bush had lied, the congressman replied, "I think the president would mislead the American people."

An American official floating unsubstantiated allegations against an American president during a visit to Baghdad would be troubling enough. But McDermott made a potentially manageable gaffe worse by insisting, despite its twelve years of verifiable prevarication, that the Iraqi regime should be given the benefit of the doubt on inspections and disarmament. Said McDermott on *This Week:* "I think you have to take the Iraqis on their face value."

As it turned out, the WMDs weren't there, and the ties to

al-Qaeda were hotly disputed. But McDermott and Bonior did their party no favor by appearing from the capital city of a hostile regime and contending that Saddam Hussein was more trustworthy than the president of the United States. This was the same president with the approval rating in the high 60s who had just gotten the country through the first year of the post-9/11 era.

As Martin Peretz, publisher of the *New Republic*, wrote after Election Day, "It evoked the craven pilgrimages of British appeasers of Hitler. Just as craven and damaging to Democrats was Gephardt's refusal to upbraid his partner in the House leadership. It wouldn't be surprising if some Americans began wondering how a person like Bonior could have risen so high in the Democratic ranks. It is not a stupid question."

Since 9/11, the Bush administration and the GOP had been making the case that terrorism was different from crime. But McDermott had specifically made comparisons, inferring that Saddam Hussein was entitled to the rights and guarantees of the U.S. criminal justice system. "They have given us assurances that there will be unfettered inspections," McDermott said at an October 2, 2002, press conference he held with Bonior after returning from Iraq. "In the United States, we have a tradition, we have a Constitution that says if there's a bad person there, we give them due process, and inspections is the due process in this example." Americans wanted to see Saddam beaten around like a villain on *24;* these prominent Democratic leaders insisted he be treated like a perp on *Law & Order.*

Ironically, one of the few prominent Democrats willing to utter a critical word of McDermott was Senator John Kerry, who said through a spokesman that he "disapproved of McDermott's comments." It was the right move, but not enough Democrats followed Kerry's lead.

Another odd aspect of the tale of the congressmen in Baghdad was that they never appeared in Republican attack ads—a dog that did not bark, spurring speculation that Gephardt's public support of the Iraq war was preconditioned on the White House and the GOP not using the congressmen in Baghdad in any campaign ads.[17]

In the end, a lot of Democratic candidates said controversial, poorly worded, and plain old stupid comments on the war on terror in the closing weeks of the campaign. Democrat Walter Mondale, the stand-in for the late senator Paul Wellstone in Minnesota, said, "Don't worry about me and terrorism," during his lone debate with Republican Norm Coleman. "I'm opposed to it." The answer was insufficient, too glib, too insubstantive a comment on the voters' top concern.

Democratic senator Jean Carnahan trivialized the terrorist threat when she said Bush had failed to get Osama bin Laden, so he was now targeting her.[18]

Democratic senatorial candidate Ron Kirk, an African-American, said that wars were fought disproportionately by low-income minorities, stating that "people who look like us" are overrepresented in the graves of the war dead but underrepresented on Wall Street and in corporate America. "Those who question our patriotic duty to make sure we have a chance to win, I wonder how excited they'd be if I get to the U.S. Senate and I put forth a resolution that says the next time we go to war, the first kids have to come from families who earn $1 million or more." Kirk said it in front of a group of veterans in San Antonio. For some reason, it didn't go over so well.[19]

Meanwhile, Bush continued to evoke the plain-spoken cowboy. "Thanks to hardworking—the hard work of our intelligence folks and our U.S. military and our friends and allies (applause)—this guy is not a problem anymore, and neither are a couple of thousand of them just like [recently captured al-Qaeda terrorist Ramzi bin al-Shibh] who have been detained. And about that many weren't as lucky."

The GOP campaign song of 2002 was not Queen's "Another One Bites the Dust," but it might as well have been.

BUSH ACES HIS MIDTERMS

Election Day 2002 was the best day for the Republicans since the takeover of Congress in 1994. By the end of the night, Democratic strategist and CNN commentator James Carville put a wastepaper basket over his head. His *Crossfire* foe, columnist Bob Novak, said that love them or hate them, you know what the Republicans stand for, but nobody knows what the Democrats stand for. Responded a clearly disgusted Carville, "You are not just right on ideology, you're right politically. The Democratic Party is a party in search of anything."

A Gallup poll conducted three days after the election showed that only 34 percent of Americans thought Democrats were "tough enough" when it came to dealing with terrorism, compared with 64 percent who thought the GOP was.

Stan Greenberg and Bill McInturff did a poll for the Vietnam Veterans of America Foundation and found that 57 percent of voters said that Bush's performance on "foreign affairs and international issues" had more of an influence on their vote than his performance on "the economy, tax cuts, and corporate corruption." The president's overall job approval among voters at the time of the election was 67 percent, and 74 percent among those voters who made up their mind within the last week before the election. More than three-quarters of voters (76 percent) approved of Bush's handling of "efforts to protect the American people," including 56 percent of Democrats and 73 percent of Independents.

Whatever Democrats had been saying about national security and terrorism in the final weeks of the campaign, the voters hadn't heard it. The Winston Group surveyed 1,000 voters in the days after the election, asking what issue they had heard each party talking about the most. Voters said they heard Democrats talking about the economy (19 percent), education (16 percent), negative campaigning (13 percent), health care (12 percent), "general negative" (12 percent), Social Security (9 percent), taxes (8 percent), employment (8 percent), and the potential war in Iraq (7 percent). Way down the list at nineteenth was terrorism, mentioned by 1 percent. Thirty-eight percent said the topics discussed made them more likely to vote for Democrats; 45 percent said it made them less likely.

By comparison, when voters were asked about what they heard Republicans talking about on the campaign trail, the answers were taxes (17 percent), defense/foreign policy (13 percent), war/Iraq (12 percent), negative campaigning (12 percent), education (12 percent), the economy (11 percent), and terrorism (10 percent). Forty-one percent said the topics made them more likely to vote for Republicans; 40 percent less likely.

As we have seen, the GOP wins of 2004 were quickly attributed to "moral values" and social issues such as gay marriage and abortion. But 2002, a consensus quickly emerged that the midterm decisive issue was protecting the country.

Anchor Aaron Brown stated on CNN: "The economy, the environment, all of those were secondary issues at best. This was an election about national security and supporting the president. . . . I think Bush made a very good argument that there are certain pieces of legislation that [he] wants—namely, bills centering on national security and homeland defense—that the only way to move them is by voting for Republican candidates. I think the White House made a compelling case."

Judy Woodruff, host of *Inside Politics,* said this: "The biggest surprise to me is that the country is ready to turn control of the Senate back to the Republicans. They are basically saying to George Bush, 'Job well done. You've led us through one of the most difficult times our country has ever been through and we have so much confidence in you we are ready to turn over to you not just the White House, but both houses of Congress.' "

In postelection interviews, Daschle and Gephardt all but admitted that the Democratic strategy was to have no coordinated party position on Iraq and to change the subject to domestic issues ASAP. They concluded that the president deserved "good credit" for the results, pointing out that he focused more on the war on terror and issues such as North Korea and Iraq, making it hard for the Democrats to break through on issues like the economy, health care, and education.

The House minority leader, Dick Gephardt (Democrat from Missouri), said, "I think some of it is related to 9/11 and the people's reactions—the people's desire to be united with the president in fighting against these issues, in trying to solve these issues."

Ultimately, Bush campaigned in 23 House races, and his candidate won in 21. Cheney campaigned in 52 districts, some repeatedly. There was one Senate seat that went from Republican to Democrat—when the GOP incumbent divorced his wife and married his much younger staffer. This is a challenging circumstance in most campaign environments; it is particularly difficult in Arkansas, as was the case here. Sometimes you have a race fall in your lap, as Barack Obama would experience two years later. Republicans held five open seats, a rare feat.

"In retrospect, the [Democrats'] emphasis on drugs and health care seemed out of place in the wake of 9/11," says GOP strategist and consultant Fred Wszolek. "But any sort of agenda-control campaign is high risk. The Democrats had a lot of equity built up in health care issues, after the 1998 and 2000 emphasis on patient bill of rights, so they figured that since they couldn't beat Republicans on national security, they should try to change the subject. And the thing about an agenda-control campaign is that you never really know whether it's going to work until after it does—or doesn't."

The one area that the Democrats didn't get walloped was in gubernatorial races, where they won Pennsylvania, Illinois, Wisconsin, Wyoming, Oklahoma, Arizona, Tennessee, and Kansas, and finished the night up three from where they had been. Why? Probably because a governor's job generally deals less with national security than with traditionally strong Democratic issues—education, health care, the environment. The governors' races were the one place that Democrats could pound away on their traditional strengths and not seem like they were dodging pressing national priorities.[20]

"Neither the party itself, in so far as it has a self, nor the individual candidates ever faced the fact that the most serious underlying issues for the country are the internal and external threats to its security," lamented Martin Peretz, publisher of the *New Republic.* "In truth, these constitute one issue, not seamless, but certainly intertwined. The nation is in danger, and Democrats avert their eyes. In this circumstance, it hardly matters whether they are right on prescription drugs for the elderly. . . . The Democratic candidates— most affecting Max Cleland in Georgia, most reflexively Fritz Mondale in Minnesota—put themselves in hock to the labor movement when they promised to support the insupportable: that a Homeland Security Department be unionized. This is tantamount to running the Air Force under a collective bargaining scheme. I am not aware of a single Democratic candidate who demurred from this mad orthodoxy."[21]

Dennis Miller, appearing on the *Tonight Show* the Wednesday after Election Day, summarized the great national changes that the election revealed: "I think that was a mandate yesterday, saying, 'Listen! We don't want these morons trying to croak us!' You know when the al-Qaeda made a big mistake? It's when they whiffed that dog on videotape. That got the liberals into it. Because they're all sitting at home with their Marmaduke day-planner saying, 'Wait a second! They croaked a puppy? Aw, now it's *on*, mother-[bleep]er!' "

SIX

Gaffes of Compounding Interest:
The Terrorism Debate
from 2002 to 2004

The Democrats didn't learn anything from the 2002 elections. Why should they learn anything from 2004?

> —*A Longtime Republican strategist nicknamed Obi-Wan Kenobi*

We all have a few memorable sayings, comments, or quotes that shape our perceptions of our leaders, parties, principles, and politics. We never really know what these statements are until we hear them; then we nod appreciatively, exclaim, "ain't that the truth," and after they take root in our brain, we repeat them when chatting with friends or debating coworkers.

Every major political figure is defined by a couple of these phrases. When people hear the name Ronald Reagan, they immediately think of "Mr. Gorbachev, tear down this wall," "Government is not the solution, it is the problem," "Are you better off now than you were four years ago," "It's morning in America," "There you go again," or "I paid for this microphone."

For Bill Clinton, the average American voter probably immediately thinks of his theme song, "Don't Stop Thinking about Tomorrow," or, "It's the economy, stupid," "change versus more of the same," "bridge to the twenty-first century," "The era of big government is over," or, less flatteringly, "I did . . . not . . . have . . . sexual . . . relations with that woman . . . Miss Lewinsky, and I never told anybody to lie." Or perhaps, "It depends on what the definition of 'is' is."

Like the months leading up to Election Day 2002, major Democratic figures spent much of 2003 and 2004 blurting out comments that seemed to define them and reinforced a reputation for weakness and indecision that was 30, perhaps 40 years in the making. Even if the following parade of gaffes, rants, conspiracy theories, and flat-out nutty comments escaped your attention, rest assured that some voter somewhere was paying attention. Bit by bit, data point by data point, the pixels formed a portrait of a party too far from the American mainstream on the life-or-death issue of fighting terrorism.

YES, TERRORISM IS A LEGITIMATE ISSUE

The 2004 campaign marked the first presidential race since the 9/11 attacks. Candidates found themselves having to make the sale on new topics, far from the usual "I'll cut your taxes" and "I'll improve little Johnny's schools." Now a successful candidate had to convince the public, "I'll stop these maniacs from killing you and your children."

After the brief and rather pleasant moment of bipartisan unity in the months after 9/11, some in the political world didn't want to see fighting terrorism turn into a partisan issue. They contended that it wasn't "fair" to claim that one party or the other would be more dedicated to fighting terrorism. We are all Americans, right? We all want to see al-Qaeda destroyed, don't we?

But the truth is, there are two parties, and they support different policies.

A political campaign is designed to give voters a choice. George W. Bush and John Kerry had different approaches to the war on terror. If one believes that different terrorism policies will bring different results, and that a better policy will bring about fewer dead terrorism victims and more dead terrorists, then it is entirely reasonable for each candidate to say, "My policy will save lives; my opponent's policy will end up costing lives."

And that's exactly what both campaigns did. On September 19, 2004, Kerry's campaign, seeking the votes of expat Americans in Australia, argued that the decision by Prime Minister John Howard to support the U.S. effort in Iraq had made them a bigger target for international terrorists. Diana Kerry, younger sister of the Democrat presidential candidate, told the *Weekend Australian* that Bush's policy choices endangered Australian lives.

"Australia has kept faith with the U.S. and we are endangering the Australians now by this wanton disregard for international law and multilateral channels," she said, referring to the invasion of Iraq. Asked if she believed the terrorist threat to Australians was now greater because of the support for the Bush administration, she replied, "The most recent attack was on the Australian embassy in Jakarta—I would have to say that."

Vice President Dick Cheney was even more direct on a campaign stop on September 7: "It's absolutely essential that on November 2 we make the right choice, because if we make the wrong choice, then the danger is that we'll get hit again, that we'll be hit in a way that will be devastating from the standpoint of the United States."

Squeamish souls shuddered upon hearing those words. When a

candidate says electing his opponent will lead to a weaker defense against terrorism and more victims of future attacks, isn't that nasty? Divisive? Isn't it committing the most unspeakable sin in American politics . . . attacking a person's patriotism?

Not in the slightest. You can be a patriot and still be wrong. You can love your country and still endorse policies that will be ineffective against a threat. In fact, that's at the heart of just about every post-9/11 military policy debate. Some of the most ardent opponents of the Iraq war contend President Bush doesn't love his country and is a Manchurian Candidate for the Halliburton Corporation. But most would say that he loves his country, wants to defend it, just has the wrong ideas about how to protect it. Similarly, most war supporters would admit that their opponents are misguided, mistaken, naive, but not America-haters.

Nonetheless, there were those who seemed to believe that any discussion of 9/11 during the campaign was off-limits. When Bush ran his first ad for the campaign, featuring an image of a flag-draped stretcher being removed from Ground Zero, the liberal online web magazine *Salon* declared the presence of a 9/11 image "surprisingly divisive."

"We came out and said, 'This is a part of our record, a big part of our record,' " said Alex Castellanos, who shaped the ad. "They came out and said, 'You can't even talk about this.' That's fine. A reaction like that says a lot to the voters. They know you don't even want anyone to bring up this issue."

THE NEXT CYCLE BEGINS

Almost immediately after the 2002 elections, the nation faced another momentous decision of war and peace: the choice to invade Iraq and topple Saddam Hussein's regime. But after two lessons—

the Left antiwar voices being spectacularly wrong about war with the Taliban and having lost the 2002 elections because they weren't hawkish enough—many Democratic voices continued to sound dovish. Or worse.

The Democrats' postelection discussion of terrorism got off to a bad start with this comment by Senator Patty Murray of Washington:

> We've got to ask, why is this man [Bin Laden] so popular around the world? . . . He's been out in these countries for decades, building schools, building roads, building infrastructure, building day care facilities, building health care facilities, and the people are extremely grateful. We haven't done that. . . . How would they look at us today if we had been there helping them with some of that rather than just being the people who are going to bomb Iraq and go to Afghanistan?[1]

Murray's comment came around the same time that a militant Islamist gunman entered a Yemen hospital and murdered three Americans, raising the question of just how highly al-Qaeda truly values "health care facilities." The mind reels at the thought of a U.S. senator who (1) is so stunningly ignorant of U.S. foreign aid projects around the world and (2) believes that bin Laden's followers revere him for his social work projects. Perhaps this reflects the thinking of a typical domestic policy–oriented senator. "Schools, roads, health care facilities, and day care facilities are popular. Osama bin Laden is popular. Thus, Osama bin Laden must be popular because he builds schools, roads, health care facilities, and day care facilities." This is to say nothing of why day care centers would be needed in a country like Taliban-era Afghanistan that didn't allow women to leave the home.

Representative Marcy Kaptur (Democrat from Ohio) almost sounded worse a few days later when she declared to the *Toledo Blade*, "One could say that Osama bin Laden and these non-nation-state fighters with religious purpose are very similar to those kind of atypical revolutionaries that helped to cast off the British crown." [2]

Yes, one could say that, if one was trying to destroy her party's reputation on this issue.

Early as it seemed, the Democrats who were thinking of running for president in 2004 began rolling out their position papers and policy speeches around this time. Many hoped for a successful topping of Saddam Hussein and no letup in the war against al-Qaeda. And then there were proposals that were not so inspiring. John Edwards, during an address on homeland security, stated:

> We need to speed up studies that will show us how to make skyscrapers safer, and the national labs should lead new R&D into improving blast- and fire-resistant designs. The administration should establish voluntary national standards for security and construction of the tallest buildings and largest arenas, including fire safety guidelines based on the advanced practices used in Europe, Australia, and New Zealand. We should provide funds for states that put those standards in their building codes, and we should encourage terrorism insurers, especially after the reinsurance bill, to give owners breaks on premiums only when they make the right improvements." [3]

Acknowledging that the speech was focusing on homeland security and not foreign policy, Edward's stance reeks of a cringe-inducing defensive posture. The problem with the World Trade Center and Pentagon was not a lack of "blast- and fire-resistant designs" or insufficient safety standards or building codes. (In fact, the WTC was designed to withstand a jet crash, and innumerable lives were saved by the fact that American Airlines Flight 77 crashed into the one side of the Pentagon that had recently completed bomb-resistant upgrades.) The problem was hijacked fuel-laden 757s crashing into them. Few buildings will ever withstand destructive impacts of that magnitude; the only real solution is to prevent the hijackings and collisions in the first place. Perhaps the only more defensive-minded proposal could have been federal funding to research more durable casing for the black boxes in airplane cockpits.

As 2003 began, the fervent opposition to invading Iraq among the Democratic grassroots fueled the candidacy of Howard Dean. Dean, along with Wesley Clark and John Kerry, managed to make statement after statement that allowed the GOP to portray its opponents as soft on national security.

On April 9, during a discussion of the toppling of the regime in Iraq, Dean declared, "We've gotten rid of him [Saddam Hussein], and I suppose that's a good thing." [4] Dean's Democratic rivals and a slew of right-of-center commentators rebuked the Vermont governor for that begrudging "I suppose."

In May 2003, Senator Bob Graham declared that a bombing in Riyadh, Saudi Arabia, "could" have been stopped, but he offered no further detail on just what policy would have stopped it. This was just one example of a continuing theme among Democratic candidates: each terrorist attack somewhere in the world signified a failure on the part of the Bush administration.

As one *New Republic* writer put it to Graham, "So, Senator, if you knew this was coming, why did you neglect to say so until afterward?" [5]

As Dean articulated the antiwar case and became the preferred candidate of much of the party's liberals, the Democratic Leadership Council, the think tank aiming to bring the party to the center, targeted him with criticism. Two leaders of that organization, Al

From and Bruce Reed, warned that he was dragging the party's image to the left.

In late May 2003, Dean told a labor audience, "[The DLC says] all my supporters are elitists and I'm catering to elitist special interest groups. Last time I looked, fifteen AFSCME [American Federation of State, County and Municipal Employees] members died at the World Trade Center. I didn't see any of the staff of the DLC at the World Trade Center."[6]

There are many moments before and after this comment when one can't help but blurt out, "What the hell was Dean thinking?" Were the union members in the audience really impressed by this oddly personal attack on the DLC, a clumsy and snide invocation of the 9/11 attacks? Is the argument that if the DLC *had* lost staffers in the attacks, their criticisms of Dean would have been valid?

Not all of the Democratic rhetoric during this era was so clumsy or insensitive. John Kerry had a moment of political courage when he told a fairly liberal Take Back America conference that the party had to be willing to use military force: "If Democrats are not prepared to make America safer, stronger, and more secure . . . we will not win back the White House, and we won't deserve to." And he went after those in the party "who reflexively oppose any U.S. military intervention anywhere, or who see U.S. power as mostly a malignant force in the world, or who place a higher value on achieving multilateral consensus."[7]

By the summer, Dean was emerging as more than an also-ran candidate—and making conservative Democrats nervous. Texas Democrat Martin Frost said, "We need a candidate who is credible on national security. I think Howard Dean has the appearance of being another McGovern."

On June 22, Dean made his debut in the political big leagues, appearing on *Meet the Press* with Tim Russert. It was not a disastrous appearance, but it did nothing to reassure Democratic hawks.

Russert asked Dean how many men and women would be on active duty under a Dean presidency. Dean said that more troops were needed in Afghanistan and Iraq. Russert asked Dean how many troops the United States currently had on active duty. Dean responded, "As someone who's running in the Democratic Party primary, I know that it's somewhere in the neighborhood of one to two million people, but I don't know the exact number, and I don't think I need to know that to run in the Democratic Party primary." (To his credit, his wide-ranging guess was correct; the number was 1.5 million.) Dean continued:

> Tim, you have to understand, and I know you do understand, that as you run a campaign and as you acquire the nomination and as you go on to be president, you acquire military advisers who will tell you these things. . . . I will have the kinds of people around me who can tell me these things. For me to have to know right now, participating in the Democratic Party, how many troops are actively on duty in the United States military when that is actually a number that's composed both of people on duty today and people who are National Guard people who are on duty today, it's silly. That's like asking me who the ambassador to Rwanda is.

Dean's answers on Iraq were both better and worse. When Russert asked directly whether the Iraqi people were better off without Saddam Hussein, Dean said:

> I think right now they are. Here's the problem. If we can't get our act together in Iraq, and if we can't build Iraq into a democracy, then the alternative is chaos or a fundamentalist regime. That is certainly not a safer situation for the United States of America. And we don't know for sure if it is or not.

> Saddam Hussein is a dreadful human being. He's a mass murderer. I think it's terrific that he's gone.

The problem was that Russert's question was spurred by Dean's comment earlier in the program, "We don't know whether in the long run the Iraqi people are better off, and the most important thing is we don't know whether we're better off."[8] To many Americans, the concept that the Iraqis could be better off under Saddam Hussein's rule was (and is) unimaginable.

There are always going to be those who would prefer to live on their knees than to die on their feet; but once someone makes the argument that the inherent "stability" of a cruel dictator and his sadistic deranged sons makes for a better life, you wonder where to draw the line. Were Germans better off under Hitler than in the initial postwar chaos? Were Russians and Ukrainians succumbing to organized famine under Stalin better off than their grandchildren in the Mafia and crime-ridden 1990s? Are sporadic attacks from warlords and dead-enders too high a price for Afghanis to pay for life without a Taliban?

Intellectuals, pacifists, and others may argue yes; most Americans—and all Jacksonians—would answer, "Hell, no." This is the country that was inspired by a founding father's demand, "Give me liberty or give me death." At that moment, the candidates were hoping to do well in the primary of a state where the license plates say, "Live free or die."

On July 7, Dean issued a press release touting his support for U.S. military intervention in Liberia. "We face a challenge to our long-term security interests in West Africa," the candidate declared. Clarifying the distinction, Dean explained, "The situation in Liberia is significantly different from the situation in Iraq. In Iraq, the administration failed to prove either a credible imminent threat to American interests or an impending humanitarian catastrophe."[9] As Lawrence

Kaplan noted, the threat to American interests in Iraq may not have been imminent, but there was certainly no less a threat from Baghdad than there was at that time in Liberia—where, aside from moral concerns, the United States had no significant national interest.

On July 15, Bob Graham suggested that the failure to find WMDs may be grounds for President Bush's impeachment.[10] He then repeated it on Sunday shows throughout the month and months later in Democratic debates. While Graham's proposal channeled the anger of the Bush-hating Democratic base and primary voters, it was way out of the mainstream of most voters. Americans would decide whether to rehire the president soon enough.

On July 22, U.S. forces achieved a significant victory in Iraq when an Iraqi tipped them off on the hideout of Saddam's sons, Uday and Qusay. In the ensuing raid, both were ixnayed. The record of the brothers reads like a demon's resume: numerous rapes, kidnapping young Iraqi women from the streets in order to rape them, masterminding the destruction of the southern marshes of Iraq to punish local Shiites, murdering numerous political activists and suspected enemies of the regime, murdering their brother-in-law after promising him amnesty for defecting to Jordan, beating and caning the soles of the Iraqi national soccer players' feet when they lost, executing thousands of political prisoners to make room in Iraqi jails, stabbing a servant to death in a drunken rage during a party thrown for the wife of Egyptian president Hosni Mubarak.

Baghdad erupted in celebration. While Saddam had yet to be captured, it was clear there would be no restoration of the Hussein regime.

The following day, Dean was asked for his reaction to the news and suggestions that it was a victory for the Bush administration. "It's a victory for the Iraqi people, . . . but it doesn't have any effect on whether we should or shouldn't have had a war," Dean said. "I think in general the ends do not justify the means."[11]

Representative Charles Rangel (Democrat from New York) made similar remarks to Fox News's Sean Hannity. "We have a law on the books that the United States should not be assassinating anybody," Rangel said. "I personally don't get any satisfaction that it takes 200,000 troops, 250,000 troops, to knock off two bums."

These comments constituted exactly the wrong tone at the wrong time. If you can't crack a smile at two bloodthirsty sadists getting shot up like Sonny Corleone at the tollbooth, then you shouldn't be running for president. Carping about "ends and means" and "assassinations" is wildly out of step with an American public that, after months of depressing news about the fight against Abu Zarqawi's insurgency, was exuberant about the chance to say, "Hasta la vista, baby" to the next generation of Baathist cruelty.

To their credit, the other Democrats running for president knew how to respond. Dick Gephardt cheered the Husseins's demise as "a good thing." Joe Lieberman called it "an important victory." And John Kerry declared, "Once again, our troops have taken an important military step towards winning the peace in Iraq."

But August brought more grim news. A suicide bomber blew up a truck bomb outside the United Nations building in Iraq, killing 20 people and injuring scores of others.

Presidential candidate Bob Graham, who had been chair and was still ranking member of the Senate Select Intelligence Committee, quickly pointed the finger at George W. Bush. "Had the president pursued the War on Terrorism prior to initiating military action against Saddam Hussein—as I advocated last year—it is likely that al-Qaeda and other terrorist networks would not have been able to take advantage of the chaos that now exists in Baghdad," Graham said in a statement. But if the United States had not invaded Iraq, the al-Qaeda and other terrorist networks wouldn't be targeting the U.N. building in Baghdad—they would be aiming for other targets. (Unless Graham believed that Bush, following his advice, would have completely shut down al-Qaeda.) The *New Republic* declared his statement "so muddled that it casts doubts on Graham's bona fides." [12]

Then, a day later, Graham said, "We have not laid a glove on Hezbollah, whose fingerprints are all over that bombing [Tuesday] in Baghdad." [13] But the Pentagon said the most likely culprit was the al-Qaeda–related terrorist group Ansar al-Islam, which was linked to a deadly car bombing earlier in the month outside the Jordanian Embassy in Baghdad.

For years, Graham advocated the U.S. taking on Hezbollah directly, and the terrorist organization does operate in Iraq. But considering how the Democratic theme for much of the year had been criticizing Bush for asserting tenuous ties between terrorism and the powers in Baghdad, it seemed an inopportune time for a Democratic presidential candidate to assert a tenuous tie between a bombing in Baghdad and a terrorist group most often associated with Iran, Lebanon, and attacks in Israel.

On September 4, the Democrats held their first presidential debate—a stunning 15 months before Election Day. The campaign had started in earnest, with the beginnings of day-to-day coverage in national papers such as the *New York Times* and the *Washington Post* and on the blogs.

Running for president makes a man (or woman) do strange things. They're surrounded by reporters, cameras, and microphones almost 24 hours a day. They're constantly being hit by questions from reporters and voters. They're expected to have coherent, compelling, simple yet detailed answers to all of these. If they're winning, they're asked whether they're in danger of peaking too soon. If they're losing, they're asked why and how soon they will leave the race. Under no circumstances, no matter how deserving, are they allowed to say, "You know, that's a stupid question," or, "Frankly, I don't give a damn about ethanol subsidies—they're about one hundredth on my priority list—and I wish you narcissistic provincial hicks would realize the rest of the country has other issues that matter more." Or whatever.

So some gaffes are natural. But the circumstances of the Democrats' 2004 presidential primaries seemed to create a perfect storm of opportunities for them to look stupid, small-minded, petty, and incoherent on the issues of terrorism, defense, and national security.

For starters, as Byron York noted, Democrats had their first caucus and primary contests among groups of voters who largely didn't think very much about terrorism. An October 27, 2003, poll—sponsored by Democracy Corps, the group founded by Stan Greenberg, James Carville, and Robert Shrum—revealed that al-Qaeda was not looming large in the minds of Democratic voters in early primary states.

In one question, pollsters read a list of a dozen topics—education, taxes, big government, the environment, Social Security and Medicare, crime and illegal drugs, moral values, health care, the economy and jobs, fighting terrorism, homeland security, and the situation in Iraq—and asked, "Which concern worries you the most?" In Iowa, *1 percent* of those polled said they worried about fighting terrorism, ranking last on the list. In New Hampshire, *2 percent* worried about fighting terrorism and *2 percent* worried about homeland security. In South Carolina, the results were the same.[14]

While primary voters weren't worrying about terrorism and national security, they were falling in love with Howard Dean and dismissing their party leaders in Washington as weak-kneed sellouts to George W. Bush. As for the president, these primary voters had concluded he was Satan, or perhaps something worse. The polls and focus groups of these voters were telling their potential nominees, "Turn left, way left, oppose the Iraq war, criticize the president in the most scathing and over-the-top terms as possible, and never, ever give Bush credit for anything, even his leadership after 9/11."

The primary voters spoke; the candidates, with the exception of

Lieberman, complied. The Connecticut senator was punished for his apostasy by the early states, and his Joe-mentum failed.

During a discussion of Iraq in that first debate, Dean declared, "Our troops need to come home." You might wonder how the U.S. troops still serving in Kosovo, South Korea, Germany, and Japan felt about Dean's timetable.

On September 9, 2003, in an interview with the *Manchester Union-Leader,* Kerry declared, "We've seen governors come to Washington . . . and they don't have the experience in foreign policy, and they get in trouble pretty fast. Look at Ronald Reagan. Look at Jimmy Carter, and now, obviously, George Bush."

Clearly, the comment was meant as a not-so-veiled attack on Howard Dean. But Kerry's comments are silly as a matter of historical record. For starters, he seems to have left off his list . . . oh yes, our most recent Democratic president. Now, Bill Clinton had his share of early foreign policy stumbles in Haiti and Somalia. And at that moment, the mission in Iraq looked particularly challenging. But to contend that Bush's record since 9/11 constituted "trouble pretty fast" while Clinton's was something to brag about stretched credibility.

On October 21, 2003, Kerry appeared on Chris Matthews's *Hardball* and said that if he were president, he might, eight months later, still be trying to get United Nations approval for the use of force. While the initial impression of this comment can be interpreted as a sign of Kerry's patience and forbearance, after a moment's thought this approach seems terrible. Michael Crowley laid out some of the objections: Keeping more than 100,000 U.S. troops amassed in the Arabian desert from January 2003 to October 2003 would have been a logistical, financial, and security nightmare. It seems hard to believe that America's diplomatic influence would have increased as the congressional authorization of force receded into memory. With Russia, France, and China all adamantly opposed to harming their client Saddam, it seems Kerry would have been waiting forever for a consensus on Saddam to emerge.[15]

Right around this time, there was the vote on the $87 billion to continue operations in Iraq. The Democratic primary voters clearly preferred candidates who voted no—with Dean and the antiwar base contending the vote was a "blank check" on the war. But with most of the primary candidates having supported the war, they faced a politically unappetizing option of voting for the war but against money to continue the fight. In the end, Gephardt supported the $87 billion, Edwards voted against it, and Kerry voted against it. It would eventually become the topic of one of Kerry's most famous gaffes.

"I think we all try to do what we think is right," Gephardt said justifyingly during an October 26 Democratic debate. "That's what I try to do. I thought the right thing to do, even though I . . . have a lot of other suggestions about where the money could come from, in the end you're presented in the Congress with a vote, up or down on the $87 billion. And I can't find it within myself to not vote for the money to support the troops, our young men and women who are over there protecting us, dodging bullets in a very tough and difficult situation. And so, I felt the right thing to do was to do that."[16]

On November 12 in a speech at Dartmouth, Wesley Clark pledged that as president he "would press Saudi Arabia to provide commandos to accompany U.S. troops in the hunt for Osama bin Laden and other al-Qaeda leaders." Specifics were lacking, and the usefulness of this idea was debatable. How skilled are Saudi commandos? How useful would they be hunting in the mountains of Pakistan and Afghanistan? How trustworthy were they? What would a President Clark do if the Saudis said no?

But at least Clark was thinking outside the box. Other candidates preferred to assert their superiority on national security without getting into specifics. On November 30, Howard Dean declared in Merrimack, New Hampshire, "I think [Bush] has made us weaker. He doesn't understand what it takes to defend this country, that you have to have high moral purpose. . . . Mr. President, if you'll pardon me, I'll teach you a little about defense." [17]

Across the fruited plain, Americans sighed in relief, secure in the knowledge that Howard Dean, with his decade of experience commanding the Vermont State Police, was prepared to instruct the commander in chief who had toppled the Taliban about how to fight terrorism. Clearly, the long struggle to break up the syrup-smuggling rings had practical applicability to the fight against al-Qaeda.

When Dean wasn't asserting his authority to teach Bush about defense, he was explaining that he had no particular opinion on whether Osama bin Laden should get the death penalty. Appearing on *Hardball* on December 1, 2003, this was the exchange with Chris Matthews:

MATTHEWS: But who would you like to, if you were president of the United States, would you insist on us trying [Osama bin Laden], since he was involved in blowing up the World Trade Center, or would you let the Hague do it [where there is no death penalty]?
DEAN: You know, the truth is it doesn't make a lot of difference to me as long as he is brought to justice. I think that's the critical part of that.

Besides ordering the embassy bombings in 1998 and the USS *Cole* attack in 2000, bin Laden had authorized, planned, and gloated over the deaths of more than 3,000 people. If those acts do not warrant the death penalty, what does? Just about every American had wanted the opportunity to strangle bin Laden with his or her bare hands since that terrible morning, yet Dean's reaction recalled Michael Dukakis's bloodless and technocratic response to a question about a criminal raping and murdering his wife. In light of Dean's declaration that he left his church over a disagreement stemming from the zoning of a bike path and his intensely fiery "scream" speech, it is bewildering what gets an emotional response from the good doctor and what doesn't.

Also in that interview, Dean stated he believed that suspected terrorists—not just Taliban fighters—being held in Guantanamo Bay deserve prisoner-of-war status and should be treated in accordance with the Geneva Conventions. But those comments were quickly lost in the shuffle, because Dean made more comments that day in a radio interview. A line of speculation would come to mark not just his campaign but would illustrate a great deal about the entire worldview of the Deaniac movement:

DEAN: There is a report which the president is suppressing evidence for which is a thorough investigation of 9/11.

DIANE REHM, WAMU (public) radio: Why do you think he's suppressing that report?

DEAN: I don't know. There are many theories about it. The most interesting theory that I've heard so far, which is nothing more than a theory, I can't—think it can't be proved, is that he was warned ahead of time by the Saudis. Now, who knows what the real situation is, but the trouble is that by suppressing that kind of information, you lead to those kinds of theories, whether they have any truth to them or not, and then eventually they get repeated as fact. So I think the president is taking a great risk by suppressing the clear, the key information that needs to go to the Kean commission.

Note the halfhearted caveats. "I think it can't be proved." (Not that he doesn't think it's true.) "Who knows what the real situation is." (That might be the real situation; it might not be; who knows.) "Whether they have any truth to them or not." (Let's keep that line of speculation open.)

Needless to say, the veiled accusation that President Bush knew the 9/11 attacks were going to occur and let the victims die caused a firestorm. Oddly, the situation did not improve when Dean said to reporters shortly afterward, "I didn't believe the theory I was putting out."[18]

Even in an intensely partisan and nasty campaign environment, for a candidate to offer that kind of conspiracy theory and make that kind of accusation against the president crossed a line. Dean's blunt talk and fiery rhetoric began to look a little wacky, and his momentum began to slow.

But it would be some time before his foes could seize the opportunity. John Kerry, in a speech at Boston University on December 2, declared, "The war on terrorism is primarily an intelligence-gathering and law enforcement operation, and we need a president who understands that. . . . This president doesn't have the experience to be commander in chief."

We will look more closely at the argument that the war on terror is "primarily an intelligence-gathering and law enforcement operation" later. But for now, let's look at the argument that Bush "doesn't have the experience to be commander in chief." Perhaps that complaint would have been compelling against Governor George W. Bush in 2000. But by this point, the American people had seen three years of the Bush presidency—a period that saw the fall of the Taliban and Saddam's regime. Few presidents execute two successful major combat operations in a three-year period.

Appearing on *Hardball* on December 8, Wesley Clark echoed Dean's assessment that Osama bin Laden deserved a Hague cell, not the hangman's noose or a firing squad:

MATTHEWS: General, do you think Osama bin Laden, if we catch him, when we catch him, should be tried here at the United States or in the Hague, the international court?

CLARK: I would like to see him tried in the Hague, and I tell you why. I think it's very important for U.S. legitimacy and for building other support in the war on terror for trying them in the Hague, under international law with an international group of justices, bringing witnesses from other nations. Remember, 80 other nations lost citizens in that strike on the World Trade Center. It was a crime against humanity, and he needs to be tried in international court.

MATTHEWS: Well, 3,000 Americans were killed here. Do you believe he should be held exempt from capital punishment, because if you send him to the Hague, he will be. They don't have capital punishment at the Hague.

CLARK: I think that's a separate issue. I think that's a separate issue.

MATTHEWS: No, it's a key issue, because the sentencing limitation, they do not execute people at the Hague.

CLARK: I think that you can adequately punish Osama bin Laden, and you've got to look beyond simple retribution against an individual. You have to look at what's in the long-term security interest in the security in America and you have to look at how we handle the war on terror from here on out.

MATTHEWS: But doesn't life in Holland beat life in a cave?

CLARK: Not in a Dutch prison. Chris, they're under water, they're damp, they're cold, they're really miserable.

While you could wonder whether those willing to die for their cause will truly be deterred by the threat of humidity, credit the general for at least spelling out the clear and intimidating message that a Clark administration would send to the terrorists: "Kill 3,000 Americans and it's a cold, damp cell for you!"

Kerry declared that the Bush administration's accord with Muammar Qaddafi to give up his weapons of mass destruction programs reflected . . . a failure of the Bush administration. Kerry said that the agreement "makes clear the shortcomings of George Bush's go-it-alone unilateralism" and revealed what negotiation, rather than force, can accomplish. Kerry's statement made it appear that the candidate could not comprehend that the United States credibly threatened force against states that sponsor terrorism or develop weapons of mass destruction. The Blair-Bush good cop–bad cop routine only works if you have a plausible bad cop. That's what makes the perp cooperate with the good cop.

On December 26, Dean jumped on the let's-not-be-too-hasty-to-execute-Osama bandwagon. "I've resisted pronouncing a sentence before guilt is found. I will have this old-fashioned notion that even with people like Osama, who is very likely to be found guilty, we should do our best not to, in positions of executive power, not to pre-judge jury trials," he told the *Concord Monitor*.

"Very likely"? Is there any chance that we have him mixed up with some other Osama bin Laden?

The new year brought only an accelerated pace of comments that must have sent the Republican opposition research teams into high-fiving spasms of joy.

Wes Clark repeatedly speculated that Bush wasn't really trying to catch Osama bin Laden: "We bombed Afghanistan, we missed Osama Bin Laden, partly because the president never intended to put the resources in to get Osama Bin Laden," he said at a January 6, 2004, appearance at McKelvie Middle School in Bedford, New Hampshire. Two days later, at Havenwoods Heritage Heights senior center in Concord, he added, "*Newsweek* magazine says he's in the mountains of western Pakistan. And I guess if *Newsweek* could find him there, we could, too, if we wanted to."

In January, Wes Clark told the *Concord Monitor* that under a Clark presidency "we are not going to have one of these incidents," refer-ring to 9/11.[19] His boast made it appear that he believed he could sign an executive order as president wishing the possibility away. Obviously, as long as there have been campaigns, there have been politicians who are willing to promise the moon. But for a presidential candidate to guarantee no terrorist attacks during his term, like Joe Namath guaranteeing a Super Bowl victory, struck a new note of outlandishness.

On January 29, 2004, Kerry made additional comments he would come to regret in the Democratic debate:

BROKAW: We're back on stage at the Peace Center for Performing Arts in Greenville, South Carolina, with the seven presidential candidates contesting for the Democratic presidential nomination. South Carolina's primary is next Tuesday. Senator Kerry, let me ask you a question. Robert Kagan, who writes about these issues a great deal from the Carnegie Institute for Peace, has written recently that Europeans believe that the Bush administration has exaggerated the threat of terrorism, and the Bush administration believes that the Europeans simply don't get it. Who is right?

KERRY: I think it's somewhere in between. *I think that there has been an exaggeration* and there has been a refocusing. . . .

BROKAW: Where has the exaggeration been in the threat on terrorism?

KERRY: Well, 45 minutes deployment of weapons of mass destruction, number one. Aerial vehicles to be able to deliver materials of mass destruction, number two. I mean, I—nuclear weapons, number three. I could run a long list of clear misleading, clear exaggeration. The linkage to al-Qaeda, number four. That said, they are really misleading all of America, Tom, in a profound way. The war on terror is less—it is occasionally military, and it will be, and it will continue to be for a long time. And we will need the best-trained and the most well-equipped and the most capable military, such as we have today. But *it's primarily an intelligence and law enforcement operation* that requires cooperation around the world—the very thing this administration is worst at. And most importantly, the war on terror is also an engagement in the Middle East economically, socially, culturally, in a way that we haven't embraced, because otherwise we're inviting a clash of civilizations.

Kerry listed exaggerations regarding Iraq's capacities. But to the majority of Democrats and antiwar voters, Iraq was completely separate from the war on terrorism. So where were the exaggerations about the threat of terrorism? Furthermore, the testament that the war on terror was "primarily an intelligence and law enforcement operation" was a direct echo of the Clinton approach in the 1990s. Americans had seen what well-meaning prosecutors could do against al-Qaeda; Coach Electorate had decided to give the ball to the Navy SEALs, air force, army, and marines.

With Democrats recognizing that their candidate would need to sound competent and experienced on terrorism, Kerry started touting his 1997 book, *The New War.* But as Michael Crowley noted, no one was calling the Massachusetts senator an oracle:

Kerry must be assuming no one will go back and actually read his [1997] manifesto [*The New War*], because his description of it is awfully selective. Yes, Kerry briefly considered the possibility of a terrorist catastrophe on American soil. But *The New War* was almost entirely focused on the threat of global crime—not terrorism. If the future Kerry predicted really had arrived, we'd currently be locked in a vicious cyberwar with CD-pirating Japanese yakuza, Chinese kidney-traders, and Italian mobsters—not hunting Islamic fundamentalists potentially armed with weapons of mass destruction. It is, of course, true that almost no one predicted a September 11–like attack, and few correctly identified Islamic terrorists as the chief post-cold-war security threat to the United States. But the ways in which *The New War* missed the mark are nevertheless revealing. They show the extent to which Kerry was influenced by the criminal investigations of his early Senate career, his preference for viewing post-cold-war security more as a matter for law enforcement than the military, and his tendency to describe problems ad nauseam without offering a clear and bold course of action.[20]

Then there was Michael Moore's oft-repeated comment from March 14, 2004, about those killing U.S. soldiers and killing hostages in Iraq: "The Iraqis who have risen up against the occupation are not 'insurgents' or 'terrorists' or 'The Enemy.' They are the REVOLUTION, the Minutemen, and their numbers will grow—and they will win."[21]

We will examine the full political impact of Michael Moore in a later chapter, but for this moment you have to shake your head at the comparison of Abu Zarqawi's thugs to George Washington.

March also brought a terrible terrorist attack in Madrid, Spain. Dean, who had slipped considerably in the primaries, apparently decided the problem was that he hadn't been accusatory enough and concluded that President Bush was ultimately responsible for the terrorist attacks in Madrid. Six days after the bombings, Dean said, "The president was the one who dragged our troops to Iraq, which apparently has been a factor in the death of 200 Spaniards over the weekend."

Thus Dean became the highest-profile advocate of the notion that al-Qaeda had become just another group protesting America's presence in Iraq. Of course, al-Qaeda and its affiliated groups had been blowing up Americans for the better part of a decade. Dean and his cohorts seemed determined to find logic and political princi-ple where there was none, refusing to see these guys as a bunch of ya-hoos who kill anybody who disagrees with them.

Finally, Kerry won the Democratic primary. It was odd to see a candidate who had been left for dead suddenly come back to win every primary except the Carolinas, Oklahoma, and Vermont.

"Once Dean imploded, the Democrats really had no plan B," concludes Patrick Ruffini, webmaster of the Bush campaign. "Kerry filled the breach by default. There was this unnatural rush back to a candidate who had been largely rejected earlier in the primary process."

(As we have reviewed the regrettable or controversial comments from the 2004 Democratic primary, note that this is not even count-ing the comments from the three never-had-a-chance candidates: Carol Moseley Braun, Al Sharpton, and Dennis Kucinich. Braun ar-gued, "Maybe by learning to work well with others, we could do a better job in defeating terrorists"; claimed Bush aimed to destroy NATO and the United Nations; accused Bush of "saber rattling that has made us hostages to fear." Sharpton claimed that he could find Osama bin Laden and suggested that Bush had a "crazy, psychologi-cal breakdown." And the candidate who unfortunately resembled Smeagol called for the establishment of a "Department of Peace" and accused the war's supporters of being motivated by secret finan-cial profits.)

GEORGE SOROS: THE SLIMMER, RICHER MICHAEL MOORE

Now that the Democrats had a candidate, the party's supporters and ideological brain trust began sharpening their attacks on the presi-dent. Billionaire George Soros, who bankrolled a great deal of the anti-Bush grassroots efforts, said while delivering the commencement address at the Columbia University School of International and Public Affairs on May 14 that Bush's reelection would be a sign that something "was wrong" with the American people. Soros explained:

> I would dearly love to pin all the blame on President Bush and his team. But that would be too easy. It would ignore the fact that he was playing to a receptive audience, and even today, after all that has happened, a majority of the electorate continues to have confidence in President Bush on national security matters. If this continues and President Bush gets reelected, we must ask ourselves the question: "What is wrong with us?" The question needs to be asked even if he is defeated because we cannot simply ignore what we have done since September 11.

Soros topped his "why aren't you agreeing with us, you stupid Americans" comments a month later by declaring that America's war on terror had claimed more innocent victims than the 9/11 attack itself. "This is a very tough thing to say, but the fact is that the war on terror as conducted by this administration has claimed more innocent victims than the original attack itself." [22]

The math is debatable, to say the least. But to make this comparison ignores a monumental moral difference between terrorists and those who resist them: The bad guys aim for innocent victims. Errors are made in war. Bombs go off course. Once fired, a bullet can't stop if a civilian steps in its path. But our enemies have no hesitation about using women, children, and the infirm as human shields. Only the morally myopic see no difference between those who aim to kill the innocent and those who aim to protect them.

Soros continued his . . . unconventional analysis of American political thought later by declaring that the Abu Ghraib prison abuse scandal was "a moment of truth" for the United States as severe as the September 11 terrorist attacks. "The picture of torture in Saddam's prison was a moment of truth for us," Soros said. "I think that those pictures hit us the same way as the terrorist attack itself. Not quite with the same force, because in the terrorist attack, we were the victims. In the pictures, we were the perpetrators and others were the victims."

There's only one way to look at Abu Ghraib: the entire scandal was an embarrassing, shameful, disgraceful black eye for the U.S. Armed Forces and the entire country. But the American military, government, and society have overcome moral failings of the past: the detaining of Japanese-American citizens during World War II, the Tuskegee Syphilis Study, My Lai, Lieutenant William Calley, Iran-Contra.

In a world where Vladimir Putin can call the collapse of Communism "the greatest geopolitical catastrophe of the century"; the latest intellectual trend in Germany is to insist that the Dresden bombing was a war crime and that Germans were victims, too; the Japanese prefer to see themselves as victims of an atomically enraged America rather than as Nanking rapists and Pearl Harbor deceivers, we can note that the United States of America has a pretty solid record of examining its failings, learning its lessons, and making amends.

The lasting effects of 9/11 on American society are deep and pervasive. Soros's status as an observer of American culture is vastly overrated if he believes that the Abu Ghraib scandal's effect on America will be as powerful and lasting as the terrorist attacks.

Soros also stated, "The coming elections are, in effect, a referendum on the Bush Doctrine, and if we endorse that doctrine, then we have to take the consequences of the mistrust and the rage that is directed against the United States." If he meant terrorist attacks, then Soros was arguing that American voters dare not re-elect Bush because America's critics overseas had deemed him unacceptable.

SUSPICION AND HATRED VEERS TO TOM RIDGE

Buried deep in a June 27 *Washington Post* story on political charges about homeland security was this scathing attack: "Kerry campaign aides who asked for anonymity because the matter is a delicate one theorize that the administration is manipulating for political impact the U.S. intelligence conclusion that al-Qaeda hopes to derail U.S. elections with new attacks."

More than a few Democrats began banging the drum on this theme, insisting that homeland security secretary Tom Ridge was doing the bidding of Bush campaign mastermind Karl Rove.

"As Ridge's appearances continued, the Kerry campaign e-mailed Democrats asking surrogates to say publicly that 'it was wrong to sit on this [terrorist threat] information so long' and expressing the hope that the administration is 'following a security schedule, not a political schedule,' in issuing the alert." [23]

In a May 26 conference call to reporters, Harold Schaitberger, president of the International Association of Fire Fighters and a frequent visitor on the campaign stump with Kerry, said the announcement by Attorney General John Ashcroft scheduled for an hour later was a trick to divert attention from Bush's political headaches.

On the same call, David Holway, president of the International Brotherhood of Police Officers—which also endorsed Kerry—said, "The administration has been sitting on information that is vital to our law enforcement. I would hope this whole [Ashcroft] press conference has not been coordinated by the Bush committee."

Moderate Democrats on Capitol Hill quickly called up Kerry

aides to warn them that they were making a mistake by suggesting the Bush administration had politicized terrorism fears.

"We told the Kerry people, 'You shouldn't be saying that. . . . A Kerry administration would say the same thing as Ashcroft,' " given the security concerns about the upcoming Memorial Day and plans for hundreds of thousands of people to visit the Mall, a Democratic staffer said. Representative Jim Turner (Democrat from Texas) said, "Based on briefings I have previously received, the information presented today [by Ashcroft and Ridge] was accurate and balanced."[24]

The charge ended up being a brief story, but it represented the kind of insane political gamble that Dean and his ilk were willing to take. Had there been a terrorist attack after prominent Democrats and Kerry surrogates had insisted the warnings were just a political game, the electoral fallout would have been catastrophic. The fact that there were no terrorist attacks could lead to the conclusion that Ridge was overstating the immediacy of the threat—but the warning may have prompted al-Qaeda to delay or change plans. When fighting a mysterious, shadowy foe that prefers to hit without warning at civilians, it is never known when a day without an attack is a result of American defenses or al-Qaeda lethargy.

FROM CONSPIRACIES TO ALL KINDS OF CRAZY TALK

As Kerry's rhetoric got more focused, his surrogates wandered far off the reservation, making tasteless comparisons and espousing bizarre conspiracy theories. "I remember after the attacks of September 11, as mayor of the city, I was very, very worried about al-Qaeda and still am. But I'm even more worried about the actions and inactions of the Bush administration." This brilliant comparison was brought to voters by Baltimore mayor Martin O'Malley.[25]

Democratic congressman Jim McDermott of Washington added this gem at a luncheon for the Confederation of Indian Industry representatives in New Delhi on July 3: "There are already rumors circulating that Osama bin Laden is being held somewhere already and it's only that they are trying to decide what day they should bring him out."

On July 8, when asked about terrorism security briefings, Kerry gave a refreshingly honest answer but a regrettable one in the context of the campaign:

KING: News of the day: Tom Ridge warned today about al-Qaeda plans of a large-scale attack on the United States. Didn't increase the—you see any politics in this? What's your reaction?

KERRY: Well, I haven't been briefed yet, Larry. They have offered to brief me. I just haven't had time.[26]

Four days later, in the swing state of Florida, a Democratic congressman compared Governor Jeb Bush's behavior after the contentious 2000 presidential recount to that of Osama bin Laden, saying the governor went into hiding.

Representative Kendrick Meek, in a conference call designed to discuss President Bush's record on issues key to black voters, said there was a "lack of accountability from the state of Florida" during the disputed recount process. "No one could find him when they had issues as it relates to so many African-American votes that were left on the floor in many supervisor of elections' offices throughout the state," said Meek, the Florida chairman for the Kerry-Edwards presidential campaign. "The governor was like bin Laden after the 2000 election."

Alia Faraj, a spokeswoman for Governor Bush, replied, "We are not even going to dignify the comment with a response."

Meek stood by his comment later in a telephone interview with the Associated Press. "I don't see the governor in any way as a terrorist," he said. "I was just saying he could not be found."[27]

The commentary and rhetoric from voices on the left veered deep into paranoia. Al Hunt, who at one point seemed like a normal liberal columnist for the *Wall Street Journal*, concluded, "Last week, the *New Republic* reported the administration has demanded the Pakistani government get bin Laden before the election, preferably during the Democratic convention this month; the story was officially denied but had a ring of authenticity."[28]

By this standard, it could be claimed there is a rumor that Al Hunt believes George W. Bush has dispatched dogs to mock him as he walks down the street. Hunt may deny the rumor, but it had a ring of authenticity.

Bin Laden wasn't caught, obviously. And you have to wonder about the intellectual seriousness of those who believe all it takes to capture the top man in al-Qaeda is for the Bush administration to pick up the phone, tell Musharraf to do it, and voilà—instant capture.

Around this time, July 2004, there was a rather revealing poll conducted by the Pew Center. The organization again asked Americans if U.S. wrongdoing may have motivated the 9/11 attacks. This time, 38 percent of respondent said yes—an increase of 5 points since a poll in late September 2001; 51 percent said no, and 11 percent said they didn't know.

Perhaps most interestingly, among Democrats, 51 percent now answered yes. Only 37 percent said no, and 12 percent said they didn't know. By comparison, Republicans rejected that notion. Only 17 percent said yes, 76 percent said no, and 7 said they didn't know. Among independents, it was nearly split: 45 percent said yes, 44 percent said no, and 11 percent said they didn't know.

Some would like to ask those 51 percent of Democrats just what wrongdoing was the motivation. Support for Israel? Foreign aid to Hosni Mubarak in Egypt? The no-fly zones and trade sanctions on Iraq?

You cannot help but suspect that the instinct that "it's really our fault" is a desire to control the situation. If our actions provoked al-Qaeda, then it follows that we can prevent further attacks by not provoking them anymore. That's an easier thought to some than facing the fact that the only thing that would placate al-Qaeda would be the mass conversion of all Americans to Taliban-style harsh and regressive Islamism.

The less generous interpretation of this conclusion is that it is simply straight-up cowardice. "Mr. bin Laden, I've always opposed my country's Middle East policy, and I think we have an exploitative relationship with Saudi Arabia over oil. I'm doing everything I can to change our imperialist policies and mindset that you are so justifiably outraged about. Please don't bomb me, as we're not as different as you might think."

A RESPITE FOR KERRY—
A PRETTY GOOD CONVENTION

Finally, July brought the official coronation of Kerry as the party's nominee at the Democratic convention. At the time, both he and the party as a whole gave what seemed to be strong performance. Kerry's speech didn't drone; his delivery that night was one of his best performances in recent memory, although many debated whether the opening line and salute, "I'm John Kerry, and I'm reporting for duty," was a bit overdone and hammy. But Bill Clinton gave one of his signature performances, spurring a *National Review* editor to conclude dejectedly, "Bush needs a good convention. I mean, a *really* . . .

good . . . convention." Illinois Senate candidate Barack Obama had his coming-out party and lived up to the hype as a rising star.

There were a few off-key notes. Jimmy Carter, who was more crippled by terrorist tactics than any other president, was perhaps the wrong man to make the case to viewers that only John Kerry could effectively fight terrorism.

You can easily second-guess the Democrats' choice to have Glenn Close leading the evening's 9/11 remembrance. Was a Hollywood star really the best choice? Were there no firefighters or other first responders available? No soldiers back from Afghanistan? Nobody who helped his officemates escape in time? Then a victim's relative addressed the convention. Again, there's nothing wrong with recalling our sadness over that day—but how about some of those other emotions: the day's determination, righteous anger, courage, and compassion for those who needed help? There was very little during the remembrance ceremonies to suggest that this was a deliberate attack and not a natural disaster.

Later in the campaign, Kerry's team had no problem using 9/11 widows like the Jersey girls as political props, outright endorsing Kerry and arguing against Bush. But during a reflective, emotional presentation, presumably aimed to be one of the less partisan moments of the convention, the Democrats' brain trust went with Close.

Senator Edward M. Kennedy gave what is likely his last major convention address, summarizing the deep-rooted loathing and fury of his party in his statement, "In the depths of the Depression, Franklin Roosevelt inspired the nation when he said, 'The only thing we have to fear is fear itself.' Today, we say the only thing we have to fear is four more years of George Bush."

Iran is building nuclear weapons, North Korea has nuclear weapons, al-Qaeda has dedicated itself to killing as many Americans as possible, some Europeans want to appease dictators, Abu Zarqawi and his band of thugs are abducting and beheading any foreigner they can get their hands on, and the senator believes that all Americans have to fear is George W. Bush?

The Democratic base and the delegates in the crowd ate it up. But it wasn't what the Kerry campaign needed to win over persuadable undecided voters or wavering Bush supporters.

KERRY'S TERRIBLE, HORRIBLE, NO-GOOD, VERY BAD AUGUST

The convention concluded, and as the calendar flipped, a very tough August for Kerry began. It started with a comment by Howard Dean on *Late Edition:* "I am concerned that every time something happens that's not good for President Bush, he plays this trump card, which is terrorism. His whole campaign is based on the notion that I can keep you safe, therefore in times of difficulty for America stick with me, and then out comes Tom Ridge. It's just impossible to know how much of this is real and how much of this is politics, and I suspect there's some of both in it." [29]

To his credit, Kerry stepped in and disavowed the accusation (merely a month after his staff reacted to earlier Ridge warnings the same way Dean did.) "I don't care what he [Dean] said. I haven't suggested that and I won't suggest that," Kerry said. "I do not hold that opinion. I don't believe that."

A few days later, addressing the UNITY 2004 Conference in Washington, D.C., Kerry pledged, "I believe I can fight a more effective, more thoughtful, more strategic, more proactive, *more sensitive* war on terror that reaches out to other nations and brings them to our side and lives up to American values in history."

A "more sensitive" war on terror? It was a poor word choice, evoking thirty years of Democratic difficulties in looking tough enough. While I joked at the time that Kerry meant "handwritten thank-you notes to informants," Dick Cheney would use Kerry's foolish word choice to devastating effect in his convention address. "He talks about leading a 'more sensitive war on terror,' as though al-Qaeda will be impressed with our softer side." (Insert the vice president's trademark half-smirk here.)

Kerry followed that up the next day by further complicating his position on Iraq, by declaring he would have voted for the congressional resolution authorizing force even if he had known then that no weapons of mass destruction would be found. With that statement, he completely undermined the most effective foreign policy argument against Bush: How could you get such a key life-or-death issue of Iraq's WMDs wrong?

On August 12, the political world was rocked by the shocking resignation of New Jersey governor Jim McGreevey, simultaneously coming out of the closet as a homosexual. Putting aside individual views on McGreevey's sexual preference, McGreevey was lambasted in the press for what appeared to be the appointment of his alleged lover in charge of the state's defense against terrorists. The appointee in question, Golan Cipel, disputed much of McGreevey's story, denying he was gay and insisting the duties of his politically appointed position were merely to act as a liaison between the governor's office and state officials with responsibility for security— at an annual salary of $110,000. Nonetheless, even by the standards of New Jersey politics, this was a jaw-dropping scandal, and the scathing media coverage further reinforced the perception that Democrats didn't take homeland security seriously.

On August 16, bloggers noted that the Kerry-Edwards campaign site touted, "Kerry is an experienced leader in the intelligence field. John Kerry served on the Senate Select Committee on Intelligence and is the former vice chairman of the committee." It is a distinguishing job on a resume; the problem was that the vice chairman was actually Nebraska senator Bob Kerrey.

Critics began to wonder just how hot Kerry's record on intel issues was. FactCheck.org, a highly regarded nonpartisan organization, researched a Bush ad claim that Kerry missed 76 percent of the meetings for the Senate Intelligence Committee. After checking the available data, FactCheck.org concluded that the amount of meetings missed or skipped by Kerry was probably *higher* than 76 percent, because Kerry refused to release records on his attendance at "closed" meetings in which sensitive intelligence is discussed.

In mid-August, both Bush and Kerry addressed the Veterans of Foreign Wars National Convention in Cincinnati. Kerry criticized the president's recent announcement of troop redeployment out of Europe and Korea. The Bush campaign shot back that just two weeks earlier Kerry was quoted as wanting to reduce the number of troops in Korea himself. After the flip-flop was pointed out, the Kerry campaign dropped troop redeployment as a campaign talking point.

At the end of a long month that had also seen the rise of the Swift Boat Vets for Truth, Kerry addressed how he would handle Iran. Kerry first outlined the idea of providing nuclear fuel to Iran in June, but his running mate, John Edwards, laid out the plan in more detail. Edwards said that if Iran failed to take what he called a "great bargain," it would essentially confirm that it is building nuclear weapons under the cover of a supposedly peaceful nuclear power initiative.

He said that, if elected, Kerry would ensure that European allies were prepared to join the United States in levying heavy sanctions if Iran rejected the proposal. "If we are engaging with Iranians in an effort to reach this great bargain and if in fact this is a bluff that they are trying to develop nuclear weapons capability, then we know that our European friends will stand with us," Edwards said.

This approach raised the question of who a Kerry administration would send to negotiate with the Iranians. The recipient of that assignment would have good reason to be wary, as the Iranians have a history of being less than fully respectful to American diplomatic personnel.

THE REPUBLICAN CONVENTION

The end of August and the beginning of September brought the Republican convention, an emotionally intense four nights in New York City, full of 9/11 reminders and imagery. The first night of the GOP convention, which was not televised on the major broadcast networks, contained one element that had been missing from the entire Democratic effort in Boston: drama. One of the Republican Party's most popular faces, John McCain, had a podium-to-press-gallery confrontation with one of the Democratic Party's most divisive faces, Michael Moore.

"Our choice wasn't between a benign status quo and the bloodshed of war. It was between war and a graver threat," the Arizona Republican said. "Don't let anyone tell you otherwise—not our political opponents, and certainly not a disingenuous filmmaker who would have us believe . . ."

Before he could finish the line, the delegates began applauding wildly. Television cameras focused on Moore, who was at the GOP convention in the press gallery writing a column for *USA Today*. Jeers and boos aimed at Moore interrupted McCain, as Moore, sporting a red baseball cap, acknowledged the outburst with waves and smiles.

For nearly a minute, the anti-Moore jeering continued and was punctuated by growing chants of "Four more years! Four more years!" All the while, television cameras stayed on Moore, who continued to laugh and wave. At one point, Moore held up his index finger and thumb in the shape of an L, the symbolic gesture for "loser."

When the noise died down, McCain deadpanned, "That line was so good, I'll use it again." To another round of cheers and jeers, he continued his reference to a "disingenuous filmmaker who would have us believe that Saddam's Iraq was an oasis of peace when, in fact, it was a place of indescribable cruelty, torture chambers, mass graves, and prisons that destroyed the lives of the small children held inside their walls."

The contrast between smiling, decorated Vietnam POW McCain and unshaven, perhaps-a-wee-bit-overweight Moore was a fantasy come true for GOP campaign strategists. Worse, while Moore apparently was giving the L-for-loser sign to the Republican delegates, to viewers at home it appeared that he was calling McCain a loser.

McCain was followed by strong speeches by Rudy Giuliani and Arnold Schwarzenegger. But perhaps the most intriguing and memorable speech of the convention came from Democratic senator Zell Miller, who had broken ranks with his party and endorsed Bush. In his fired-up barn burner of a keynote address, Miller just kept whacking at Kerry like he was a piñata:

> The F-14A Tomcats, that Senator Kerry opposed, shot down Khadifi's Libyan MIGs over the Gulf of Sidra. The modernized F-14D, that Senator Kerry opposed, delivered missile strikes against Tora Bora.
>
> The Apache helicopter, that Senator Kerry opposed, took out those Republican Guard tanks in Kuwait in the Gulf War. The F-15 Eagles, that Senator Kerry opposed, flew cover over our Nation's Capital and this very city after 9/11.
>
> I could go on and on and on: Against the Patriot Missile that shot down Saddam Hussein's scud missiles over Israel,

against the Aegis air-defense cruiser, against the Strategic Defense Initiative, against the Trident missile, against, against, against.

This is the man who wants to be the Commander in Chief of our U.S. Armed Forces?

U.S. forces armed with what? Spitballs? . . . John Kerry, who says he doesn't like outsourcing, wants to outsource our national security.

The delegates loved it; but some conservatives, including *National Review* editor Rich Lowry, feared it might be "too hot" and too angry for television. The anger was the centerpiece of the Democratic response.

Terry McAuliffe commented on Zell Miller: "I don't think I've ever seen such a hateful speech in my life. He scared people. It was like one of those Jason movies. I think a lot of parents needed to move their children out of the room so that they wouldn't hear it." [30] (Note that McAuliffe sees no distinction between anger and hate.)

The Democratic Party and Peter Jennings's reaction to Zell was essentially that the Georgia senator's speech was "too mean." Perhaps to them—but to many Americans, Miller articulated perfectly the instinctive urge of parents to protect "the cubs," and he looked like just the type of mean SOB you want defending your kids from a threat. The kinder, gentler, "I feel your pain" Clinton style was perfect for the 1990s, when America was at peace. But America was no longer at peace, and a significant chunk of the country wanted the government run by some tough-as-nails cranky former marine with a mean streak a mile wide whose idea of dealing with threats included a crowbar, duct tape, and a hill of fire ants. You know, like Zell.

The focus group gathered by pollster Frank Luntz on MSNBC appeared to like Zell's speech better than Cheney's. They described it as, "stronger . . . focused on the family . . . dead on, convincing coming from a Democrat."

Miller's "spitballs" line got a big laugh, and in the discussion afterward, the focus group seemed to like the line, and many thought it illustrated a serious point well.

Cheney's line about "as though al-Qaeda will be impressed with our softer side" did well with Luntz's group, and in particular, Cheney's argument, "He [Kerry] declared at the Democratic convention that he will forcefully defend America after we have been attacked. My fellow Americans, we have already been attacked," made all the lines on the instant-response graphs take off. Even the Democrats agreed with that line and liked it.

In the final count, 11 out of 17 liked the speeches and said they were more likely to support Bush.

THE FALL CAMPAIGN

The weeks following the Republican convention were marked by a rapid succession of big emotional stories. Former president Bill Clinton was suddenly hospitalized. In Beslan, Russia, Chechen terrorists massacred hundreds of schoolchildren. A *60 Minutes II* story on memos about Bush's National Guard service proved to be based on a hoax. A vigilant band of bloggers pointed out that the memos looked exactly like Microsoft Word and nothing like any document generated by a typewriter of the early 1970s. Rather and the producers behind the story ignored several forensic document examiners who said they could not authenticate the memo and selectively edited an interview with a handwriting expert to make his equivocal assessment of the signature a full-throated endorsement of the entire document's veracity.

Yet ultimately the Sauronic Eye of CBS was felled by the Pajamahadeen, and CBS anchor Rather was forced to admit that the network could not authenticate the origin of the memos—about as close to a retraction as anyone could get from the stubborn, computer-illiterate, axe-grinding fossil.

Meanwhile, Kerry gave the country a taste of the sophisticated, nuanced diplomacy his administration would enact. When then Iraqi prime minister Awad Allawi visited America and expressed appreciation for the coalition's efforts in rebuilding his country, senior Kerry adviser Joe Lockhart said, "The last thing you want to be seen as is a puppet of the United States, and you can almost see the hand underneath the shirt today moving the lips." Reporters on the Kerry beat never quite cleared up whether Lockhart was moonlighting as a message consultant with the Moqtada Sadr militia at the time.

The campaign continued to focus heavily on which man would make a better commander in chief in a dangerous world. Among the hawkish Democrat voters most likely to swing, certain bloggers made the argument that President Kerry would be a lot tougher on terrorism than his rhetoric.

Joe Katzman wrote on the Winds of Change Web site:

> "Cicero," like Jeff Jarvis, Armed Liberal, and many other centrist bloggers these days, isn't undecided—he's unhappy. So he tries on Michael Totten's approach and attempts to convince himself that while he favours Bush, electing Kerry would finally force the Democrats to face reality. . . .
>
> In response, I get a vision of Owen Wilson's character in *Shanghai Knights*. Cornered and in deep trouble, with only one difficult means of escape, he looks incredulously over at Jackie Chan and says:
>
> "What in our history together makes you think I'm capable of something like that?"

These bloggers looked at John Kerry's record in and out of public life and concluded there was nothing in his history to suggest he was capable of becoming a hawkish president.

His remarks on Iran suggested he would normalize relations with that state while the mullahs attempted to undermine Iraq and Afghanistan, offer them nuclear fuel, propose sanctions that the Europeans will drag their feet on, in order to stop a late-stage nuclear program that's impervious to sanctions, anyway, and oppose both missile defense and the nuclear bunker-buster weapons. He seemed inclined to get American troops out of Iraq as quickly as possible and invite international organizations with spotty records to help out in Afghanistan. In Kerry, many warbloggers saw Chamberlain, not Churchill.

By October, Kerry had failed to change the minds of the persuadables, the voters willing to see if he would be an improvement from Bush on this issue. He compounded his mistakes by making one of his most harmful gaffes. In an interview with *New York Times Magazine*, Kerry said:

> We have to get back to the place we were, where terrorists are not the focus of our lives, but they're a nuisance. As a former law-enforcement person, I know we're never going to end prostitution. We're never going to end illegal gambling. But we're going to reduce it, organized crime, to a level where it isn't on the rise. It isn't threatening people's lives every day, and fundamentally, it's something that you continue to fight, but it's not threatening the fabric of your life.[31]

This was the opening the Bush campaign had been waiting for. The president and his surrogates hit this weak spot with everything they had. As usual, Rudy Giuliani, New York's mayor, had the most powerful and devastating response:

> I'm wondering exactly when Senator Kerry thought they were just a nuisance. Maybe when they attacked the USS *Cole?* Or when they attacked the World Trade Center in 1993? Or when they slaughtered the Israeli athletes at the Munich Olympics in 1972? Or killed Leon Klinghoffer by throwing him overboard? Or the innumerable number of terrorist acts that they committed in the 70s, the 80s and the 90s, leading up to September 11?
>
> This is so different from the President's view and my own, which is in those days, when we were fooling ourselves about the danger of terrorism, we were actually in the greatest danger. When you don't confront correctly and view realistically the danger that you face, that's when you're at the greatest risk. When you at least realize the danger and you begin to confront it, then you begin to become safer. And for him to say that in the good old days—I'm assuming he means the 90s and the 80s and the 70s—they were just a nuisance, this really begins to explain a lot of his inconsistent positions on how to deal with it because he's not defining it correctly.
>
> As a former law enforcement person, he says 'I know we're never going to end prostitution. We're never going to end illegal gambling. But we're going to reduce it.' This is not illegal gambling; this isn't prostitution. Having been a former law enforcement person for a lot longer than John Kerry ever was, I don't understand his confusion. Even when he says 'organized crime to a level where it isn't on the rise,' it was not the goal of the Justice Department to just reduce organized crime. It was the goal of the Justice Department to eliminate

organized crime. Was there some acceptable level of organized crime: two families, instead of five, or they can control one union but not the other.

The idea that you can have an acceptable level of terrorism is frightening. How do you explain that to the people who are beheaded or the innocent people that are killed, that we're going to tolerate a certain acceptable [level] of terrorism, and that acceptable level will exist and then we'll stop thinking about it? This is an extraordinary statement. I think it is not a statement that in any way is ancillary. I think this is the core of John Kerry's thinking.[32]

At the time that New York's mayor was pretty much calling Kerry a wimp, his campaign was increasingly convinced that they were doing just fine on the terrorism issue and that it was time to play to their strengths on traditional Democratic issues. As Dotty Lynch, political editor of *CBS News,* noted, 62 percent of the Kerry campaign's paid advertising in the last week of September and the first week in October was on health care.[33]

"Democrats genuinely misperceive what the pecking order of issues is," says Bush's webmaster, Ruffini. "Yes, people are concerned about prescription drugs, but it's not necessarily what people are going to vote on."

When Kerry did turn to national security and threats to American lives, it generally was in the context of American military casualties in Iraq. Throughout the entire election, casualties in Iraq were believed to be politically damaging to the Bush campaign. And the Kerry campaign was convinced that stories of National Guard troops being called up and deployed to Iraq hurt the president's standing. Not so, says Bush campaign spokesman and message man Steve Schmidt.

"I think the conventional wisdom is mostly wrong," Schmidt said after the election. "Someone with a family member who's serving a second tour of duty in Iraq right now, the overwhelming majority of military families believe in the mission, in the war on terror and Iraq, and are proud of their relative's services, so when a story appears in the paper about the deployment of National Guard troops, military families in the community aren't angry about those stories, those aren't negative stories. They think that the American people have a very realistic view that we're a nation at war. What are the reasons that we're fighting, but particularly those families, the overwhelming majority of them are proud of their relative's service, and I don't think those families view those stories as negative." [34]

PREELECTION PUNDITRY
FROM OSAMA BIN LADEN

Kerry was boosted by three strong performances in the presidential debates. Even most Bush partisans concede the president appeared tired and uninspired in his first outing. But the campaign wasn't terribly worried.

"We were confident that we had a better narrative, compared to the litany of complaints the other side had," says one Bush campaign staffer. "I mean, was the election really going to turn on the argument that the president had not done enough on distributing the flu vaccine? All these standard microissues? No. That's why Kerry did well in the debates. He could mouth off about the smallest minutia and sound competent. In that forum, he did well. But that's not the formula for connecting with people. Our model and assumptions probably just had a better understanding of this than theirs did."

But the first post-9/11 presidential election had one remaining huge curveball. The afternoon of the Friday before Election Day, a videotaped statement by Osama bin Laden was released to al-Jazeera and shown around the world. Like a vision out of a nightmare, bin Laden appeared in robes, older but not terribly wounded, quiet, less blustery:

> And we never knew that the commander in chief of the American armed forces would leave 50,000 of his people in the two towers to face those events by themselves when they were in the most urgent need of their leader. He was more interested in listening to the child's story about the goat rather than worry about what was happening to the towers. So, we had three times the time necessary to accomplish the events.

Both campaigns suddenly had to respond and account for an appearance by America's archnemesis, gloating, and seemingly attempting to influence the election—although there was strong disagreement on how.

The Kerry campaign was divided. A senior strategist told Arianna Huffington:

> Stan Greenberg was adamant that Kerry should not even mention Osama. He insisted that because his polling showed Kerry had already won the election, he should not do anything that would endanger his position. We argued that since Osama dominated the news, it would be hard for us to get any other message through. So a compromise was reached, according to which Kerry issued a bland statesman-like statement about Osama (followed by stumping on the economy), and we dispatched [former U.N. ambassador Richard] Holbrooke to argue on TV that the reappearance of bin Laden proved that the president had not made us safer.[35]

In the end, both candidates made statements that were appropriate, perhaps even understated. "Earlier today, I was informed of the tape that is now being analyzed by America's intelligence community," Bush said. "Let me make this very clear. Americans will not be intimidated or influenced by an enemy of our country. I'm sure Senator Kerry agrees with this. I also want to say to the American people that we are at war with these terrorists, and I am confident that we will prevail."

"In response to this tape of Osama bin Laden, let me just make it clear, crystal clear, as Americans we are absolutely united in our determination to hunt down and destroy Osama bin Laden and the terrorists," Kerry said. "They are barbarians, and I will stop at absolutely nothing to hunt down, capture, or kill the terrorists wherever they are, whatever it takes, period."

But once again, while Democratic officeholders were cautious about mishandling the situation, the angry liberals at the grassroots offered comments of praise for bin Laden that were political cyanide and arguably treasonous. That evening, on his live show on HBO, comedian Bill Maher discussed the tape with his guests. His audience's reaction is incomprehensible to most Americans:

MAHER: All right, I want to start with this bin Laden tape. When I read this today, it reminded me of Ted Kaczynski, because I remember when Ted Kaczynski, the Unabomber, put out his manifesto—we all thought, Ted Kaczynski, of course he should die; he's a terrible guy; he's been killing people—but if you read his manifesto, there were some things in it that you kind of agreed with. Listen to some of the stuff from bin Laden's tape today. I swear to God, this is stuff that could have come out of the Democratic National Committee or a Kerry speech. He says, "Bush is still deceiving you and hiding the truth from you."

GENERAL WESLEY CLARK: [overlapping] I'm not sure I agree with that.

MAHER: I'll read it. "Bush is still deceiving you and hiding the truth from you. And, therefore, the reasons are still there to repeat what happened." That's what Kerry has been saying. "Bush and the administration resemble the regimes in our countries ruled by the military and by the sons of kings. They have a lot of pride, arrogance, greed, and thievery."

The audience then *applauded* this comment from Osama bin Laden.

MAHER: I've heard people say that. "Bush adopted the crushing of freedoms and called it the Patriot Act under the guise of combating terrorism."

The audience again applauded the words of the world's most wanted terrorist, the biggest mass murderer of our time, because he was criticizing the Patriot Act.

MAHER: I'm just quoting. And I'm saying, I've heard this. I'm not saying that the Democrats—
RICHARD BELZER: No, no, your point is well taken.

Maher later added, "Sometimes you can agree with an evil person. I mean, Hitler was a vegetarian."

Later in the program, Maher interviewed hyperbolic conservative columnist Ann Coulter. Discussing Bush's immediate reaction in the Florida classroom to the terrorist attacks, Coulter said, "What? Do you want the president to run out of the school and say, 'Let the planes hit me first?' " The audience cheered that thought, prompting Coulter to respond, "I hope a lot of people are watching this. Those are your supporters, Bill."

On the Daily Kos Web site, a reader posted, "[bin Laden] couldn't believe that Shrub stayed in a classroom reading a book about a goat to kids while his country was being attacked. SMACK-DOWN from OBL." Another wrote, "Well, I guess I have to agree with the man." Yet another stated, "It drives me INSANE that OBL can offer more insightful analysis than our pundit-ocracy." "OBL slammed shrub [Bush] on my pet goat. That's pretty bad."

When you're applauding Osama bin Laden for his assessment of the Patriot Act and references to *Fahrenheit 9/11,* you're so far from the political mainstream that the light from the mainstream takes several minutes to reach you. (And can we agree that once you stand up and cheer for a guy who killed thousands of Americans, it's okay to question your patriotism?)

The following day, Stan Greenberg added a question about the videotape to his planned poll and mentioned it in a conference call with reporters. The Bush-Cheney campaign seized on that bit of news, and Vice President Cheney declared, "The thing I find most amazing about it is John Kerry's first response was to go conduct a poll. It's as though he didn't know what he believed until he took a poll. George Bush doesn't need a poll to know what he believes, especially about Osama bin Laden. . . . I feel strongly about it. Ever since I heard about the poll, I've been agitated about it."

It was an unfair criticism; the call was Greenberg's, not Kerry's, and the job of a pollster is to measure the public's reaction to events.

There were others on the right who used the video for a last-minute attack, a move of dubious propriety. Fox News Channel anchor Neil Cavuto quipped that bin Laden was wearing a Kerry button—spurring a righteously furious reaction from the Kerry campaign.

It's not so clear that the tape was a help to the Bush campaign. (Kerry would later blame the tape for his defeat.) In the four tracking polls released on October 30, roughly one-third of the pollsters' calls were made after the release of the bin Laden tape. In Zogby's, Kerry moved up 1 point. In Rasmussen's, Kerry moved up 1 point. In WaPo/ABC, Kerry moved up 2 points. In Tipp, Bush moved up 2 points.[36]

No one in the political world quite knew how to calculate this last-minute geopolitical bombshell. Your humble author concluded it would take a middling Bush victory and turn it into a landslide. The longtime GOP operative nicknamed Obi-Wan Kenobi had his doubts.[37]

"It might freeze things in place as the voters mull over new information—and the bin Laden tape was a big piece of new information," he said the Monday before Election Day. "While some folks are focusing on what bin Laden said, a certain segment of voters were and are just reacting to the reappearance of bin Laden. Their reaction to what he said will come after they have 'digested' the fact that he is alive. This digestion starts over the weekend and continues as they come back to work on Monday, talk around the water cooler, listen to the radio, talk to coworkers, etc."

Bush had enjoyed a lead of 4 to 7 points in many of the polls over the last month, but he finished with a 3-point margin in the popular vote. It could easily be argued that the bin Laden tape actually hurt Bush.

If the Republican policies and rhetoric on terrorism was so in tune with dominant public sentiment, and the Democratic policies and rhetoric so lacking, you can justifiably ask why Bush only won by 3 percentage points. Obi-Wan suspects (and I concur) that voters know the course that Bush has charted is hard and will have hard moments. They know that bringing democracy to the Middle East and crushing militant Islamists, rogue states, and terrorism is going to have frustrations, setbacks, and casualties. If the world didn't need this task done, Americans would prefer to stay home and relive the 1990s.

But Americans know the world changed.

The day before Election Day, Moore wrote,

To George W.:

I know it's gotta be rough for you right now. Hey, we've all been there. "You're fired" are two horrible words when put together in that order. Bin Laden surfacing this weekend to remind the American people of your total and complete failure to capture him was a cruel trick or treat. But there he was. 3,000 people were killed and he's laughing in your face. Why did you stop our Special Forces from going after him? Why did you forget about bin Laden on the DAY AFTER 9/11 and tell your terrorism czar to concentrate on Iraq instead?

There he was, OBL, all tan and rested and on videotape. (Hey, did you get the feeling that he had a bootleg of my movie? Are there DVD players in those caves in Afghanistan?)[38]

Moore's comments about bin Laden's apparent citing of a scene from *Fahrenheit 9/11* seemed oddly . . . proud. Could you imagine seeing your work cited by the world's most wanted terrorist in the middle of a threatening statement? Wouldn't you be screaming bloody murder?

In the middle of his preemptive gloating over Bush's imminent defeat, could Moore have spared a word to say something—anything—negative about bin Laden? After all, Moore found the time to observe that bin Laden looked "tan and rested."

Nonetheless, the Bush campaign wasn't reacting to the tape with horror. On the Halloween edition of *Inside Politics*, CNN's Judy Woodruff said, "This is what a Bush/Cheney campaign official is saying today about the bin Laden statement, the bin Laden videotape that came out late on Friday. He said, 'We want people to think terrorism for these last four days and anything that raises the issue in people's minds is good for us.' "

"No one wanted the last week to be about health care or prescription drugs," said Bush campaign ad man Castellanos. Half a year after Election Day, Castellanos laid out just how intense the emotional power of the terrorism issue was and continues to be, referring to the work of the famous Russian scientist Ivan Pavlov.

Pavlov's experiment is widely known. By ringing a bell every time he fed a hungry dog, he conditioned the dog to associate the ringing of the bell with food. With time, the ringing of the bell prompted the dog to salivate, because the sound of the ring was now strongly associated to food.

Once, severe storms resulted in flooding near Pavlov's labs. He and his assistants were only able to save some of the dogs; when they returned to their experiments, they found that all of the surviving dogs had lost their conditioning. The trauma of the flood—seeing other dogs die, fearing death themselves—wiped the dogs' minds clean of everything they had learned.

The dogs were eventually retrained, but Pavlov began to wonder about the effects of the flood. So after the lab was closed for one day, he poured water underneath the door, mimicking the first sign of the flood. The next day, the scientists found that the dogs had lost their conditioning again. Just the sight of the water coming in under the door was enough to retrigger the trauma and wipe out the conditioning.

"9/11 was the flood," Castellanos said. "And every time we went back—went back to New York, to Giuliani, to terrorism—that was water coming in under the door. And any time we did that, our numbers went up."

WHEN DOES CAMPAIGNING BECOME EXPLOITATION?

Comparing voters' reaction to terrorism to Pavlov's dogs is certain to spur charges of exploitation. But as we saw in the beginning of this chapter, politics is about policy differences. There is no way to have a presidential campaign without the candidates discussing what separates them. It is not merely legitimate but right to say, "These are my policies and this is why they are right; here is why my opponent's policies are wrong." Both Bush and Kerry did it on the issue of terrorism; the alternative is to declare 9/11 and the issue of fighting terrorism too sensitive a topic to be discussed publicly.

That is cowardice, and a position unfit for a great democracy. The American people are grown-ups. They can handle it.

This is not to say that the 2004 campaign was entirely devoid of exploitation. No, to see a textbook example of this phenomenon of emotional manipulation, we have to look at both parties' relentless and unseemly use of 9/11 widows, firefighters, and other heroes and victims of that day.

At the Republican National Convention, delegates heard from Tara Stockpile, the widow of a New York City firefighter, Debra Burlingame, the sister of the captain of the American Airlines plane that crashed into the Pentagon; and Deena Burnett, the wife of a passenger of the United Airlines flight that crashed into a field in Pennsylvania. On September 15, 2004, the group of 9/11 widows known as the "Jersey Girls" held a press conference at the National Press Club to announce their endorsement of Kerry. One of them, Kristen Breitweiser, joined Kerry and Edwards on the campaign trail for several days in September.

Every American's heart aches at the thought of what these men and women have been through. But a harrowing hardship does not make someone a policy expert; just because I sympathize with you and pray that God eases your suffering does not mean I care about your endorsement. Essayist Noemie Emery described the unspoken theme of the phenomenon she calls "grief-centered politics": *We are suffering, so you owe it to us to give us what we ask for. If you don't do what we ask you, you don't care that our loved one is dead.*

No journalist with an ounce of compassion wants to challenge a widow. But the result of this natural sympathy was that the Jersey Girls offered outlandish conspiracy theories in television interviews and the hosts simply nodded.

One of the Jersey Girls, Lorie Van Auken, declared on the April 8, 2004, episode of Chris Matthews's *Hardball,* "We also know that people stopped flying domestically. Ashcroft stopped flying. Pentagon officials stopped flying the day before September 11. They were warned not to fly on September 11. We think San Francisco mayor Willie Brown was told not to fly."

"You're talking about before 9/11 they were warned?" Matthews asked.

Van Auken responded, "Yes. Yes, right."

Matthews merely moved on, asking, "What about the July briefing that was on domestic agencies?"

To be clear, under the scenario Van Auken describes, the national security leadership of the Bush administration felt it was necessary to warn the mayor of San Francisco, but not Barbara Olsen, wife of the solicitor general Ted Olsen, or anyone at the Pentagon.

On April 9, 2004, Katie Couric interviewed Breitweiser, who was urging the Bush administration to declassify all of the presidential daily briefs received in the summer of 2001. Couric asked, "Are you making too much, do you believe, Kristen, out of the summer of threats?" Breitweiser responded:

> Here's an easy thought. They design cars now with an autopilot function that if the car gets too close to the car in front of

them, it's diverted. Why didn't over the past ten years we try to install something like that on a plane, that it couldn't crash into a building, couldn't crash into a mountain? The pilots, you know, they simply could have told the pilots these Middle Eastern men knew how to fly planes. The pilots would have behaved differently. They wouldn't have just acquiesced. They would have fought back, but these pilots—and I've spoken to their wives—thought that these Middle Eastern men needed the pilots, so they just sat there and listened and did what they were told.

This cringe-inducing moment was quickly brushed over and forgotten. Where to begin? The suggestion that the pilots "did what they were told" and crashed into the targets? Every indication we have is that hijackers killed or incapacitated all of the pilots and crashed the planes themselves.

Yes, today's cars have sensors that can detect an object; they beep when an unseen object such as a branch or a child is too close. They don't seize control of the vehicle from the driver and divert the car, as Breitweiser describes. Similar technology *does* exist on passenger jets today, warning pilots of a mountain ahead if they are low and in fog, and even guiding pilots to the runway in instrument landing conditions with a computer voice stating "500!" "300!" feet as the plane descends to land.

But there is no technology that will bring back to life a dead captain in the cockpit; nor is there technology that will seize control of the plane from any pilot and steer it around whatever danger is ahead, especially if a terrorist is at the controls and has overridden the autopilot functions, anyway.

Whoever sent Breitweiser out for that appearance, so thoroughly misinformed about the topics she was opining on, ought to be flogged. *That* is exploitation.

SEVEN

Who Is Your Face?

> Four years ago, the face of the national Republican
> leadership was Newt Gingrich, Dick Armey and
> Trent Lott—legislators with relatively high nega-
> tive ratings among voters nationwide. But this elec-
> tion, the face of the GOP leadership was George W.
> Bush, Richard Cheney, Colin Powell, Donald Rums-
> feld and Rudy Giuliani—executives with very
> strong positive ratings. This new GOP face reas-
> sured many previously skeptical swing voters.
> —*Ron Faucheux, editor in chief of* Campaigns & Elec-
> tions, *Dec. 2002 issue*

Perhaps the simplest reason that the Democratic Party has been
beaten like a red-headed stepchild since 2001 is their absolute inability to control who represents them—which individuals get to cast
themselves as the face of the party. At any given time, voters associate
a political party's identity and values with a half-dozen to a dozen
faces—leaders who define what the party is.

The president is always the de facto leader of his party. After the president and vice president, a party's identity is shaped by congressional leaders, high-profile members of the president's cabinet, and perhaps a few governors of the larger states.

For the party out of power, there are the Senate and House minority leaders, some committee ranking members, the party chairman, maybe a governor or two. Sometimes a party will have a legislator with a unique history, popularity, or accomplishments—like New York's Senator Hillary Rodham Clinton.

And then there are the folks who aren't elected to office who either want to be the face of their party or who become the face of their party due to the circumstances of their popularity and their stances. On the right, these would include Rush Limbaugh, Sean Hannity, Ann Coulter, perhaps a celebrity associated with gun rights like Charlton Heston or Tom Selleck. You could argue that their counterparts on the left are Al Franken, Alan Colmes, and Rosie O'Donnell.

Some journalists and political columnists, whether they like it or not, often become associated with the party they prefer. Many on the right see Maureen Dowd and Paul Krugman as faces of the Democratic Party, even though their official affiliation is with the *New York Times*. To many voters on the left, the *Weekly Standard*'s William Kristol and *National Review*'s Jonah Goldberg are stand-ins for the GOP.

Certain individuals, like Michael Moore, aspire to be one of those unelected faces, and the filmmaker clearly succeeded in 2004. However, like many of those public figures whose fame derives from Hollywood instead of actually winning elections, Moore only appeals to a very distinct and very limited minority of the voting public.

Too many of the Democratic Party's faces have no appeal outside core Democratic areas of big cities and university towns: Moore, Howard Dean and his scream, Al Sharpton, Jesse Jackson, Jeanine Garafalo. This category should also include Jimmy Carter—in voters' minds, he is associated more with America's impotence during the Iranian hostage crisis than with his noble work for Habitat for Humanity. Whatever else one thinks of the Nobel Peace Prize winner, he is undoubtedly the last man the Democrats should have arguing against Bush's policy on Iran. At times, the man speaks as if he's trying to hurt his party's image; Carter did Kerry no favors when two weeks before Election Day 2004, he argued that "the Revolutionary War could have been avoided. It was an unnecessary war." [1]

When Democratic leaders like Carter suggest that George Washington's fight for independence from the British monarchy was a mistake, the whole party loses credibility. This is not to say that Democrats don't have some appealing faces. Barack Obama. Edwards and Kerry both had their good moments. Ken Salazar of Colorado looks like a rising star. A lot of Republicans would pull the lever for Joe Lieberman, and Evan Bayh isn't too far behind him.

In fact, looking at the Democratic governors, you can find a slew of figures who would make appealing faces for the party. Pennsylvania governor Ed Rendell exudes a *Sopranos*-esque charm, and New Mexico governor Bill Richardson always seems to project a professional, serious aura of leadership. Michigan governor Jennifer Granholm is often described as telegenic, which is a polite way of saying she is strikingly attractive *and* knows what she is doing while leading her state. Cam Edwards, host of NRANews.com, often raves about two pro–Second Amendment southern Democratic governors: Phil Breseden of Tennessee and Michael Easley of North Carolina.

Perhaps one of these figures will emerge as a promising Democratic presidential candidate in 2008. Of course, governors have limited ability to influence national security policy. Their jurisdiction is essentially limited to homeland security, a topic that forces them to focus on how the United States can play defense against the terrorists, not stay on offense.

The Democratic Party also has several nonelected faces who help the party. James Carville and Paul Begala come to mind.[2] Both men are dedicated partisans, and while many on the right may grind their teeth at the sound of Carville's Cajun accent, few would doubt these two men represent smart strategists.

The Hollywood types who often jump into Democratic Party politics are often a mixed bag. The Democratic Party's base probably loves Barbra Streisand and her public memos to Dem leaders, Ben Affleck showing up on *Crossfire*, and Martin Sheen portraying the alternative reality presidency of Jeb Bartlett on *West Wing*. But the ostentatious wealth, often crass style, and less than fully informed policy statements alienate a certain segment of middle America— and fail to impress voters who don't seek political leadership from movie stars.

Whether Democrats like it or not, Michael Moore became their face in 2004.

THE POLITICAL ALBATROSS
THAT IS MICHAEL MOORE

In the previous chapters, we have seen a few of Michael Moore's greatest hits. But it is hard to overstate:

- Moore's distance from mainstream American political thought
- His ability to generate these controversial comments about the war on terrorism so spectacularly regularly that you can set your clock by him
- How uniformly and intensely the Democratic Party embraced him in the last presidential election year.

"No Terrorist Threat"
If Karl Rove were designing his ideal icon of weakness that he wished to associate with the opposing party, he probably would want

a fool willing to argue, even after 9/11, that the terrorism threat doesn't exist. Surely, no Democratic elected official is foolish enough to make such a wrongheaded statement.

If people wished to argue that God is a Republican, the first piece of evidence would be His divine generosity to the Bush administration by sending them Michael Moore. From a chapter added in 2001 to Moore's 2000 book, *Stupid White Men:*

> What if there is no "terrorist threat?" What if Bush and Co. need, desperately need, that "terrorist threat" more than anything in order to conduct the systematic destruction they have launched against the U.S. Constitution and the good people of this country who believe in the freedoms and liberties it guarantees?[3]

Lest one think this is a one-time utterance by Moore, this has in fact been a continuing theme in Moore's post-9/11 work. From page 95 of Moore's 2003 book, *Dude, Where's My Country?:*

> There is no terrorist threat.
> You need to calm down, relax, listen very carefully, and repeat after me:
> There is no terrorist threat.
> There is no terrorist threat!
> There . . . is . . . no . . . terrorist . . . threat!

A page later, Moore admits that more terrorist attacks are inevitable but that his point that the chances of each individual being killed by a terrorist is small. He audaciously points out that no Americans were killed in terrorist attacks in the United States in 2000, 2002, or 2003. (It appears Moore is ignoring or oddly classifying the LAX shooter on July 4, 2002, and the D.C. sniper. And while he is accurate about "in the United States," the argument may be less than fully compelling to the sailors on the U.S.S. *Cole*, attacked while docked in Yemen.)

Moore further argues that the chances of an American dying of a terrorist attack in 2001 were 1 in 100,000.[4]

Well, okay, then.

The chapter has another, more valid, point that the media sometimes overhypes the likelihood of a terror attack. But by then the damage is done. Moore has epitomized the liberal who refuses to see the dangers of a worldwide effort by militant Islamists to kill infidels and especially citizens of the Great Satan.

While appearing on *60 Minutes,* Moore continued to make comments that are hard to interpret as anything but a downplaying of the threat of terrorism. "Three thousand Americans were killed. There's 290 million Americans, all right? The chance of—of any of us dying in a terrorist incident is very, very, very small."[5]

Again, lest you think these are merely quotes taken out of context, let us examine Moore's October 7, 2003, appearance on the *Today* show. "Let's talk about the war on terror," said host Lester Holt. The resulting exchange:

MOORE: We're being manipulated with fear. . . . There is no terrorist threat to this country.

HOLT: Well, there's a body of evidence that suggests you're wrong—about two miles from here.

MOORE: It was a horrible tragedy, but there's been no threat since then.[6]

During a speaking engagement at Michigan University in October 13, 2003, Moore declared, "There is no terrorist threat in this country. This is a lie. This is the biggest lie we've been told."[7]

A year after 9/11, Moore was part of a panel discussion on BBC-

TV's *Question Time* show that aired live in the United Kingdom. During the warm-up before the studio audience, Moore said something along the lines of "I don't know why we are making so much of an act of terror. It is three times more likely that you will be struck by lightning than die from an act of terror."[8]

Since 9/11, Democrats have been trying to persuade the public that the "mommy party" is tough enough and serious enough to deal with a dangerous world. And Moore, accusing Bush and the Department of Homeland Security of scaremongering, leaps way beyond logical and persuasive rhetoric into arguing America's fears of another terrorist attack are irrational.

In late 2002, almost a year after 9/11, Christopher Hitchens had an onstage debate with Michael Moore at the Telluride Film Festival. In the course of this exchange, Moore stated his view that Osama bin Laden should be considered innocent until proven guilty. This was, he said, the American way. The intervention in Afghanistan, he maintained, had been at least to that extent unjustified.[9]

And yet, within a few months, Moore was no longer publicly doubting bin Laden's guilt. He was now offering a new theory, shared on HBO's *On the Record* with Bob Costas, on May 12, 2003:

COSTAS: You think they know where Osama bin Laden is and it's hands off?

MOORE: Absolutely, absolutely.

COSTAS: Why?

MOORE: Because he's funded by their friends in Saudi Arabia! He's back living with his sponsors, his benefactors. Do you think that Osama bin Laden planned 9/11 from a cave in Afghanistan? I can't get a cell signal from here to Queens, all right, I mean, come on. Let's get real about this. The guy has been on dialysis for two years. He's got failing kidneys. He wasn't in a cave in Afghanistan playing—

COSTAS: You think he's in Saudi Arabia, not Afghanistan, not Pakistan.

MOORE: Well, could be Pakistan, but he's under watch of those who have said put a stop to this because—

COSTAS: Including, at least by extension, the United States, he's under the protective watch of the United States?

MOORE: I think the United States, I think our government knows where he is, and I don't think we're going to be capturing him or killing him anytime soon.[10]

In the account of columnist Yasmin Alibhai-Brown in London's *Independent*, Moore "went into a rant about how the passengers [of the hijacked flights on September 11] were scaredy-cats because they were mostly white. If the passengers had included black men, he claimed, those killers, with their puny bodies and unimpressive small knives, would have been crushed by the dudes."[11]

Mind you, Moore had made all of these comments before *Fahrenheit 9/11* was released.[12]

Moore's fan base in the post-9/11 era quickly proved to be global. While being tried by Indonesian authorities in August 2003, Imam Samudra, a supporter of the Bali nightclub bombing that killed 202 people, quoted Moore's *Stupid White Men* in a rambling defense that justified terrorism as part of the Islamic struggle for freedom and respect.[13]

We saw Michael Moore's first comments after 9/11, lamenting the number of Gore voters who had died. His tone did not shift significantly during the week. On September 13:

But GET A GRIP, man. "Declare war?" War against whom? One guy in the desert whom we can never seem to find? Are our leaders telling us that the most powerful country on earth cannot dispose of one sick evil f—wad of a guy? Because if that is what you are telling us, then we are truly screwed. If you are unable to take out this lone ZZ Top wannabe, what on earth would you do for us if we were attacked by a nation of millions? For chrissakes, call the Israelis and have them do that thing they do when they want to get their man! We pay them enough billions each year, I am SURE they would be happy to accommodate your request. . . .

Keep crying, Mr. Bush. Keep running to Omaha or wherever it is you go while others die, just as you ran during Vietnam while claiming to be "on duty" in the Air National Guard. Nine boys from my high school died in that miserable war. And now you are asking for "unity" so you can start another one? Do not insult me or my country like this!

In a September 15 dispatch, Moore stated in an online column,

No one wants to talk about politics right now—except our installed leaders in Washington. Trust me, they are talking politics night and day, and those discussions involve sending our kids off to fight some invisible enemy and to indiscriminately bomb Afghans or whoever they think will make us Americans feel good.

I feel I have a responsibility as one of those Americans who doesn't feel good right now to speak out and say what needs to be said: That we, the United States of America, are culpable in committing so many acts of terror and bloodshed that we had better get a clue about the culture of violence in which we have been active participants. I know it's a hard thing to hear right now, but if I and others don't say it, I fear we will soon be in a war that will do NOTHING to protect us from the next terrorist attack. . . .

Three days ago, I learned from someone at ABC News

that ABC had videotape—an angle of the second plane crashing into the tower—that showed an F-16 fighter jet trailing the plane at a distance. I have not shared this with you as I had not personally witnessed that tape myself and did not want to contribute to all the unsubstantiated rumors. It just came across on the TV that the government admitted they did dispatch fighter jets when they knew the planes were off course.

From this point, I will pass on any censored information to those of you in the mainstream media who are being blocked from reporting.

Is it becoming more clear now that the plane that went down in Pennsylvania was shot down to prevent it from attacking its destination?

The truth is harrowing, unbearable—but it must be told to us. A free people cannot make an informed decision if they are kept in the dark. Let's hear ALL the truth NOW.

In the first days after the attacks, a lot of Americans said a lot of things that look foolish in hindsight. (The day after the attacks, Vermont governor Howard Dean told reporters that the attacks "require a re-evaluation of the importance of some of our specific civil liberties. I think there are going to be debates about what can be said where, what can be printed where, what kind of freedom of movement people have and whether it's OK for a policeman to ask for your ID just because you're walking down the street.")[14] But it's interesting to note Moore's immediate conclusions, from which he hasn't deviated all that much in the years since then:

- There is no point in declaring war on terrorists.
- Bush is a coward, draft-dodger, and is the one seeking to start a war—not al-Qaeda.

- The military's strategy is to "indiscriminately bomb Afghans."
- America is "culpable in so many acts of terror and bloodshed."
- The government is lying to us.
- The government is censoring the press, and the press is apparently cooperating without complaint.
- The government could have shot down the plane before it hit the tower but chose not to, resulting in the deaths of thousands.

Notice where all of that anger is focused. Not on the perpetrators of the attacks—at Bush, at the U.S. military, at the American government.

Fahrenheit 9/11

Moore's first splash in the 2004 campaign occurred when he appeared on stage with Wes Clark at a rally during a presidential campaign. During his appearance, Moore accused President Bush of being a "deserter." The press seized on this statement—after all, desertion is a crime that used to be punishable by death. Clark, perhaps due to his character or his political inexperience (or both), could not bring himself to repudiate Moore, either at the event or later on the campaign trail.

First, could you imagine a major Republican presidential candidate appearing on the trail with right-of-center bomb-throwers like Ann Coulter or Michael Savage? It's hard to recall a Republican candidate for office sharing a podium with even the comparably mild Rush Limbaugh or Sean Hannity.

Second, if the parties were reversed and Coulter declared, say, that liberals ought to be shot for treason, could you imagine any serious Republican officeholder refusing to repudiate her comment? Most GOP officials with presidential aspirations would probably seize the "Sister Souljah moment" and the opportunity to look high-minded, standing up for polite and respectful public debates. Reagan did a similar tack when the John Birch Society endorsed him, emphasizing that he welcomed their votes but didn't endorse their statements.[15]

The inaccuracies of Moore's film *Fahrenheit 9/11* have been discussed at length in other arenas. Among the most egregious—and most central to the discussion of America's two political parties and their reaction to terrorism—are:

- Moore got a lot of mileage out of Bush's apparent slow reaction to word of the planes hitting the towers. But few Americans beyond Bush's usual detractors could find it in themselves to hold those seven minutes against him when they entered the voting booth. Again, as focus groups revealed, every American remembers exactly where they were when they heard the news, and many felt paralyzed by shock, fear, and disbelief. To complain about Bush's reaction in the first seven minutes—and to overlook his leadership in the days, weeks, and months afterward—seems petty. The principal of the school, Gwendolyn Tose-Rigell, praised Bush's action: "I don't think anyone could have handled it better." Lee Hamilton, the vice chair of the September 11 Commission and a former Democratic representative from Indiana, said, "Bush made the right decision in remaining calm, in not rushing out of the classroom." Also unmentioned in *Fahrenheit 9/11* was the fact that as Bush was being informed, White House press secretary Ari Fleischer was in the back of the classroom holding up a legal pad with the words, "Don't say anything yet."

- The film showcases former counterterrorism czar Richard Clarke, using him as a critic of the Bush administration. Yet in another part of the film, Moore rips members of the Bush administration for permitting members of the bin Laden family to fly out of the country almost immediately after 9/11. What the film does not mention is that Richard Clarke says that he approved the departure of those flights. "I think Moore's making a mountain of a molehill," Clarke said.

- Moore is half correct for arguing that U.S. policy has been too kind to the House of Saud for way too long. But as Christopher Hitchens observes, "Why did Moore's evil Saudis not join 'the Coalition of the Willing'? Why instead did they force the United States to switch its regional military headquarters to Qatar? If the Bush family and the al-Saud dynasty live in each other's pockets . . . then how come the most reactionary regime in the region has been powerless to stop Bush from demolishing its clone in Kabul and its buffer regime in Baghdad?" If this is a conspiracy, this is a strikingly contradictory and divided one.

- Moore claimed that the Bush administration "supported the Taliban," based on an envoy's visit in March 2001. But the envoy was rebuked for supporting al-Qaeda, not handing over bin Laden, and was told that the U.S. government did not recognize them as legitimate rulers of Afghanistan.

- Perhaps most widely derided has been Moore's thesis that the Afghanistan war was solely for a Unocal pipeline and to distract attention from Saudi Arabia. He minimizes or ignores the fact that the U.S. military eliminated al-Qaeda training camps in Afghanistan, removed a government that did whatever al-Qaeda wanted, and killed or captured two-thirds of the al-Qaeda leadership.

- There are several scenes involving Oregon state troopers who patrol coastal areas in the state. The troopers are presented as underfunded and spread far too thinly. The film never states that their funding is from the state government, not the federal government. The film also ignores the additional resources devoted to the mission by the U.S. Coast Guard and the U.S. Navy.

- Moore says Saddam "never threatened to attack the United

States." On November 25, 2000, Saddam declared in a televised speech, "The Arab people have not so far fulfilled their duties. They are called upon to target U.S. and Zionist interests everywhere and target those who protect these interests." Moore also conveniently chooses to say nothing of Hussein's regime repeatedly firing on U.S. planes enforcing the no-fly zones.

- Moore portrays Iraqi daily life with children flying kites before suddenly cutting to bombs destroying buildings at night. The footage he uses of U.S. bombing is the Iraqi Ministry of Defense in Baghdad. It seems unlikely that Iraqi children flew kites there.

- With repeated portrayals of civilian casualties of the U.S. invasion, the "insurgent" side is presented in this film as justifiably outraged. Saddam Hussein's 30-year record of war crimes and repression and aggression is not mentioned once.[16]

The GOP was able to mitigate whatever influence Moore might have had with non-lefty voters with a single, devastating rejoinder from Rudy Giuliani: "I haven't seen it. I don't really need Michael Moore to tell me about September 11th."

While Moore's fan base loved him, most Americans felt the same as Rudy. They had lived the horror of that day; they didn't need to hear the conspiracy theories.

The Democratic Embrace
Any Democrat with any sense of the electorate would have quickly determined that Moore's movie was political poison, a skillfully created but over-the-top cinematic spittle-emitting rant that would repulse and repel the kind of voters the Democrats needed to attract. And Bush voters who had previously seen the Democrats as merely gullible or naive about national security issues concluded the opposition party had become jaw-droppingly reckless and had to be

stopped at all costs. *Fahrenheit 9/11* was a brilliant motivator—for the Republicans.

Yet Democrat after Democrat didn't just embrace this movie; they snuggled with it.

On June 24, 2004, Moore had a VIP screening of *Fahrenheit 9/11* at Washington, D.C.'s Uptown Theater. Almost every prominent Democrat attended: Senators Tom Daschle, Bob Graham, Barbara Boxer, Tom Harkin, Max Baucus, Ernest Hollings, Debbie Stabenow, Bill Nelson, Representatives Charles Rangel, Jim McDermott, September 11 Commission member Richard Ben-Veniste, strategist Paul Begala, and DNC chairman Terry McAuliffe.

When asked by *National Review*'s Byron York if he believed that the Afghanistan war was not to destroy al-Qaeda but to benefit the Unocal Corporation, McAuliffe responded, "I believe it after seeing that. . . . I think anyone who goes to see this movie will come out en masse and vote for John Kerry." [17]

Florida senator Bob Graham noted that while he had only seen "half the movie," he "thought it was accurate." Harkin told the Associated Press that all Americans should see the film. "It's important for the American people to understand what has gone on before, what led us to this point, and to see it sort of in this unvarnished presentation by Michael Moore."

The New York premiere audience consisted of not just credulous movie stars but top-of-the-line editors, First Amendment lawyers, and sober-suited Democratic Party donors. It was left to Tina Brown to observe,

> Nobody raised a question about his film's wacky insinuations that Bush let Taliban thugs escape because of some previously concocted deal in Texas or let Osama bin Laden get away because of deep Bush connections to the bin Laden

family. In Moore's version of Iraq, nobody was hanging from a meat hook in Saddam Hussein's jails. Baghdad was a happy city where children frolicked in the streets until boom! We blew them away. The invasion of Afghanistan? That was just a cover for running an oil pipeline across the country. . . . This crowd feels that they're entitled to some lefty exuberance after biting their tongues through a week of Republican mythmaking [the recent funeral for President Ronald Reagan]. Their Bush-loathing is so intense there is a pent-up longing for excess, a desire to be swept with emotions the cautious Democratic nominee can't arouse. They were so jazzed by Moore's rip-snorting assault, the discussion on the sidewalk afterward was about just one thing: Will it help with the swing vote?[18]

The National Education Association showed the film to its 11,000-plus members at its annual convention, and the NAACP did the same at its convention in mid-July. The Congressional Black Caucus organized a series of events around *Fahrenheit 9/11* at black churches across the country. Even a comparative moderate, Louisiana Democratic senator Mary Landrieu, declared, "It's been out there for three weeks, and there is not one criticism of that film that hasn't been backed up substantially because of the fact checks."

During the Democratic convention, Moore received an award from the Congressional Black Caucus. He spoke before a packed house at an event organized by the Campaign for America's Future, did an interview with Larry King, appeared on MSNBC with Ron Reagan, and chatted on ABC's *Good Morning America* from the floor of the convention. Recently defeated California governor Gray Davis told interviewers he likes Michael Moore, respects him, and thinks there is "a lot of truth" in *Fahrenheit 9/11*.

And, of course, in what was widely interpreted as the highest-profile endorsement of Moore, there was his appearance sitting next to former president Jimmy Carter's box at the opening night of the Democratic convention. There is some dispute as to how extensive an invitation was offered by the former president; according to one account, Moore and his entourage were looking to find a different skybox they were invited to and someone in the Carter box pulled them in. Nonetheless, by every account, Moore was thrilled to meet Carter, and the feeling appeared to be mutual. Carter later told an interviewer that *Fahrenheit 9/11* was one of his two all-time favorite movies, sharing the top spot with *Casablanca*.

Whether the invitation was impromptu or planned, the high-profile seat next to one of the party's icons was widely interpreted as the Democratic Party's official seal of approval of the man, the movie, and his highly controversial message. A prominent political strategist close to the Bush White House says that "having Michael Moore with President Carter in the box," was a key moment of the 2004 campaign. "It was a fairly symbolic moment, to have an ex-president sitting with the leader of a left-wing movement, to have Moore so embraced by him and by them."

Asked after the election about the image of Moore and Carter sitting together at the convention, Joe Lieberman concluded it was a self-inflicted electoral chest wound. "This guy doesn't speak to me about what's patriotic and good about America. I thought it was a terrible signal to people watching. We lost a lot of voters in that one frame." [19]

All of this occurred after the film industry publication Screendaily.com reported that as *"Fahrenheit 9/11* was preparing to debut in Syria, Lebanon, Jordan, Egypt, the United Arab Emirates, Kuwait, Qatar, Oman and Bahrain, it was getting a marketing 'boost from organizations related to Hezbollah.' " [20] In late summer 2004, the Iranian government scrapped the films scheduled to play at the Farabi Cinema in Tehran and showed *Fahrenheit 9/11,* timing the release to coincide with the three-year anniversary of the 9/11 attacks.[21]

Take a moment to consider under what circumstances you would accept money from the Iranian government.

The Moore Fallout

Did Michael Moore cost Democrats at the ballot box? Hell, yes.

In 2004, Virginia Schrader ran as a Democrat in the congressional race for the 8th District of Pennsylvania, located in suburban Philadelphia and the Delaware River Valley. The seat became open when Jim Greenwood, a relatively liberal pro-choice Republican, retired. Schrader screened *Fahrenheit 9/11* at a fund-raiser, prompting the Republican National Congressional Committee to distribute a flyer labeling her as the candidate of "The Hate America Crowd" and calling Moore "her running mate." After losing the campaign, Schrader showed polling data to the *American Prospect*, suggesting that 12 percent of those who saw the flyer were affected by it, and persuaded some to vote against her. Republican Michael Fitzpatrick ended up winning rather easily, ruining one of the best open seat opportunities the Democrats had that year.[22]

The flyer and screening weren't the sole reasons for Schrader's defeat, but they gave the GOP candidate an emotionally powerful issue with which he could paint his opponent as extreme and anti-American.

"The Democrat you don't want to run against is the one who's respected, who shares your values, respects your family, respects your business," says Alex Castellanos. "When you see somebody who is the embodiment of the antithesis of these values, well, Michael Moore is the perfect poster child for that."

Governor Mike Johanns, a Nebraska Republican, said that each time Michael Moore spoke up for John Kerry, Mr. Kerry's support in Nebraska took a dive.[23] The average Moore supporter may scoff; Nebraska is hardly a swing state. But Democratic senator Ben Nelson and any Democrat who would wish to challenge Johanns or Senator Chuck Hagel or run for the state's three congressional seats *do* care about how Moore shaped the party's image in that state.

Former Clinton chief of staff Leon Panetta concluded, "The party of FDR has become the party of Michael Moore, and that doesn't help the party."

More than a few political observers saw Moore as a heavyweight factor in the Democrats' awful year. "Michael Moore, I think, actually had a very major impact—a negative impact—on the Democratic Party," Cokie Roberts said in a postelection appearance on Chris Matthews's *Sunday* show, "because I think he exemplified all of the things people hate about Democrats."

"They don't shave?" joked the host.

"His physical appearance did not help," she agreed, "and the fact that [Moore's] *Fahrenheit 9/11* was a 'Hate America First' movie, and people think that that's what the Democrats stand for. That hurts the Democrats every time."[24]

A certain number of Americans love Moore; thus, his future films are guaranteed hits. But a larger percentage hates him. He was booed during a postelection appearance on the *Tonight Show*, and it seems a certain chunk of the middle is repelled by him. On balance, he has done the Democrats more harm than good.

Peter Beinart, editor of the *New Republic*, gamely tried to make the case that Moore hurts liberals, in a widely discussed postelection essay, "A Fighting Faith":

Today, most liberals naively consider Moore a useful ally, a bomb-thrower against a right-wing that deserves to be torched. What they do not understand is that his real casualties are on the decent left. When Moore opposes the war against the Taliban, he casts doubt upon the sincerity of liberals who say they opposed the Iraq war because they wanted to win in Afghanistan first. When Moore says terrorism should be no greater a national concern than car accidents or pneumonia, he makes it harder for liberals to claim that their belief in civil liberties does not imply a diminished vigilance against Al Qaeda.[25]

The general reaction from Beinart's readers was that Moore wasn't the problem with the Democrats; underhanded tactics by the Republicans are. The grassroots commentators on Daily Kos denounced Beinart as an "alleged Democrat."

Kevin Drum of the *Washington Monthly* offered a stunning and perhaps revealing response:

> What [Beinart] really needs to write is a prequel to his current piece, one that presents the core argument itself: namely, **why defeating Islamic totalitarianism should be a core liberal issue. . . .** The fact is that compared to fascism and communism, Islamic totalitarianism seems like pretty thin beer to many. It's not fundamentally expansionist, and its power to kill people isn't even remotely in the same league. . . . Bottom line: I think the majority of liberals could probably be persuaded to take a harder line on the war on terror—although it's worth emphasizing that the liberal response is always going to be different from the conservative one, just as containment was a different response to the Cold War than outright war. But first **someone has to make a compelling case that the danger is truly overwhelming. So far, no one on the left has really done that.**

If you don't see the need to defeat Islamist totalitarianism by now, you probably never will.

There is no equivalent figure to Michael Moore on the Right—and that's a good thing for Republicans. No matter how off-base Rush Limbaugh's assessment of Donovan McNabb is, he's never stuck his foot in his mouth as deep as Moore has, and he certainly doesn't create controversies as frequently. Ann Coulter and Michael Savage are verbal bomb-throwers of the Right, but it is unlikely either will be seated next to George H. W. Bush or Gerald Ford at a future Republican convention.

And liberals do themselves a disservice if they respond to this argument by pointing to shrill voices on the Right and insisting they're worse. For starters, it's exactly what Moore would do. Whatever flaws the Coulters and Savages of the world have, the GOP makes sure that their gadflies never get in a position to cost the party votes.

The Democrats will never win a majority so long as Michael Moore is seen as one of the animating spirits of the party. His criticisms of President Bush are often laced with inaccuracies and distortions, and he has a blind spot for excusing America's enemies. His books and longer works just pile up "Bush messed up" assertions one after another, a litany of complaints that offer no real solutions or ideas on the war on terror, economics, or any other issue.

Despite Moore's short-lived combed and shaved postelection look, he will remain a lead roadblock to Democratic efforts to bring their party's image back to the center.

THE (MOSTLY) PITCH-PERFECT FACES
OF THE GOP

Meanwhile, most of the most prominent GOP faces in recent years have been perfect for an era of the war on terror.

Besides Bush's landing on the USS *Abraham Lincoln* that evoked the closing scene of *Top Gun,* perhaps the most cinematic image of the post-9/11 administration came in an Annie Liebovitz photo that ran on the cover of *Vanity Fair.* The dramatic portrait showed the top level of the administration—Bush, Cheney, secretary of state Colin Powell, former national security adviser Condi Rice, secretary of defense Donald Rumsfeld, CIA director George Tenet, and White House chief of staff Andy Card—clad in black and appearing cool, calm, and in control. All they lacked were the dark sunglasses of the *Men in Black.*

Outside the administration, the Republican Party has been quick to maximize the political advantage of four of its biggest stars: Rudy Giuliani, John McCain, Mitt Romney, and Arnold Schwarzenegger.

"The Republicans and Democrats have a different idea of who their stars are," says Patrick Ruffini. "There are a large number of people who like Arnold but are not necessarily going to go to the barricades for him. The GOP's stars are mainstream figures who are generally liked by a lot of people and not really disliked at all. They have a bigger net favorability. The Democrats' stars generate this strong anger and also this strong sense of excitement among a very small, very vocal segment of population."

You may wonder if Ruffini is underestimating the popularity of these figures. Rudy Giuliani is an incomparable figure in American politics today. He was called "America's mayor" after 9/11, was named *Time*'s "Man of the Year" for that epoch-changing year, and is one of the few politicians who earned the adjective "Churchillian." If, as is widely believed, Rudy has presidential aspirations, he has serious advantages and has not hesitated to put his prestige on the line to help the Republican Party.

In 2002, Giuliani filmed commercials for 24 GOP candidates and took more than 30 political trips on their behalf. He ignored whatever ideological differences he had with social conservatives like

Jim Talent of Missouri and even paleocon Bob Smith of New Hampshire. Bush extensively used Giuliani to bolster his own reelection campaign, joining him frequently on the campaign trail. The RNC and Bush-Cheney 2004 campaign rapid-response e-mails to reporters often included quotes from the former mayor. Giuliani was part of a GOP team dispatched to Boston during the Democratic convention to ridicule the record of John Kerry. Giuliani called Kerry "an indecisive candidate with an inconsistent position on the war on terror." [26]

Arizona senator John McCain evokes somewhat similar feelings to Giuliani. He has a stunning personal story, surviving years of brutal abuse as a POW in Vietnam and rejecting offers of early release that were meant to hurt the morale of other American prisoners. When the late-night comedy shows reappeared after *9/11*, McCain was one of the first guests, able to offer traumatized audiences just the right tone of sympathy, inspiration, and determination.

"We send cruise missiles and then we think everything's all right or we try to bring them to trial," McCain said. "My friends, this time they've gone too far. This time we're serious. This time we won't quit until they are gone, completely gone from the face of the earth. . . . To the guilty, may God have mercy on you . . . because we won't."

He even offered a bit of humor for the circumstances.

McCAIN: Dave, do you know what Osama bin Laden is going to be on Halloween?
DAVID LETTERMAN: I don't know, what?
McCAIN: *Dead.*

Even at the gubernatorial level or lower, certain Republicans have staked out positions that demonstrate a hard-nosed approach to the war on terror.

Massachussetts governor Mitt Romney ruffled feathers in September 2005 when he said in a speech at the Heritage Foundation, "How about people who are in settings—mosques, for instance—that may be teaching doctrines of hate and terror? Are we monitoring that? Are we wiretapping? Are we following what's going on?"

Civil libertarians were aghast, and vocal Muslim groups declared the suggestion "an affront to American values." But mosques where radical imams preach the message of jihad are the exact places where we're most likely to find Islamist extremists and aspiring terrorists. Despite vocal protests, Romney defended the idea as "common sense" and refused to retract his comments or apologize.

Perhaps Romney's tough-mindedness comes from his experience managing the 2002 Winter Olympics in Salt Lake City, held four months after the attacks. It's easy to forget today, but many feared a terrorist attack at those games, a global target on American soil with the world's media watching—with even the president on site for the opening ceremony. Romney's record in Salt Lake and his first years as governor of the Bay State were strong enough to spur widespread speculation that he would succeed Tom Ridge as the second Secretary of Homeland Security, a position that ultimately went to Michael Chertoff.

The instinctive knock on governors is that they generally lack foreign policy experience and nuts-and-bolts familiarity with counterterrorism policy. Romney would be an exception to that rule.

And in the California special election of 2003, the Republican Party got its biggest and most important gift from Hollywood since Ronald Reagan: the Austrian bodybuilder-turned-megastar-turned-lawmaker Arnold Schwarzenegger. While the position of California governor isn't quite central to the war on terror, the emergence of Ah-nuld as one of the GOP's most high-profile figures only reinforced the characteristics the public associated with the party: masculinity, strength, toughness, and the occasional Reaganesque wise-crack.

In a time when, as the satirical Web site the Onion put it, "American Life Turns into Bad Jerry Bruckheimer Movie," the GOP's biggest figure outside Washington is the action hero who's been blowing away bad guys on the silver screen for decades. The only way Arnold could be any better for the party's image is if he were *actually* a time-traveling cyborg impervious to bullets sent from the future to protect the innocent.

Arnold had one of the most significant addresses at the 2004 Republican convention, and not just because he made the counterintuitive declaration that he found Richard Nixon to be "a breath of fresh air." This movie star, who had enormous likability and respect from millions of Americans who don't follow politics, made the case for the president's leadership on the war on terror, the common sense of Republican values, and the optimistic sense that America had rebounded from the pain of 9/11 and was, as he is famous for saying, . . . *back*.

> My fellow Americans, make no mistake about it: Terrorism is more insidious than communism, because it yearns to destroy not just the individual, but the entire international order. The President did not go into Iraq because the polls told him it was popular. As a matter of fact, the polls said just the opposite. But leadership isn't about polls. It's about ma—It's about making decisions you think are right and then standing behind those decisions. That's why America is safer with George W. Bush as President. He knows—He knows you don't reason with terrorists. You defeat them. He knows you can't reason with people blinded by hate. You see, they hate the power of the individual. They hate the progress of

women. They hate the religious freedom of others. And they hate the liberating breeze of democracy. But ladies and gentlemen, their hate is no match for America's decency.

Next, Arnold focused on an explicit sales pitch for the party, not just for himself or the president, aimed at a lot of young male voters who don't usually pay attention to politics:

Now, many of you out there tonight are "Republican" like me—in your hearts and in your belief. Maybe you're from Guatemala. Maybe you're from the Philippines. Maybe you're from Europe or the Ivory Coast. Maybe you live in Ohio, Pennsylvania, or New Mexico. And maybe—And maybe, just maybe, you don't agree with this Party on every single issue. I say to you tonight that I believe that's not only okay, but that's what's great about this country. Here—Here we can respectfully disagree and still be patriotic, still be American, and still be good Republicans.

My fellow immigrants, my fellow Americans, how do you know if you are a Republican? Well, I['ll] tell you how.

If you believe that government should be accountable to the people, not the people to the government, then you are a Republican.

If you believe that a person should be treated as an individual, not as a member of an interest group, then you are a Republican.

If you believe that your family knows how to spend your money better than the government does, then you are a Republican.

If you believe that our educational system should be held accountable for the progress of our children, then you are a Republican.

If you believe—If you believe that this country, not the United Nations, is the best hope for democracy, then you are a Republican.

And ladies and gentlemen—And ladies and gentlemen, if you believe that we must be fierce and relentless and terminate terrorism, then you are a Republican!

Now there's another way you can tell you're [a] Republican. You have faith in free enterprise, faith in the resourcefulness of the American people, and faith in the U.S. economy. And to those critics who are so pessimistic about our economy, I say: "Don't be economic girlie men!"

That last line got a standing ovation from Dick Cheney. Finally, the grand finale:

Let me tell you about a sacrifice and the commitment that I have seen firsthand. In one of the military hospitals I visited, I met a young guy who was in bad shape. He'd lost a leg; he had a hole through his stomach, and his shoulder had been shot through, and the list goes on and on and on.

I could tell that there was no way he could ever return to combat. But when I asked him, "When do you think you'll get out of the hospital?" he said to me, "Sir, in three weeks." And you know what he said to me then? He said he was going to get a new leg, and then he was going to get some therapy, and then he was going to go back to Iraq and fight alongside his buddies. And you know what he said to me then? He said, "Arnold, I'll be back!"

Well, ladies and gentlemen—ladies and gentlemen, America is back.

Perfect post-9/11 rhetoric. It takes the horror and fear of that day and tells of both a wounded veteran and all Americans overcoming all of that, becoming as tough, relentless, and unbeatable as any one of Arnold's action hero personas.

There is always a scene in action movies where the villain believes he has triumphed and then learns that the hero he thought he had defeated is back—and the hero comes back and defeats him. Years after 9/11, the country is still yearning for a moment where we could see Osama bin Laden cackling in hubris, and then turning around and gasping as he sees the American he thought was dead is alive, well, and about to defeat him. We may never get that moment. But seeing Saddam Hussein dragged out of the spider hole was a nice consolation prize.

This is one of the reasons that for all the casualties, carnage, chaos, and sense of unexpected problems in Iraq, the conflict there never emerged as a winning issue for Democrats in 2004. While anti-war Democrats were left to make the case that Saddam Hussein never represented that serious a threat to Americans, the voters knew what they saw. Previous televised images of Saddam had shown him in his military uniform, reviewing troop parades, firing a shotgun in the air, and denouncing America, threatening "the mother of all battles" and gloating over the 9/11 casualties. He was a classic villain, and Americans were not inclined after the trauma of the attacks to dismiss this guy or his deranged sons as no big deal.

Reportedly, Saddam spat at an American G.I. as he was arrested. *Time* magazine reported that the soldier promptly slugged him, offering a bare-knuckle introduction to the differences between the life of a dictator and the life of a prisoner. There was also a disputed story that the first words of the U.S. troops to Saddam were, "President Bush sends his regards." Maybe that exchange didn't happen, but the described scene is wonderfully cinematic. Were the same to occur with Osama being dragged out by U.S. troops somewhere in Afghanistan or Pakistan, America could psychologically roll the credits on their real-life Bruckheimer movie.

Of course, Republicans don't always pick out the right face to represent the party. But they seem to have a keener sense of the risks. Following Newt Gingrich's ouster in 1998, then-majority whip Tom DeLay—perhaps the most polarizing Republican in Congress—rejected a House speakership that was his for the taking.[27] Aware of the harm he might inflict on his party by becoming its public face, he instead installed his deputy, a quiet, little-known Illinois congressman, Dennis Hastert, in his place. Hastert's job was to be the anti-Gingrich—uncontroversial, bland, downright boring, even.

But the temptation to come out from behind the scenes and into the spotlight, and the opportunity to be a face of the party, is hard to resist. After the 2002 elections, DeLay became House majority leader and assumed a much more high-profile role, and has since caused the party more than their share of headaches. DeLay decided to resign from Congress in 2006.

The key lesson: The party that has the more appealing faces wins the election.

EIGHT

Even If You Say Michael Moore Isn't Your Face, the Other Guy Is Telling People That He Is

GENERAL RICHARD MYERS: And I just—let me just add, Mr. Secretary, it was effective. I mean, we've been on the ground and it had the desired effect.
REPORTER: Which was what? What was the desired effect?
MYERS: The desired effect was to kill al-Qaeda.
REPORTER: What sort of results are you aware of? What did your people on the ground see?
MYERS: Dead al-Qaeda.
  —*Pentagon briefing, Dec. 11, 2001*

We have the right to kill four million Americans—
two million of them children—and to exile twice as many and wound and cripple hundreds of thousands. America can be kept at bay by blood alone.
  —*al-Qaeda spokesman Suleiman Abu Gheith, June 2002*

> **Sept. 11 was not an unprovoked, gratuitous act. . . .
> Though dismissed widely, the best strategy for the
> United States may well be to acknowledge and ad-
> dress the collective reasons in which Al Qaeda an-
> chors its acts of force. Al Qaeda has been true to its
> word in announcing and implementing its strategy
> for over a decade. It is likely to be true to its word in
> the future and cease hostilities against the United
> States, and indeed bring an end to the war it de-
> clared in 1996 and in 1998, in return for some degree
> of satisfaction regarding its grievances.**
> —*Mohammad-Mahmoud Ould Mohamedou, associate di-
> rector of the Program on Humanitarian Policy and Con-
> flict Research at Harvard University, Friday, Sept. 16,
> 2005*

Democrats can insist that nobody elected Michael Moore to anything, and that no one outside of Vermont and the DNC committee
elected Howard Dean to any office. Yet Democrats rarely publicly
fight, criticize, or denounce these controversial figures, often out of
party solidarity.

The rise of a conservative-friendly alternative media ensures that
while Democrats may want to sweep these controversial figures
under the rug, FOX News and the gang will make sure they are front
and center.

The only way the public could have gotten the message that
Michael Moore only speaks for himself, and not for the Democrats,
would be for Democrats to denounce his unwiser comments. In
2004, they didn't dare. And they paid the price.

And when mainstream Democratic officials make gaffes or comments that come across as less-than-fully-hawkish, the conservative
media notices it and trumpets it as much as it can.

John Kerry may not have thought he was hurt by:

"I voted for the $87 billion before I voted against it."

"The war or terror is primarily an intelligence and law enforcement operation."

"I think the threat of terrorism has been overstated."

"We need to get terrorism down to the level where it is manageable, like organized crime or prostitution."

"[9/11] didn't change me much at all."

But the alternative media made sure as many voters as possible heard those remarks. The overall message was clear: Kerry is too weak and indecisive to lead a serious war on terror, and his presidency would mean four years of "duck and cover" from al-Qaeda attacks.

Take, for example, this October 2004 statement by Kerry adviser and former Clinton administration official Richard Holbrooke: "We're not in a war on terror, in the literal sense. The war on terror is like saying 'the war on poverty.' It's just a metaphor."[1]

As Holbrooke said this, roughly 140,000 members of the U.S. Armed Forces were in conflict or tracking al-Qaeda, Baathists, insurgents, and affiliated groups in Iraq, with an additional 30,000 soldiers estimated to be operating in Kuwait and other areas of the region supporting operations in Iraq. Another roughly 20,000 were continuing operations in Afghanistan, hunting for al-Qaeda and helping secure the newly elected Afghani government.

Besides the two high-profile military operations, the Pentagon had also deployed 100 special operations forces in Yemen to track al-Qaeda members, and 1,000 troops and special operations forces to help fight al-Qaeda–related groups in the Philippines. In 2002, U.S. Special Operations Forces were sent to the former Soviet republic of Georgia to train Georgian troops to fight rebels using terrorist tactics from Chechnya. And an unknown number of U.S. forces were also providing assistance to the Pakistanis in patrolling and hunting on their side of the border for Osama bin Laden, Ayman al-Zawahiri, and other al-Qaeda leaders. (These are just the ones we know about. Covert military action in Syria or Iran is not unimaginable.)

The war seemed plenty literal to these men and women in uniform.

Keep in mind Holbrooke was widely believed to be a leading candidate for secretary of state in a Kerry administration. To the *New York Times Magazine* writer who conducted the interview, the "metaphorical war" comment was nothing particularly newsworthy; it was simply one of many in an extraordinarily detailed 7,600-word look at Kerry's comments, views, and policy proposals on terrorism. But Holbrooke's assessment that the war on terror was merely a "metaphorical war" was widely circulated by Rush Limbaugh and other radio talk show hosts, the *Washington Times*, the *American Spectator*, the blogs, columnists Dick Morris and Jeff Jacoby, and Fox News. Max Boot described Kerry's approach as a rehash of Clinton's insufficient policies and labeled Kerry "The Man Who Was Unchanged" by 9/11. The web satirist Scrappleface suggested that Kerry's terrorism plan was to organize a "do-not-terrorize" list, akin to the recently formed "do-not-call" list.

The Republican National Committee spotlighted the quote. Finally, Bush himself began noting the comments in his stump speech. "Senator Kerry's top foreign policy adviser has questioned whether this is even a war at all. Here's what he said, and I quote, 'We're not in a war on terror in the literal sense. It is like saying 'the war on poverty,' it is just a metaphor.' End quote," Bush said during a campaign stop in Mason City, Iowa, on October 21, 2004. "Confusing food programs with terrorist killings reveals a fundamental misunderstanding of the war we face, and that is very dangerous thinking."

Presumably, Richard Holbrooke thought he was helping Kerry when he agreed to be interviewed by *Times* reporter Matt Bai. This comment, be it merely clumsy wording or his genuine thoughts, provided the Bush campaign with a handy stick to beat Kerry over the head. It didn't matter that Bai didn't spotlight it or that other major mainstream media sources didn't give it much play. Bush, the GOP, and the alternative media saw it as a revealing insight into the strategy of a Kerry administration and made sure as many voters as possible heard those words. The era when an (often Democratic) official could count on a friendly media to brush his gaffes and politically unwise comments under the rug was over.

Kerry didn't say that "the war on terror is just a metaphor," but he might as well have.

Upon this conclusion, the wail of many Democrats can be heard: "It's the right-wing noise machine!" "It's that damnable FOX News, propagandizing America into Rove's desired state of fearful subservience!"

But Holbrooke actually said it. And Moore actually said, "There is no terrorist threat." And Howard Dean really speculated that President Bush was warned about 9/11 by the Saudis and chose to let it happen. And so on. When a Democratic candidate or his adviser makes a comment that sounds wimpy on terrorism, it reinforces a message that has been built—by Democrats and their supporters themselves—for years, if not decades. All the Republicans have to do is call attention to their opponent's words.

When a Democrat fumbles, the new alternative media takes the ball and runs with it. It's not a matter of orders from Rove or an agenda to portray Democrats as more dovish than they are. It's that the conservatives who work in these organizations largely believe that every Democrat *really is* a spineless wimp when it comes to military force, and thus electing them is akin to national suicide. The alternative media doesn't see their reporting and commentary as painting the Democrats in false colors; they see it as revealing their true nature.

"The rise of the non-MSM is very much responsible for the fact that the statements of left liberals don't get buried and forgotten," says John Podhoretz, a man connected like few others in conservative media. He is a FOX News Channel contributor, a twice-weekly columnist for the *New York Post*, a weekly columnist for *National Review Online*, a contributing editor to *Weekly Standard* magazine, and a consulting editor at ReganBooks. He explains:

> The way people used to remember them was this: Two months after somebody said something, a compendium article in *Commentary* or *NR* or the *American Spectator* on some subject would gather all the statements made on a given topic and then the really bad ones would become memorable, quoted samizdat-like and remembered. Now we don't have to wait two months. More important, the theoretical audience for the circulation of these quotes is infinite, as opposed to the universe of a magazine with 50,000 subscribers who tell others and then over time it leaches downward into the popular culture. . . . The Internet has been a kind of reality check, a watchdog, a way of ensuring that the most extreme statements of what are generally held left liberal positions don't vanish into the ether, which is then reflected in FOX, etc.

"I think blogging (and the other alternative media) are really picking up where the National Conservative Political Action Committee left off," says Mike Krempasky, former political director for American Target Advertising, a conservative direct mail firm founded by conservative activist pioneer Richard Viguerie. He cofounded several blogs including RedState.org, Rathergate.com, and NotSpecter.com.

"In Viguerie's 'America's Right Turn,' he tells the whole story of going out to the country and telling voters what Democrats were really voting for in Washington. Now the Democrats have learned a little more about how to vote, but they keep spouting off—and instead of telling those folks in South Dakota some bad vote—we can tell them about chumming about with Michael Moore—and do it instantly, with documentary evidence."

Viguerie himself points out that 2004 was the first presidential election framed by the new and alternative media—cable TV, talk radio, the Internet, and political direct mail.[2]

It can be argued that the alternative media now is actually more influential and effective than the mainstream media.

SAFE DISTRICT DEMS HURT
PURPLE-STATE DEMS

So why do Democrats keep committing acts of political self-immolation? Why have they rarely been able to go a month without someone in the party saying something stupid and providing the GOP with fresh ammunition that the conservative alternative media spotlights? Perhaps it is the echo chamber phenomenon.

Too many Democrats reside, work, and spend almost all of their daily life in very "blue" environments—that is, they have to make an effort to encounter someone who disagrees with them. They represent blue states and blue districts, read the *New York Times* and the *New Yorker,* never click the channel to FOX News, and chat with friends in the party's support structure in environmental groups, civil rights organizations, unions, antiwar groups, and trial lawyers. There's nothing wrong with any of that—but if these Democrats wanted to hermetically seal off their lives from any interaction with red state America, it would be effortless.

There is an echo-chamber phenomenon on the right as well, but it's nearly impossible for a Republican to work in politics and have no exposure to blue-state America. Even the alternative media of FOX News, talk radio, the blogs, and such are often reacting to what they see as poor reporting in the mainstream media. They're often up in arms about the latest statement by John Kerry, Howard Dean, or Hillary Clinton. Republicans may not necessarily hang out with Democrats (though they probably ought to), but it's impossible to not know what the Democratic assessment, spin, or thinking is on any given issue.

(In fact, there is a bizarre phenomenon of extreme attentiveness to lefty comments in righty circles. Conservative bloggers, in particular, seem to have this intense interest in what the fringiest of the left fringe is saying about the political news of the day. When a big event shakes up the political world, like Iraq news or a Supreme Court justice retiring, the first reaction of certain right-of-center bloggers is to look at the reaction from the hard left sites—DemocraticUnderground.com, the commenters on Daily Kos, AmericaBlog, the HuffingtonPost, etc.)

For an example of a well-meaning Democratic leader trapped in a deep blue echo chamber, look no further than House minority leader Nancy Pelosi. Most of her Republican critics will concede that she is passionate, hardworking, and loves her country. But a legislative career spent representing San Francisco has made her tone-deaf to appealing to red states or even purple districts. (One example: She opposed the 1991 Gulf war partly on the grounds that it could create an "ecological disaster of the first order" in the Persian Gulf. The environment is an important issue, and the first Gulf war had its risks. But if your argument against taking on Saddam centers around egret health, a lot of Americans will tune you out.) Until she became minority leader, Pelosi never needed to appeal to centrists, because there just aren't that many in her district.

In 2002, the *New Republic* didn't welcome her leadership because they saw her as even less capable of winning over red America than her predecessor: "In the most recent election cycle, the Democrats' decision to go to the mat for labor by stalling a homeland security bill wound up costing them at least one Senate seat—and, perhaps, two or three. Neither Dick Gephardt nor Tom Daschle, both of whom hail from swing states, saw this disaster coming. Is there any reason to believe Pelosi, who has never in her own races had to reflect on the inclinations of swing voters, wouldn't do even worse?"

The magazine found that none of Pelosi's allies would even consider the possibility that their opposition to the president's Iraq policy had hurt them in the 2002 elections. Massachusetts representative Barney Frank scoffed that operatives with polling data showing the war to be a campaign liability were peddling "bulls—t." California's Anna Eshoo said questions about the party's national security image amounted to "Beltway think." [3]

Well, of course they think the party's doing fine on the issue; their stances were and are popular in New Bedford and Palo Alto. The problem is for the southern and midwestern Democrats who cannot win if the party has the Pelosi-Frank-Eshoo stance as its face.

THE LURE OF THE BASE'S LOVE

There's another phenomenon affecting Democrats with national aspirations. If you're Bill Clinton, an extraordinarily gifted politician, you can pretty much set your own course and bring the party with you. If you want welfare reform, NAFTA, or a war in Kosovo, you can persuade your party to support those policies. If you want tax increases, you can persuade the country that they're necessary. The entire time, your raw charisma will keep both the party and the public behind you, even if you have other factors complicating your political leadership. To take a random example, let's say, getting caught suborning perjury and lying under oath after doing the horizontal mambo with an intern during working hours in the Oval Office. You have the love of the party and the public, and you'll keep it.

But if you're not such a great politician, you really don't have much chance to get that love. You'll always be vaguely appreciated. You'll get periodic appearances on the Sunday morning shows, and luncheons at think tanks, and the usual perks of Washington life. But you will never be revered and will rarely have much opportunity to set the course for your party. And you won't be scandal-proof, as former California congressman Gary Condit learned.

These second- and third-tier officeholders know they will never head a movement. Their names will never become an adjective (Reaganesque/Clintonesque), their ideas will never become a philosophy (Clintonism/Reaganism), their staffers and followers will never be labeled by their leader (Clintonite/Reaganite). . . . Their autobiographies will be minor sellers at best, and they'll be quickly forgotten after their retirement.

But also-rans and never-weres have a chance for a form of greatness . . . if they embrace the party's base. If you're a mediocre Democratic officeholder who goes out there to the hard left—if you adopt their policies, and their rhetoric, and serve the base voters a steady diet of red meat, they'll love you. The center will think you've gone nuts, but whenever you need to, you can show up on a college campus, or at a MoveOn.org rally, or at an antiwar protest or some other event, and the teeming multitudes of the Democratic left will treat you like a rock star.

Embrace the base, and suddenly you're Elvis, Malcom X, and Harry "I give 'em the truth and they think it's hell" Truman rolled into one. Air America will fawn over you. Liberal bloggers will label you their dream presidential candidate. Even the officeholder who never tries to climb that political Everest will become a kingmaker in the party, a leader with followers who must be courted. Embracing the scathing rhetoric, raw anger, out-there policies, and conspiracy theories is a sure route to a finite but addictive amount of power. As Bush's web guru Patrick Ruffini put it:

> Remember the Al Gore 2000 campaign. Back then, Al was a dry, boring technocrat—able to spit out poll-tested lines that kept him in the game—but ultimately unloved. Then he fell into what he calls "that little known third category." And instantly, legions of left-wing activists rose up to proclaim him their president; people were still waving his signs along the inaugural parade route. Suddenly, this conventional pol became the most remembered and beloved loser in the history of modern Presidential politics. And no thanks to the DLCers [centrists at the Democratic Leadership Council]— who even then chafed at Gore's left turn in the 2000 election, replete with a Shrumian "people vs. the powerful" motif. It was the MoveOn crowd, not the DLC, who finally made Gore a star, and he owed them.
>
> Fast forward to a little known former Governor of Vermont, a man with an unimpressive resume who nonetheless stirred "passion" and "energy" in his audiences wherever he set foot. And the Deaniacs bent the Democrats so far out of shape that even some mainstream observers wondered whether this "passion"—of which the Internet money was an outgrowth—was a prelude to true success. Here again, the Left transforms a pedestrian figure who panders to their interests into a cult leader—so much so that the internal culture of the Dean campaign held that victory in 2004 was secondary to building some transcendental "movement."[4]

Even besides unelected buffoons like Michael Moore, the Democrats have two other unappealing groups competing to be their face: blue-state Democrats who don't care about appealing to the center and insecure formerly centrist Democrats who lust after the love of the party's angry base voters—neither of which will help the party win back any red states.

To a certain extent, this phenomenon occurs on the right. It could be argued that Spiro Agnew, Richard Nixon, George H. W. Bush, and Bob Dole were establishment Republicans who veered right and embraced their party's base when they deemed it politically advantageous. But looking at the post-9/11 era, it is hard to recall a second-tier Republican who once had centrist credibility inside the beltway throw it away and grew more conservative in office.

REPUBLICANS EXPEL THEIR GUYS WHO LOOK STUPID

Credit the Republicans for weeding out and denouncing their members who make controversial or unpopular statements. Some of this is pure political calculation—Republicans know they can't afford the electoral price of sticking by the politically radioactive in their midst.

Ann Coulter had her column dropped by the *National Review* after calling for forced conversions to Christianity. Ari Fleischer said Representative Cooksey should watch what he says and that there's "never a time" for his comments. Falwell and Robertson lost whatever influence they had outside the core of the religious Right.

While not related to the war on terror, Trent Lott was quickly ditched as Senate majority leader after declaring, "I want to say this about my state: When Strom Thurmond ran for president [in 1948, on an explicitly segregationist platform], we voted for him. We're proud of it. And if the rest of the country had followed our lead, we wouldn't have had all these problems over all these years, either." That brought a scathing criticism from many within his own party, and conservative publications like the *National Review*, and finally a direct presidential rebuke.

Perhaps the greatest example of this phenomenon is the near-complete marginalization of the "paleocon" school of thought in the Republican Party. A longtime Republican who departed the party in 2000, Pat Buchanan offered this explanation of 9/11 during a debate on Chris Matthews's *Hardball* on September 30, 2002: "9/11 was a direct consequence of the United States meddling in an area of the world where we do not belong and where we are not wanted. We were attacked because we were on Saudi sacred soil and we are so-called repressing the Iraqis and we're supporting Israel and all the rest of it."

This, and a slew of other comments by a group of right-of-center columnists, thinkers, and writers often labeled "paleoconservatives" spurred the *National Review* to essentially call for their excommunication from the conservative movement, not just the Republican Party.

In a scathing cover story titled, "Unpatriotic Conservatives," contributing editor David Frum called out Buchanan and syndicated columnist Robert Novak, as well as lesser-known figures such as Llewellyn Rockwell, Samuel Francis, Thomas Fleming, Scott McConnell, Justin Raimondo, Joe Sobran, Charley Reese, Jude Wanniski, Eric Margolis, and Taki Theodoracopulos. The Frum argument, in a nutshell:

Now it is time to be very frank about the paleos. During the Clinton years, many conservatives succumbed to a kind of gloom. With Bill Bennett, they mourned the "death of outrage." America now has non-metaphorical deaths to mourn. There is no shortage of outrage—and the cultural pessimism of the 1990s has been dispelled. The nation responded to the terrorist attacks with a surge of patriotism and pride, along with a much-needed dose of charity. Suddenly, many conservatives found they could look past the rancor of the Clinton years, past the psychobabble of the New Age gurus, past the politically correct professors, to see an America that remained, in every important way, the America of 1941 and 1917 and 1861 and 1776. As Tennyson could have said: "What we were, we are."

America has social problems; the American family is genuincly troubled. The conservatism of the future must be a social as well as an economic conservatism. But after the heroism and patriotism of 9/11 it must also be an optimistic conservatism.

There is, however, a fringe attached to the conservative world that cannot overcome its despair and alienation. The resentments are too intense, the bitterness too unappeasable. Only the boldest of them as yet explicitly acknowledge their wish to see the United States defeated in the War on Terror. But they are thinking about defeat, and wishing for it, and they will take pleasure in it if it should happen.

They began by hating the neoconservatives. They came to hate their party and this president. They have finished by hating their country.

War is a great clarifier. It forces people to take sides. The paleoconservatives have chosen—and the rest of us must choose too. In a time of danger, they have turned their backs on their country. Now we turn our backs on them."[5]

The nonpaleoconservatives knew, and argued, that there would be severe political consequences for letting Pat Buchanan be one of the faces of the party or conservatism itself. (It is worth noting that "Pitchfork Pat" officially cut his ties to the GOP in 2000 to run on the

Reform Party ticket.) Chris Matthews once wrote that presidential elections are always won by "the guy with sun on his face"—the one whom you can picture, beaming in bright sunlight, smiling before a crowd outside. The GOP brain trust treats the paleocon's dour defeatism as a poison to be avoided at all costs.

DON'T EVEN TRUST HAWKISH DEMOCRATS

When conservatives aren't spotlighting the dovish gaffes of Democrats, they're making the case that even a hawkish Democrat can't be trusted to enact hawkish policies. Sometimes this argument is put quite directly—that even hawkish-appearing Democrats can't be trusted because of the influence of the party's dovish wing. Stanley Kurtz explained how even Joe Lieberman, perhaps the most hawkish figure in the party, a supporter of the Iraq war whose views are diametrically opposed to the party's base, could not truly be expected to take an aggressive stance were he ever to be elected president:

> The Sixties-inflected antiwar wing of the Democratic party makes the party untrustworthy on critical issues of war, peace, and national security. Even with the best of intentions, any Democratic hawk elected to the presidency is going to be subjected to tremendous pressures from within his own party to back down. The example of Tony Blair shows that it is possible to lead a party or a country, in such a situation. But the British case also shows how perilous it is to be a hawk in a dovish party. After all, Tony Blair came very close to being ousted. A lesser man than Blair might have buckled under the pressure and found an excuse to join the doves. And whatever he'd done, Blair might simply have lost and been replaced. . . . Any prominent hawkish Democrat, be he pundit or pres-

ident, is going to be subjected to almost unbearable pressure from the [Nancy] Pelosi wing of the party. Until that changes, it's going to be tough to trust a Democrat in the White House.[6]

At a Bush rally on the campaign trail in Muskegon, Michigan, Representative Pete Hoekstra, the chairman of the House Select Committee on Intelligence, contended that Michael Moore is one of Kerry's principal foreign policy advisers.[7]

"Democratic Party apologists want to persuade the public that their pacifist caucus can be contained and kept from the levers of power, but that never happens," wrote conservative radio talk show host, blogger, and author Hugh Hewitt. "The government is too vast, the demands for patronage for the activists, too strong. . . . The 'blame America first' impulse is alive and dominant in the Democratic Party, and unless and until it is rooted out, the Democrats cannot be trusted with the country's national security."[8]

Hewitt continued, "The theme of 2004 is simple: the Democrats aren't serious about terrorism. They talk a good game, but they don't fight a good war. Their hearts aren't in it, and they'd rather have the UN manage such stuff. They don't like the idea of killing people. Period. And they have been suspicious of the military since Vietnam."[9]

This message isn't limited to conservative columnists and writers. A staple of Bush's campaign rhetoric in 2004 was to state, "You cannot negotiate with these people. You cannot hope for the best from them. You cannot hope they'll change their ways." The unspoken subtext is that there is some dangerous faction of Democrats who wanted to sign a treaty with al-Qaeda.

A *New Republic* writer picked up the message in that first night of the Republican convention: "Listening to McCain, you'd have thought Michael Moore was on the short list to be John Kerry's national security adviser. Listening to Giuliani, you'd have thought John Kerry's approach to fighting terrorism was to capture the terrorists and then let them go after a couple of hours, maybe after a stern talking to about how terrorism is mean."[10] The pounding of this message, day after day, from hawkish officeholders and hawkish columnists and at kitchen tables and barstools around the country, cumulatively had an effect.

The volume and intensity of the antiwar wing's message means it doesn't matter if you're a hawkish Democrat. A significant chunk of the voting public that supports hawkish policies just won't trust you.

IT'S GETTING WORSE—NEW UGLY DEMOCRATIC FACES

The supremacy of the issue of fighting terrorism, the historical weakness of Democrats on this issue since Vietnam, the political consequences of sounding dovish in a time of war, the importance of controlling the face of your party—none of these are state secrets. And yet, despite the supremely illustrative case study of the 2004 elections, there are many indications that the Democratic Party has exacerbated its problems in recent years, instead of taking steps to solve them.

The faces of this year's party aren't that much better than they were in 2004. In the world of blogs, there is no more prominent or influential voice on the left than Markos Moulitsas and his site/discussion board, Daily Kos. Mention this to conservatives and probably the first thing they will mention is Moulitsas's April 1, 2004, response to the savage murder of four American contractors in Fallujah: "I feel nothing over the death of the mercenaries [sic]. They are there to wage war for profit. Screw them."

Two days after the 2004 election, Kos shared the good news with his readers: the "big silver lining" to Bush's victory was that America will lose the Iraq war on Bush's watch:

> The big silver lining, and it's significant, is that Kerry won't be tarred for cleaning up Bush's mess. Had Kerry gotten us out of Iraq, he would've been blamed for "losing the war." Now Bush will ineptly lose it for himself. Kerry would've been forced to make sense of a mess of a budget. Now Bush will be responsible for his own half-trillion dollar deficits.

Declaring an American military defeat as a "silver lining" and a good thing is the sort of comment that can make Democratic strategists induce a concussion by banging their head against the wall in frustration.

Fascinatingly, since the 2004 election in which Kos endorsed Dean (who lost), Clark (who lost), Kerry (who lost), and 15 House members (who *all* lost), the site has gone mainstream. (In 2004, Moulitsas raised more than $500,000 through his Web site to assist the campaigns of those 15 House candidates.) Not in the sense of moderating its message to appear to the middle—but it has become a major venue for Democrats to communicate with the grassroots. Lawmakers who have posted to the site, often lavishing the Kos community with thanks and praise, include Senators Barbara Boxer of California, John Kerry of Massachusetts, Jon Corzine of New Jersey, Barack Obama of Illinois, and Russ Feingold of Wisconsin, as well as Representatives John Conyers of Michigan and Louise Slaughter of New York.

The passion of the Daily Kos community is credited with generating a great deal of momentum for Howard Dean's election to the chairmanship of the Democratic National Committee. Some senior

Democratic operatives told the *Los Angeles Times* that unease about a Dean chairmanship is widespread among congressional leaders and many governors. But almost none of those grumbling privately expressed their concerns publicly—in part, because they fear crossing the ardent grassroots, Internet activist community still backing Dean.[11] The headline on Daily Kos after this report was published? "They Finally Fear Us."

Kos has laid out a "litmus test" for the kind of Democratic candidate he will endorse and support:

> Does the candidate "distance himself" from the party and/or its leaders, or is he proud to be a Democrat?
>
> Does he talk like a bureaucrat or like a regular person?
>
> Does she make it clear that she opposes Bush and the Republicans?
>
> Does she back down when the corporate press/media or Republican pundits attack her, or does she stand by her words?
>
> Does he sleepwalk through the campaign, or does he act like he wants to win?[12]

Kos adds, "Notice the complete lack of ideology"—that is, it is not about the policy positions; the Kos endorsement is all about the attitude and the anger. Anger and attitude sell terrific in Moulitsas's hometown of Berkeley, California. They don't sell well where Democrats need to compete—Ohio, Florida, Colorado, Nevada. So the most powerful emerging grassroots-rallying, fund-raising phenom within the Democratic Party has pledged to only endorse candidates who have the exact opposite attitude that they need to win in swing states.

MOVEON.ORG

One of the most influential activist groups making up the Democratic Party's base is MoveOn.org, which organizes and informs an online community estimated at more than 3 million people. The group, founded as an effort aimed to persuade Congress to "move on" from impeaching President Bill Clinton, runs a Political Action Committee, voter registration drives, and political advertising particularly in swing states. The group spent $30 million in 2004.

At times, MoveOn.org seems like the organizational equivalent of the bumbling employee who keeps "falling upward" to higher positions. It was founded to persuade the House to move on from impeachment, which passed on a mostly party-line vote. Its petition regarding September 11 called for "justice, not escalating violence." The country rejected the Gandhi approach to al-Qaeda and the Taliban. It opposed the recall of California governor Gray Davis, the war in Iraq, congressional redistricting in Texas, and the reelection of President Bush. Passed, passed, passed, won. The MoveOn Political Action Committee endorsed 27 candidates for the House or Senate in the 2004 election; 5 won.

As one liberal critic observed, "The group declares its actions to be a success when it organizes its members to call a congressional office every five minutes, or to circulate an e-mail, instead of when one of its political aims is achieved. MoveOn has turned itself into a perpetual motion machine, one that's great at inspiring its members to engage in the political version of treadmill running but never goes anywhere."[13]

Unfortunately, the group's unofficial motto seems to be "passion first, results . . . eventually." Time and again, MoveOn's leadership has demonstrated a refusal to compromise or water down its message that evokes a Leninist insistence for purity.

The group ran a contest during the 2004 presidential election in which people were invited to create and submit political TV ads critical of the Bush administration; apparently no one there seemed to recognize that a member-submitted TV ad comparing President George W. Bush to Adolf Hitler could be considered a wee bit controversial. (If the RNC Jewish Outreach Committee didn't send a handwritten thank-you note, they should have.)

Another campaign ad portrayed an American troop sinking into quicksand and appearing to surrender. Apparently the metaphor and image of a suffering U.S. soldier inspired enthusiastic smiles and high-fives at the group's HQ, but the over-the-top image wasn't such a big hit with viewers. The organization ran a full-page ad attacking the Gallup polling organization, a move that we will look at more extensively in a later chapter.

In September 2005, Ben Brandzel, the group's advocacy director, told *USA Today* that the group would air an ad featuring images of poverty-stricken victims of Hurricane Katrina to raise questions about the civil rights record of John Roberts, the nominee for U.S. chief justice, during the confirmation hearings in the Senate. Brandzel described an ad that would use images of African-American evacuees and suggest that Roberts might not be sensitive to the plight of the poor—including, presumably, those desperate evacuees. The next day, the organization suddenly denied that it had any plans for that ad, and "we regret any misunderstanding that may have arisen because of anything that our staff member might have told *USA Today*'s reporter."

In an e-mail to MoveOn members after the 2004 election, Eli Pariser, the executive director of MoveOn.org, wrote, "It's our party. We bought it, we own it and we're going to take it back." That's great news if you love covering flashy, controversial ads that call attention to MoveOn.org; bad news if you're a Democrat and you would like to win a close race before the end of the decade.

THE LOONS AT THE GRASSROOTS

This is all looking at elected officials, celebrities, or armchair strategists blogging their philosophies on the Internet. But when ordinary members of the party behave badly, it also reflects badly on the whole.

Take, for example, a postelection rally in San Francisco on Wednesday, November 3, the day after the election.[14] Many Democrats were devastated by the election results in 2004; it's understandable that the emotions would be raw.

But the manifestations of that disappointment and anger suggested that these angry liberals hated not merely Bush but Bush voters and were looking for a way to lash out at them. The crowd waved signs reading, "F—k Middle America"; "Can we secede already?" "I'm ashamed to be an American"; "Bush = Satan"; "The flag is not a blindfold: Investigate the CIA for 9/11."

As the protest continued into the evening, someone started burning George Bush in effigy. After torching the effigy, the angry crowd ignited an upside-down American flag and cheered its consumption by the flames. Bloggers took photos. Middle America noticed.

For another vibrant example of how ordinary liberals can shape the Democratic Party's image to its detriment, examine the 256-page picture book *Sorry, Everybody* that costs $14.95. The book declares itself to be "an open letter of apology from America to the rest of the world."

Shortly after the election, James Zetlen, a neuroscience student at the University of Southern California, created the Web site SorryEverybody.com, declaring, "Some of us—hopefully most of us—are trying to understand and appreciate the effect our recent election will have on you, the citizens of the rest of the world. As our so-called leaders redouble their efforts to screw you over, please remember that some of us—hopefully most of us—are truly, truly sorry. And we'll say we're sorry, even on behalf of the ones who aren't."

The entries speak for themselves: "I'm not sure how or why it happened. I thought our country was literate. I'm rather ashamed of the 51%." "Half of Ohio is really, really sorry. Don't hate us." (One wonders from the almost groveling, fearful tone, is the apology intended for French elites or al-Qaeda?)

The creators and contributors to SorryEverybody.com display a fascinating concept of sovereignty, in which it is somehow rude or inappropriate for Americans to elect a chief executive disliked by groups of foreigners. SorryEverybody is the sort of thing that right-of-center bloggers and talk show hosts love to spotlight, mock, and get angry about. It reinforces their belief that left-of-center Americans are not merely mistaken but weak-willed, hopelessly kumbaya types who wish to grovel before the moral authority of France, China, Russia, and the autocrats of the Middle East.

To right-of-center Americans, terrorism is "almost certainly the issue on which the campaigns of 2006, 2008, and beyond ought to be conducted."[15] No matter what the economic or social conditions are, terrorism will be on voters' minds when they enter the voting booth in the coming years. And when they see the D next to an official's name, they won't see the candidate's stances and rhetoric—or at least not exclusively. They'll see Michael Moore, and Daily Kos contributors, and MoveOn.org protesters.

"Right now, a lot of money, energy, and activism in the Democratic Party is with the hard left," says a senior Republican strategist close to the White House. "I think they're in a pickle. I think on a national level, they realize they will have a hard time winning as an antiwar party. But they have their base so energized on this issue. Their danger is that they have begun to believe the caricature of the president that they created. They get so filled with fever, hatred, and rage at the president that they begin to believe their own rhetoric. They don't understand that they come across as fringe elements. You get the sense they can't help themselves."

"The influence of new media on their side has not been a good one," says Ruffini, who managed the Bush campaign's Web site in 2004. "It has created a false sense of energy and drive on the left. If your primary criteria for a candidate is excitement, then the only type of candidate you're going to run is a Howard Dean. Politics isn't always supposed to be exciting—especially in an off year. You don't always need to be activating a frenzy among the die-hard members of your base. Sometimes it's worthwhile to be calm and take a step back and think about what's best in the long term—what's going to win votes on Election Day, not just win applause lines today."

"THE PARTY OF TERRORISTS' RIGHTS"

One of the oddest and most potentially disturbing trends among Democrats is their accelerating sense that there is political advantage to be had by shining a spotlight on incidents of prisoner abuse. Periodically in the war on terror, the national media has spotlighted reports of abuse. Sometimes the reports are accurate and disturbing, as in the case of Abu Ghraib. Sometimes they are unconfirmed and illusory, like *Newsweek*'s report of a Koran being flushed at Guantanamo. Despite the attention to these stories, they have had a limited impact on the public's political views.

The short answer for this phenomenon is that very few Americans lose sleep over the treatment of captured al-Qaeda operatives in Gitmo. These guys want to kill our children. The public's attitude toward interrogations is, "Do whatever you have to do to learn everything about them you can."

Ironically, recent years have seen a plethora of pop culture antiheroes who don't hesitate to beat answers out of the bad guys, concluding the ends justify the means when lives are at stake. The heroic counterterrorism agent Jack Bauer makes Abu Ghraib look like a tea party every week on *24*. Before then, Detective Andy Sipowicz could be counted on to at least threaten a severe beating to a perp to get him to confess on *NYPD Blue;* on *The Shield,* Vic Mackey wouldn't hesitate to pulverize a kidnapper to get him to reveal the victim's location. Back in early 2002, on *Saturday Night Live,* Jimmy Fallon asked why the Red Cross is so fixated on al-Qaeda detainees' living conditions: "They're suicide bombers. They hate living conditions."

For whatever legitimate concerns a lawmaker may have about the treatment of prisoners, it is worth noting that there are few if any votes to win by making the case for nicer treatment of aspiring mass murderers. And an argument that always sees U.S. troops as potential abusers until proven otherwise sets up the Democrats to be the reflexively antimilitary party, reinforcing 30-some years of unpopular dovishness. As columnist Mark Steyn put it, "You can't claim [as Democrats do incessantly] to 'support our troops' and then dump them in the same category as the Nazis and the Khmer Rouge." [16]

Steyn was referring, of course, to Illinois Democratic senator Dick Durbin, who found himself in hot water over these comments on the Senate floor:

> Let me read to you what one FBI agent saw. And I quote from his report:
> On a couple of occasions, I entered interview rooms to find a detainee chained hand and foot in a fetal position to the floor, with no chair, food or water. Most times they urinated or defecated on themselves, and had been left there for 18–24 hours or more. On one occasion, the air conditioning had been turned down so far and the temperature was so cold in the room, that the barefooted detainee was shaking with cold. . . . On another occasion, the [air conditioner] had been turned off, making the temperature in the unventilated room well over 100 degrees. The detainee was almost unconscious on the floor, with a pile of hair next to him. He had apparently

been literally pulling his hair out throughout the night. On another occasion, not only was the temperature unbearably hot, but extremely loud rap music was being played in the room, and had been since the day before, with the detainee chained hand and foot in the fetal position on the tile floor.

If I read this to you and did not tell you that it was an FBI agent describing what Americans had done to prisoners in their control, you would most certainly believe this must have been done by Nazis, Soviets in their gulags, or some mad regime—Pol Pot or others—that had no concern for human beings. Sadly, that is not the case. This was the action of Americans in the treatment of their prisoners.[17]

If we capture bin Laden, Zawahiri, Zarqawi, or any other al-Qaeda operatives, America wants the interrogations handled by the real-life equivalents of Jack Bauer, Andy Sipowicz, or Vic Mackey. After 9/11, a common quote among the warbloggers was George Orwell's "We sleep safe in our beds because rough men stand ready in the night to visit violence on those who would do us harm." In the war on terror, lives are on the line every day and there are plenty who would do us harm; the American people want their rough men to start their violent visits ASAP.

Ted Kennedy may have thought he had a good applause line when he declared, "Saddam's torture chambers have opened up under new management," but most Americans, no matter how horrified by Abu Ghraib pictures, don't like hearing their sons and daughters compared to Hussein's ghouls and Uday and Qusay.

After bombings of the London Underground in July 2005, New York City began searching bags of subway commuters. The New York Civil Liberties Union opposes all bag searches. Someone on Air America, the liberal talk radio network, suggested that riders carry many bags to confuse and irritate the cops.[18]

In a speech at the Brookings Institution, historian Fred Siegel said that the Democrats, pegged as the party of criminals' rights, are in danger of becoming the party of terrorists' rights.[19]

NYAH, NYAH, I DISPUTE THE RANK OF YOUR CAPTURED TERRORIST

The Left also exhibited a weird, creepy glee in May 2005 when debate arose concerning whether captured al-Qaeda terrorist Abu Farraj al-Libbi was the number three man in the organization or was several ranks lower in the hierarchy. David Brock's left-of-center organization, Media Matters for America, berated news organizations for not mentioning the claims of some terror experts that al-Libbi was merely a "middle-level leader." They fumed that not enough articles mentioned claims that Pakistan and American authorities "completely overestimated his role and importance." They repeated claims of an unnamed source that al-Libbi's role constituted "grade inflation."

The *Village Voice* declared, "He is a nobody and won't be much help in the search for bin Laden." Liberal bloggers labeled al-Libbi "an al-Qaeda has-been." On Daily Kos, a common line of speculation was that the arrest was a ruse designed to help Tony Blair in an upcoming election.

From the bitter, snippy tone in these fever swamps of the Left and how eagerly the doubts of al-Libbi's importance were trumpeted, it could easily be concluded that these folks were hoping America and its allies *hadn't* captured a major terrorist. (As if most Americans cared what his job title was—the bottom line was, one less aspiring mass murderer walking around free.) Thankfully, Senate Democratic leader Harry Reid rejected this defeatism and had the good sense to call the arrest "an important accomplishment in the fight against the al-Qaeda extremist threat. . . . Americans should also be proud of the men and women of our military, our intelligence community, and other government agencies for their contribution in bringing this terrorist to justice and for all of their efforts in the war on terror. Today's capture is a success for them and for all Americans."

Some U.S. and European intelligence analysts claimed the man arrested was in fact Anas al-Liby, another Libyan involved in the global jihad, but those claims were shown to be false. While it still remains unclear whether Libbi was the replacement for previously captured number three man Khalid Sheik Mohammed, it now appears he was a high-ranking al-Qaeda leader, far from the "nobody" the Left was eager to label him. The number two man in al-Qaeda, Ayman al-Zawahiri, writing to Abu Zarqawi, al-Qaeda's top man in Iraq, declared, "The enemy struck a blow against us with the arrest of Abu al-Faraj, may God break his bonds."

LET'S NEGOTIATE WITH THOSE PLOTTING TO MURDER US

Cases of outright calling for appeasement of al-Qaeda are rare but not unheard of. The quote at the beginning of this chapter, from Mohammad-Mahmoud Ould Mohamedou, urges a dialogue with al-Qaeda and for the United States to provide "satisfaction" for al-Qaeda's "grievances." Mohamedou made these comments in an op-ed in the *Boston Globe* four days after the four-year anniversary of 9/11.[20] When readers examine his proposal for ceasing hostilities with and making concessions to mass murderers who have pledged to kill 2 million American children, which side of the political spectrum will they associate him with? Conservatism?

"Once a party picks up a defining characteristic, it takes something very major . . . and probably some blundering from the other party . . . to shake that definition," says Republican consultant Fred

Wszolek. "The GOP became defined as anti–Social Security a long, long time ago, and we're still living that down. We will almost have to have a complete generational turnover in the population for that perception to lessen. I think the Democrats might be in the same bind now on national security. To shake the Michael Moore/Barbra Streisand/Howard Dean/Sean Penn/And So On positioning, it will take quite a bit more than a Sister Soljah moment, à la Bill Clinton and Jesse Jackson. And the price a Democrat would have to pay for staging such a moment has grown tremendously as their moonbat base becomes more vocal and organized."

Do "Moonbats" control the Democratic Party? Howard Dean's pre-"YEEEAARRRGH" third-place finish in the Iowa caucuses would suggest no. However, they are assuming more and more of the spotlight and taking a higher-profile role in shaping the party's image, particularly on national security. More and more, they're becoming the face. And the alternative media is helping them along, every step of the way.

NINE

A Handicap Masquerading
as an Advantage

The big picture is, Bush has the momentum and is
playing offense, while Kerry is on the defensive
going into Election Day. A key panic button moment for the Kerry campaign came on Friday, when
the candidate lectured the American people to
"wake up!"
> —*A GOP source, quoted by Jim Geraghty, Oct. 30, 2004*

Jim Geraghty is sounding more and more like a
man in a cocoon rather than a man in the know. . . .
I think Kerry is [the] 44[th president]. [Bob]
Shrummy wins!
> —*The blogger PunditChick, Oct. 31, 2004*

Bush 286, Kerry 252
> —*Final Electoral Vote Tally*

In addition to their squeamishness about military action and other
weaknesses laid out earlier, Democrats are held back by a serious

problem that many in the political world have mistaken for an advantage: the widespread perception is that at least a solid chunk of the mainstream media reports the news with liberal bias. Probably a million books, articles, and blog postings have been written on this topic; many liberals insist that the largest media organizations are actually biased in favor of conservatives.

Let's begin by acknowledging that arguments about media bias are often oversimplified. Many conservatives depict the mainstream media (or, to use the blogger vernacular, MSM) as a giant monolithic bloc that wakes up every morning asking, "How can I hinder Republicans today?" and receives hourly instructions from their masters at the Democratic National Committee.

Any fair-minded conservative would admit that's a caricature. News organizations are made up of many individuals, and their political views and ability to remain fair and/or objective are likely to range as well. An organization can employ both Mary Mapes, the infamous unverified-memo-story producer who spent five years digging into President Bush's Texas Air National Guard records looking for a story, and the crotchety but usually fair Bob Schieffer. MSNBC can be a home to both Tucker Carlson and Joe Scarborough on the right and Keith Olbermann on the left.

Assume for the sake of argument that at least a slim majority of the reporters, editors, producers, and anchors at institutions like the *New York Times*, the *Los Angeles Times*, *Newsweek*, *Time*, CBS, ABC, CNN, and National Public Radio are at least a smidgen more sympathetic to the arguments and policies of the Democratic Party than the GOP. And assume, just for now, that these beliefs consciously or subconsciously are reflected in their coverage, be it headlines, word choice, labels, the order of quotes, or just their selection of which stories warrant extensive coverage and which can be relegated to briefs in the back pages.

The result is that a good number of the most influential newspaper, magazine, and television reporters sympathize with liberal goals. And these reporters, particularly when covering campaigns, will often report and forecast the best-case scenario for the Democratic Party. The reporters want to emphasize the good news for Democrats and downplay the bad news; the net cocooning effect leaves Democrats blind to their weaknesses and unpopular positions. Every Election Day, Democrats are shocked to find their candidates and initiatives underperforming the media polls and their confident predictions.

One of the first on the Right to observe how this helped the GOP was Washington lawyer J. Peter Mulhern, in an essay for the now-defunct *Washington Weekly*.[1] Mulhern argued that so much of today's political journalism consisted of "cheerleading for the Democrats" that members of the party have to go out of their way to hear a dissenting view. The party's elected officials, campaign strategists, and message gurus "exist in an ideological cocoon," which leads them to believe that their ideas and policies are widely popular when in some cases the opposite is true.

By comparison, he noted, the press never lets the Republicans forget their political vulnerabilities. The religious Right is scary. They're seen as a bunch of old white men in suits. Women don't trust them. They're seen as cold-hearted misers cutting off aid to the poor.

While Republicans know the Democratic strategy from day one—"their playbook is splashed all over the editorial pages of the *Washington Post* and the *New York Times*"—Democrats rarely get a sense of the winning themes of their opponents. Mulhern offered the example of President Clinton's ill-fated attempt to make the military stop expelling gay and lesbian soldiers, sailors, and pilots. The Pentagon and many military families reacted with howls of outrage, and the Clinton administration was caught by surprise. What had been a minor agenda item became one of the first massive fights for the administration, settling on the "don't ask, don't tell" compromise.

Mulhern chuckled, "It never occurred to the Democrats that many people don't accept homosexuality as a morally neutral lifestyle choice or that many people view the military as a bastion of traditional virtues."

Mulhern's essay mostly focused on domestic matters, contending that the coverage of the *Washington Post* makes it easy to suppose that the people are clamoring for more taxation to support new and better government programs, when Walter Mondale's 1984 run had demonstrated the political consequences of promising tax increases. Then House minority leader Dick Gephardt had recently promised tax increases if the Democrats retook the House in 2002, a lapse in political judgment that Mulhern attributed to "surrendering to his delusions."

But the phenomenon has continued, with clear effects in recent elections. A terrific example of this phenomenon came on the final Sunday before Election Day 2002, when the *New York Times/CBS News* released their final poll. They found that after months of Democrats and Republicans running neck-and-neck on the "generic ballot" question, the GOP had jumped to a 47 percent to 40 percent advantage.

The lead? "The battle for control of Congress moved into its final stretch with Americans unsettled about conditions at home and threats from abroad, but saying that Democrats and Republicans have failed to offer a clear vision about how they would lead the nation."

The article (headlined "In Poll, Americans Say Both Parties Lack Clear Vision") declared there was "mixed evidence" on whether Bush's campaigning helped GOP candidates. "About 40 percent said the president was not a factor in their vote, while 31 percent said they considered their vote to be one of support for Mr. Bush and 19 percent considered their vote to be in opposition to him."

Six paragraphs in, *Times* reporter Adam Nagourney addressed the Republicans' 7-point bounce:

> That question, known as a generic ballot question, is a measure of national sentiment, and does not necessarily reflect how Americans will vote in the governor's races around the country and in the handful of close Senate and House races that will ultimately determine the control of Congress. The concern among Democrats about the nation's direction and the economy *suggests that Democratic voters might be more motivated to cast their ballots on Tuesday* and respond to the ambitious get-out-the-vote drives that have been organized by the Democratic Party, aimed in particular at voters who are distressed about the economy.[2]

The *Times*'s poll was declaring, if not shouting, that Republicans had built a significant single-digit lead—but the message from the accompanying article in one of the most important papers in the country to the Democrats was, "Don't worry, you're set for a good Election Day." Similarly, the Election Day assessment of the political staff of *ABC News,* in their funny and insightful daily roundup of news and gossip called "The Note," was "Democrats start this day with . . . a bit more mojo in the tight contests."

As we have seen, since 9/11, the mainstream media largely downplayed the pacifist or simply foolish statements by Democratic figures on the war on terrorism. But a thriving and flourishing conservative alternative media movement makes sure that this message does get out to voters. So a candidate like John Kerry can believe that a comment like "I think the threat of terrorism has been overstated" or "We need to get terrorism down to the level where it is manageable, like organized crime or prostitution" won't be too damaging, because it gets little play in the *New York Times*, the newsweeklies, the network news, and so on. In fact, a Democratic candidate may not even recognize that such a statement is damaging at all.

Thoughout the 2004 campaign, the widespread sense throughout much of the media was that whatever flaws Kerry had as a candidate, the "fundamental dynamics" of the race were against Bush. Another good example of this phenomenon comes from *ABC News*'s "The Note." Periodically, "The Note" would feature allegorical and humorous coverage of meetings of "the Gang of 500"—the 500 reporters, editors, television producers, network anchors, writers, and talking heads who have the largest influence on coverage of the campaign.

While these 500 reporters don't actually get together, imagining the meeting allows "The Note" writers to suggest the sorts of discussions and conventional wisdom circulating through the political press corps. On August 9, 2004, "The Note" "reported" on a Gang of 500 meeting at the Washington Mexican restaurant Lauriol Plaza, in which:

> With only three dissenting votes, the [*Journalist*] Division agreed that until weapons of mass destruction are found in Iraq (thus restoring Mr. Bush's credibility) John Kerry's best attempts to come off as a Gore-like grasping, exaggerating, pandering, slashing equivocator would not be noticed—or at least, not be allowed to define coverage of the Democratic nominee.
>
> So Kerry's inexplicable attack on the President for staying in the classroom on 9/11? Ignore it. (Ignore what Mrs. Heinz Kerry said earlier in defending the president's actions.) And Kerry's equally inexplicable blurting out to NPR that he would significantly reduce the number of troops in Iraq in his first year in office? Ignore that too.

Even ignore the wacky explanation given by one of his aides to the *Washington Post*, courageously on background: Kerry's "pledge to reduce troops came in response to a question and did not mark a new policy, rather a hope for improved conditions in Iraq."

On this point, the Division did raise an orange juice toast of agreement with the absent Mr. Mehlman, endorsing his view that, until and unless the press starts holding the non-incumbent accountable for such statements, the president probably can't win."

And then two days later, "The Note's analysis was even more emphatic:"

This is now John Kerry's contest to lose.

Forget the hemorrhaging of manufacturing jobs (and Team Bush's inability—so far—to enunciate a second-term jobs/growth agenda or find a compelling Rubinesque spokesperson on the economy).

Forget the fact that we still can't find a single American who voted for Al Gore in 2000 who is planning to vote for George Bush in 2004.

Forget the fact that California, New York, Illinois, and New Jersey (sorry, Matthew) aren't in play and never were.

Forget the latest polling out of Ohio (and perhaps Florida . . .).

Forget the extraordinary anti-Bush energy that exists on the left and the "how-do-we-whip-our-folks-up?" dilemma that exists on the right.

Forget the various signs that the Democratic challenger is playing in battleground areas for the middle and the president seems geographically and issues-wise to be still shoring up the base.

Forget the persistence of the Democratic advantage on the congressional generic poll question.

Forget the current ad spending advantage the DNC/anti-Bush 527s have over BC04RNC—while John Kerry pinches pennies.

But remember the poisonous job approval, re-elect, and wrong track numbers that hang around the president's neck to this day and then consider the very smart, mustest-of-read essay by Charlie Cook, in which the Zen Master surveys the troubling (and consistently so . . .) poll numbers of the incumbent and renders this spot on verdict: "President Bush must have a change in the dynamics and the fundamentals of this race if he is to win a second term. The sluggishly recovering economy and renewed violence in Iraq don't seem likely to positively affect this race, but something needs to happen. It is extremely unlikely that President Bush will get much more than one-fourth of the undecided vote, and if that is the case, he will need to be walking into Election Day with a clear lead of perhaps three percentage points."

Almost all reporting involves some degree of subjective interpretation. But a press corps, optimistic about a Kerry victory, kept looking for good signs for Kerry, and wrote their articles and produced their television segments accordingly. Even body language and staffers joking with reporters were interpreted as a signal of campaign momentum. One of the last campaign updates filed by *Slate* magazine reported:

The Kerry campaign staff is confident, and it appears to be genuine, rather than bluster. "I never told anyone in 2000 that Al Gore was going to win by 6 points," Bob Shrum—taking a shot at Karl Rove's record in election forecasting—told reporters on the campaign plane. For the past week or two, the campaign has spoken confidently of winning "big states"—presumably Florida, Ohio, and Pennsylvania—that would assure Kerry the presidency.

By Monday evening, reporters from news organizations that have colleagues traveling with Bush started saying that the Bush folks have clammed up, or that they seem unusually tight. Kerry's final events had a giddy air. The traveling press credentials for the night's last "major rally" in Cleveland featured a head shot of longtime Kerry spokesman David Wade, who gladly autographed a few. To the New York *Daily News* reporter, he wrote, "At least you're not the *Post.*" And to the *New York Post*, he tweaked the paper's veep "scoop" by writing, "Go Kerry-Gephardt!" [3]

It's neat to see this sort of behind-the-scenes fun and games—but it demonstrates a naive and unwarranted optimism about Kerry's standing in the polls that the campaign and the reporters covering the candidates reinforced. There are some smart observers of politics who reject this theory. One senior strategist close to the Bush White House dismisses the idea, stating, "If the Democratic Party is making their judgments based on what they read in the papers, then they're in worse shape than I thought."

But at times the 2004 Kerry campaign *was* using the headlines of the mainstream media as their primary measuring stick of whether their campaign was performing well. Kerry senior adviser Chad Clanton stated after the election:

An interesting little insight into our war room, we'd wake up very early every morning, get in and look at the newspaper and decide sort of what our message of the day was and by the end of the day and a lot of cheeseburgers and pizza and Dr. Pepper, whatever it took to get through the day, we would watch the evening news and that was kind of how we kept score. . . . We perhaps naively thought we had put together a pretty good string of evening news and newspaper reports for the last five weeks of the campaign. . . . I'm still a little in shock and awe probably like a lot of the rest of our campaign, that it wasn't quite enough.[4]

Steve Schmidt, lead spokesman for the Bush–Cheney campaign, said that the Republican strategy assumed that the power of certain newspapers is overstated:

I think the overwhelming majority of Americans and real folks in Ohio don't read the *Washington Post*, for example. I think the *New York Times* drives news coverage all across the country, and I think people all across the country read *USA Today*, but the *Los Angeles Times* and the *Wall Street Journal* and the other national newspapers are not read widely by average Americans in their local communities. So it's much more important to have positive news coverage in the *Columbus Dispatch*. One of the things that on the Bush campaign we were very cognizant of is that the President's speeches had synergy with our paid advertising message.[5]

After the election, political junkies remembered this and started wondering how the conventional wisdom that had driven so much of the election coverage could have been so spectacularly wrong. "I've obsessively sniped at ABC's 'The Note' for its declaration on August 11 that it was 'Kerry's contest to lose,' " wrote Mickey Kaus of *Slate*. He explained:

The whole point of ABC's "Note" is that its put out by the smartest, most knowledgeable and nuanced political insiders around, which it is. And the whole point of it being "Kerry's contest to lose" was that these experts were telling us that the underlying dynamic of the campaign favored Kerry because of Bush's "poisonous job approval, re-elect, and wrong track numbers." But we now know that this considered judgment of the smartest, most knowledgeable insiders was wrong—it was Dem wishful-thinking spin. Kerry in fact did pretty well in the final months of the campaign. He won the debates. He didn't commit many gaffes. He raised tons of money and successfully turned out record numbers of Democratic voters. And he still lost. Why? Because the underlying dynamic of the campaign didn't actually favor him at all. It favored Bush, despite the supposedly tell-tale "wrong track numbers." . . . How could brilliant genuine experts like Mark Halperin & Co. get it wrong? Because at some level they were conned by their peers and their Dem campaign sources (who were probably conning themselves) in a way I doubt they could be conned by Republican sources. . . . And Halperin is known as a relatively non-partisan straight-shooter. What does this tell you about the rest of the press corps?"[6]

There is a mutual con job going on in political coverage: Democrats con reporters into believing that the campaign is working, that the message is resonating, that all the indicators look good, and the reporters turn around and tell Democratic campaign staff that the indicators look good, that they're winning the news cycle, that they have the momentum, and so on.

In the final days of the campaign, groupthink intensified within the campaign press corps. "The journalists were convinced Bush would lose," *Newsweek* reported:

Backstage at rallies, reporters plugged the latest poll numbers into electoral math calculators on the Web. Kerry came out ahead every time. They gossiped about Bush's performance on the stump. "Doesn't he seem a little off?" a newspaper reporter asked me as we stood watching one of Bush's final rallies in Albuquerque, N.M. On Election Day the early exit polls seemed to bear out the correspondents' predictions: Bush was losing Florida and Ohio and was getting demolished in Pennsylvania."[7]

For as long as there have been campaigns, there has been a certain chumminess between campaign staffers and the reporters covering their bosses. But the press deals with the two parties differently.

A member of the elite press put it this way: "Democrats and reporters think of one another, 'Oh, you're a friendly soul. You're the kind of person I might be friends with outside of the campaign.' . . . Whereas Republicans just know that you're a Democrat and you work for whatever God-forbid big liberal media entity and you're not going to be sympathetic."[8]

A veteran political reporter stated, "My overall sense is that Democrats expect reporters to be sympathetic with them and not be as tough on them. . . . And, when you are, they get squirrelly and can freeze you out in certain ways."[9]

Meanwhile, Republicans are making sure the local coverage is good, advertising under the Democrats' radar; taking the "temperature" of the electorate much more thoroughly and deeply and laying the groundwork for massive turnout on Election Day.

Few political minds have studied the electorate like Fred Wszolek, a well-connected Republican consultant and founder of TargetPoint Consulting. In 2004, TargetPoint studied massive amounts of consumer purchase data to find new ways to reach naturally conservative voters. (Among their findings, likely GOP voters watch college football, drink Coors and bourbon, watch FOX News, and are more likely to have caller ID.)

TargetPoint's research truly paid off in its ability to match likely voter lists with the issues that were most likely to move those groups of voters. If the data suggested that you were likely to be pro-life, your direct mail writers, phone bank callers, and door-knocking volunteers were forearmed, and knew to focus on that issue. The net result was an exponentially more effective get-out-the-vote effort. Wszolek says:

> I think the left was very shocked with the outcome of the 2004 election, because they consume "their" media, and to them it was simply unimaginable that their guy could lose. Our coalition is now firmly convinced that the media is hopelessly biased against our side. But we're close to re-entering the era of "party newspapers." I was struck by the survey I saw that said among listeners to NPR, they thought the network was very fair and balanced, and non-listeners, of course, didn't really have much of an opinion. When you combine the fact that younger people (who are getting older) don't watch much network news or read daily newspapers and older people, who do watch the news and read newspapers are dying off, I'm wondering if the relevance of the MSM isn't going to, at some point soon, just fall off the cliff. By the next presidential election, I'm wondering if the issue of media bias is going to be LESS powerful because people simply don't pay any attention to them anymore. If not 2008, then certainly by 2012.

SECURITY MOMS

Sometimes this media-Democratic groupthink goes well beyond denying poll numbers or signs of momentum to denying the significance of groups of voters. Take, for example, the "security mom" phenomenon.

Democratic pollster Anna Greenberg put considerable effort into making the case that security moms didn't exist, at least in any politically significant way. Noam Schieber of the *New Republic* called them an "urban myth" and complained that the typical security mom story—variations of which appeared in the *Washington Post* (twice), the *New York Times,* the *Chicago Tribune,* and the *Philadelphia Inquirer,* as well as on CNN, ABC, and NPR—relied on anecdotal evidence. A Kerry pollster named Diane Feldman aggressively set out to knock down the security mom "meme" (an idea spread virally). So did Media Matters for America, *Boston Globe* columnist Ellen Goodman, and a slew of liberal bloggers.

It's hard for a party to correct its problems when some of its members keep insisting that the problems don't exist. When the gender gap disappeared on Election Day 2004, Democrats were blindsided and stunned to learn that, by golly, some women *were* shifting to Bush because of his strong stand on terrorism. The exact number and share of the electorate can be disputed, but the phenomenon cannot. And whatever the exact number, it was consequential.

FEELING DOWN? CHECK OUT ZOGBY!

There has always been some variance among pollsters tracking major campaigns, and the political world is often buzzing about whether this guy's numbers are more accurate than the other guy's, and whether a surprising result is a sign of genuine movement or just statistical noise.

In recent years, the variance has become so great, and pollsters have become such prominent talking heads and celebrities in the political world, that a market has emerged for the poll guru who tells each side what it wants to hear.

Enter John Zogby. After striking successes in 1996, when he accurately projected Bill Clinton's margin of victory as much narrower than other pollsters were expecting, and 2000, when he picked up on the late Gore surge, Zogby established himself as a brand name in polling. Ironically, after Zogby refused to buy the Clinton hype in 1996, he became a favorite of the Right—touted by the *New York Post*, FOX News, and Rush Limbaugh. Conservatives may not have liked his assessment of the last-minute swing to Gore in 2000, but it's tough to argue with accuracy.

But somewhere along the line, whatever "secret sauce" Zogby was using in his weighting of demographics and calculations of likely voters went sour. In 2002, his final polls were pretty lousy. In Minnesota, Zogby predicted Democrat Walter Mondale over Republican Norm Coleman by 6 points; Coleman won by 3. In Colorado, Zogby picked Democrat Ted Strickland over GOP incumbent Wayne Allard by 5; Allard won by 5. In Georgia, Zogby picked Democrat Max Cleland over Republican Saxby Chambliss by 2; Chambliss won by 7. In Texas, Zogby's final poll had Republican John Cornyn over Democrat Ron Kirk by 4 points; Cornyn won by 12. Zogby's final poll in the Florida gubernatorial race had Jeb Bush winning by 15, but only three weeks earlier he had Bush winning by only 3; Bush won by 13 points.

In 2002, Zogby got the winner wrong more often than any other pollster according to the National Council on Public Polls' Polling Review Board. Those results were quickly forgotten by the media, and Zogby was able to keep dining out on his reputation as the Polling Hero of 1996 and 2000.

In 2004, Zogby became the pollster of choice for Democrats, as he always seemed to have some morsel of good news for them— good news that escaped the eyes and surveys of his colleagues. In May, he boldly declared the race was Kerry's to lose, touting the myth that Kerry was a "good closer." Month after month, Zogby kept finding reassuring news for Kerry that somehow eluded other pollsters. He conducted dubious Internet-based polls of self-selected web users and found all kinds of good news for Democrats: leads for Kerry in Arkansas, Tennessee, Missouri, Nevada, and Florida outside the margin of error. "Don't expect any real bounce after the Republicans convene in New York later this month," he wrote in early August. Some polls found a Bush lead of 10 or 11 points after the convention, although that lead did erode as time passed.

Late afternoon on Election Day—awfully late for a final call— Zogby predicted that Kerry would win Florida, Ohio, Iowa, and New Mexico (0 for 4!) and get at least 311 votes in the Electoral College, while Bush was assured only 213. (The remaining 14 electoral votes were too close to call.)

There's no other way to say it: The Big Z's final polls were garbage. His final poll had Colorado too close to call; Bush won by 7 points. He had Florida by a tenth of a percentage point for Kerry and "trending Kerry"; Bush won by 5 points. Zogby had Bush winning North Carolina by 3; the president won John Edwards's home state by 13. Zogby had Bush leading Tennessee by 4; the president won by 14. Zogby called Virginia a "slight edge" for the GOP; Bush won by 8. In West Virginia, Zogby predicted a Bush win by 4; the president won by 13. And in the vital swing state of Wisconsin, Zogby had Kerry up by 6; the final margin was 1 point.

No wonder John Kerry never figured out what was wrong with his campaign. One of the highest-profile pollsters was insisting that he was winning by a wide margin. Why fix what you erroneously conclude isn't broken?

While the public and even some politicians may buy into dubious survey results, political professionals do keep track of pollsters' accuracy.

"Zogby? Is he still in business?" asks Wszolek.

GALLUP JOINS THE VAST RIGHT-WING CONSPIRACY?

Democrats and like-minded organizations have become quick on the draw when someone tells them news they don't want to hear. On September 28, MoveOn.org, a liberal advocacy group, paid $68,000 to run a full-page ad in the *New York Times*. Titled, "Gallup-ing to the Right," MoveOn.org declared:

> Gallup's methodology has predicted lately that Republican turnout on Election Day is likely to exceed Democrats' by six to eight percentage points. But exit polls show otherwise: in each of the last two Presidential elections, Democratic turnout exceeded Republican by four to five points. That discrepancy alone can account for nearly all of Bush's phantom 14-point lead. . . .
>
> This is more than just a numbers game. Poll results profoundly affect a campaign's news coverage as well as the public's perception of the candidates. . . .
>
> George Gallup Jr., son of the poll's founder, was the longtime head of the company and now directs its non-profit research center. Why hasn't he pushed for an update of the company's likely voter modeling, which his own father pioneered in the 1950s? Gallup, who is a devout evangelical

Christian, has been quoted as calling his polling "a kind of ministry." And a few months ago, he said "the most profound purpose of polls is to see how people are responding to God."

In retrospect, Gallup's numbers during that time were just measuring the traditional postconvention bump. Bush had a larger than expected one. Perhaps they oversampled Republicans a bit, and their model of predicting what percentage of the electorate would be Republican or Democrat was off, no doubt. While the GOP didn't have higher turnout than the Democrats, it evened up for the first time in years.

George Gallup Jr., who retired in May 2004, was not involved in the company's political polling and made those comments in reference to his specialty and main interest: polling people on their religious beliefs. Frank Newport, the editor in chief of the Gallup Organization, said of MoveOn.org, "We have a group that doesn't like that their candidate is behind in most polling, if not all polling, and therefore they're shooting out at the messenger." [10]

Democratic pollster Mark Blumenthal wrote on his blog that he "was somewhat taken aback by the ad's ferocity. . . . Whatever doubts I have about Gallup's model, I don't believe for a minute that they are intentionally 'Gallup-ing to the Right,' as MoveOn loudly charges. . . . I have admired MoveOn's efforts, but I have to ask, is it now so flush with cash that it can afford to buy a full page ad in the *New York Times* a few weeks before 'the most important election of our lifetimes' attacking a polling company? Do swing or less-than-likely voters really care? Wouldn't it be better to spend that money, say, making a case against George Bush or just turning out the vote?"

But this is the problem with the conventional thinking of the Democratic Party today: when someone offers a warning that the Democrats may do badly in a coming election or that their message is falling flat, there is always a true believer willing to shriek, *"Lies, all lies!"*

If you're a Republican, this emerging and accelerating trend is great news: you never seem to face a foe who knows where his or her vulnerabilities lie. Your opponents hear nothing but good news, they think all of their opinions are widely popular, and they think your values, policies, and ideas are shared by only a fringe.

ONE LAST EXAMPLE OF SELF-DELUSION

This doesn't quite fall under the heading of media, but it is another fascinating example of reinforcing self-deluding messages, among the Democratic grassroots in this case. This posting was on the Web site DemocraticUnderground.com, an online home for the hardest of the hard Left. Among their readers, this e-mail was widely circulated and cited by several Lefty bloggers. The e-mail is dated October 30, 2004:

> my friend in the kerry campaign spoke late last night with mark mehlman of the bush team. mehlman was a roomate of my friend when they were both at the harvard law school. they are at opposite ends of the political spectrum, but are very good friends. mehlman says the bush team is in "major melt down" because their polling has them losing in ohio and florida, so they are in a mad dash to pull something out in the upper midwest. michigan isn't really in play. he called it a "head fake". wisconsin is slipping away. bush spoke in green bay today to less than 5,000 people (kerry drew 80,000 in madison on thursday). iowa has the numbers potentially but they've focused on it way too late, after the dems had a mas-

sive absentee push, so iowa is unlikely. they can't win with minnesota alone and even that state doesn't look good.

mehlman says that there is incredible discord at the top. cheney is absolutley livid with rove on the overall strategy ("we peaked too soon you bastard") and with karen hughes for not adequately preparing bush for the debates ("he looked like a g** d**** mental patient"). cheney is apparently a "real monster". the rnc doesn't know what to do because they can't get any clear direction from the top.

mehlman says that bush's slide in their polls began about three weeks before the debates when kerry went into attack mode with major foreign policy speeches at nyu and at a national guard convention, the day after bush spoke. the slide accelerated big time after the debates, "everyone was as bad as the first with no let-up in free fall" according to mehlman. cheney freaked during the first debate, convinced that bush " 'lost the f****** election in front of 65 million people". Now they simply don't have the numbers to win in Florida, have not got their ducks in a row to "deflect" the massive number of early voters and are having real trouble maintaining the base in Florida and elsewhere ("our people are just turning away"). in ohio they've been simply overwhelmed with the new voter registrations and have been unsuccessful in court challenges. bush's number actually go now when he visits ohio after Treasury Secretary Snow's comments in the state that job losses were a "myth". Additionally many repubs are pissed about the financial profligacy of Bush and Cheney and their incompetence in Iraq, so a lot are simply going to "take a pass", read not vote. bush apparently has been totally "out of it" believing Rove and Hughes that everything was fine and that victory was assured, but is finally and slowly catching on that he might lose this thing. yesterday morning when made aware of the bin laden tape in nh, simply said. "It's over."

maybe all this can be chalked up to mehlman having a tough week.

Absolute nonsense, obviously. For starters, *Ken* Mehlman was Bush's campaign manager; *Mark* Melman was a pollster for the Kerry campaign. Disinformation has been around almost as long as there have been campaigns, but in this case, it ended up convincing a portion of the Democratic base that Kerry was well on his way to an LBJ-versus-Goldwater landslide. Did it lead to overconfidence? Or, one wonders, was either side's Election Day effort affected by the early exit poll numbers showing a Kerry landslide (including Kerry winning South Carolina, North Carolina, and Virginia)?

Bush ad man Alex Castellanos attributes the insane numbers to a simple dynamic:

Often when it comes to exit polls, people self-select. We knew that to a lot of people in this election, Bush wasn't the cool guy. You watch the media, and they tell you Kerry is the cool guy. If people have an exit pollster come up, they want to tell them they're voting for the cool guy, and the cool guy isn't Bush. The Kerry voter is proud to say who they're voting for.

The Bush voter said, "Get out of my face."

TEN

You Can't Win If You're Angrier at Halliburton Than Osama bin Laden

It is customary in democratic countries to deplore expenditure on armaments as conflicting with the requirements of the social services. There is a tendency to forget that the most important social service that a government can do for its people is to keep them alive and free.

—*Sir John Cotesworth Slessor, marshal of the Royal Air Force, 1954*

But the worst came with the final speaker, a woman by the name of Sherry Wolf, a member of the editorial board of *International Socialist Review*. She talked, and talked, and talked; terms like "architects of the slaughter," "war criminal," and "Noam Chomsky" wafted about the room; my eyes grew so bleary that I ceased taking notes. But then she brought up the insurgents in Iraq. Sure they were bad, she admitted: "No one cheers the beheading of journalists." But, she continued, they had a "right" to rebel against occupation. Then she read from a speech by the activist Arundhati Roy: "Of course, [the Iraqi resistance] is riddled with opportunism, local rivalry, demagoguery, and criminality. But, if we were to only support pristine movements, then no resistance will be worthy of our purity." In sum, Wolf said, the choice boiled down to supporting occupation or resistance, and we had to support resistance. So there it was. I even forgot about the Constitution Ball for a minute. Apparently, we were to view the people who set off bombs killing over 150 peaceful Shia worshippers in Baghdad and Karbala as "resistance" fighters. And the audience seemed entirely fine with this. These weren't harmless lefties. I didn't want Nancy Pelosi talking sense to them; I wanted John Ashcroft to come busting through the wall with a submachine gun to round everyone up for an immediate trip to Gitmo, with Charles Graner on hand for interrogation.[1]

—*An account of protesters at Bush's second inauguration,
2005*

Republican base voters are passionately motivated and intensely driven because they think Democrats secretly want to lose the war on terror. They see their foes on the left as so consumed by Bush hatred that they want to see America suffer. They suspect the opposition party wishes for another Vietnam. They conclude that liberals want a humbled, scarred, crippled America.

Thomas Friedman, often a critic of the Bush administration but a supporter of toppling Saddam Hussein, writes, "Liberals don't want to talk about Iraq because, with a few exceptions, they thought the war was wrong and deep down don't want the Bush team to succeed."[2] Further back, he tried to hold in his own anger at British protesters during President Bush's visit to London. They were so focused on the irredeemable evil of Bush and Blair that they couldn't spare any fury for the al-Qaeda operatives who blew up the British Consulate in Istanbul, Turkey, that day:

> Just a few hours earlier, terrorists in Istanbul had blown up a British-owned bank and the British consulate, killing or wounding scores of British and Turkish civilians. Yet nowhere could I find a single sign in London reading, "Osama, How Many Innocents Did You Kill Today?" or "Baathists—Hands Off the U.N. and the Red Cross in Iraq." Hey, I would have settled for "Bush and Blair Equal Bin Laden and Saddam"—something, anything, that acknowledged that the threats to global peace today weren't just coming from the White House and Downing Street.
>
> Sorry, but there is something morally obtuse about holding an antiwar rally on a day when your own people have been murdered—and not even mentioning it or those who perpetrated it. Watching this scene, I couldn't help but wonder whether George Bush had made the liberal left crazy. It can't see anything else in the world today, other than the Bush-Blair original sin of launching the Iraq war, without U.N. approval or proof of Iraqi weapons of mass destruction. . . .
>
> "In general," says Robert Wright, author of "Nonzero," "too few who opposed the war understand the gravity of the terrorism problem, and too few who favored it understand the subtlety of the problem." [3]

Some liberals objected to Friedman's conclusion, pointing out that antiwar protesters did discuss the Istanbul attacks that day—and found the ultimate responsibility for the bodies blown apart and the tears of the families laid with—wait for it!—George W. Bush and Tony Blair. Damon Albarn, lead singer of the rock group Blur, addressed the bombings in his speech to the gathering: "That's going to happen increasingly *because of the policies of the Western world*. The attacks in Turkey and Bush's visit to Britain were no mere coincidence."[4]

The folks in the London crowd may or may not be registered members of the Democratic Party; there were probably only a few Americans among them. But they are of "the Left," and people outside the Left see the movement as one big, noisy, angry, drumbeating, giant-puppet-waving blob with some serious issues regarding personal hygiene. Centrists and conservatives don't see the London "It's all Bush and Blair's fault" crowd as all that distinct from American antiwar protesters and antiwar lawmakers and Democrats as a whole. Only if U.S. Democratic officials come out and say, "Friedman is right, these are morally obtuse morons," will the link in voters' minds be broken.

In a war against bloodthirsty maniacs, the rest of the political spectrum doesn't have much patience for this. As widely cited warblogger Bill Whittle puts it, maybe fighting the rhetorical fight to support the war, the troops, and the administration prosecuting it represents the small task that the ordinary guy can do in the war on terror:

> I tried to enlist on September 12th, 2001. I knew a little about airplanes; maybe the Air Force would trust me to wash them or something so as to free up useful people. They asked how old I was, thanked me, and told me they'd give me a call if they needed me.
>
> So here I am: feeling useless. But President Bush warned that this was going to be a different war—something unlike anything we had ever seen. The front line now, at this critical

time, is in the hearts and minds of our own people. That's where the real battle is now. That is our weakest point, our breach, our point of failure. We have not made the case to enough people and time is running out.

So maybe now, at this absurd point in this new kind of war, we're the crack troops, we old and useless pajama patriots reduced to printing up pamphlets to sell war bonds to the weary, to make the case for holding on to an unglamorous, uninspiring, relentless grind because that—not Normandy and Midway—is the face of war in this gilded age of luxury and safety and plenty.

Maybe that's our job. Maybe we can help cover some small gap in the lines. We'll see. But for now, I will take up the sword of the pajamahadeen, and rise up: just another citizen-wordsmith, trying to put words and ideas where they are needed: into the stumbling gaps, exasperated expressions and defensiveness of a brave and exhausted man under a lot of pressure.[5]

To the GOP grassroots, supporting their president and their party *is* their war effort. Hugh Hewitt points out that GOP activists are working like their lives depend on it, because deep down, they really do believe their lives depend on it.

Where would Bush's supporters get the idea? Well, President Bush himself has said to his cabinet that at least some elements of the mainstream media do not want victory or act as if they do not. Speaking at an October 26, 2001, meeting of his national security principals, Bush said, "Look, we're entering a difficult phase. The press will seek to find divisions among us. They will try and force on us a strategy that is not consistent with victory. . . . We've only been at this [bombing Afghanistan] for 19 days. Be steady. Don't let the press panic us."[6]

"The public wants leaders who will take care of this threat— leaders who are strong and responsible," says a White House strategist. "When you see or hear the president, you can tell this is something he feels deeply in his bones, and that this is the dominant issue on his mind every day. One thing you can say about President Bush is that he is an authentic person. He is easy to read, and it is easy to tell what he cares about. It seems less clear that the Democrats care about this in the same way."

This discussion raises a fundamental question: Do Democrats want to lose the war on terror? No.

Do liberals? Well, for a few on the fringe . . . yes, they *do* want us to lose.

Nicholas De Genova, a Columbia University assistant professor of anthropology and Latino studies, said so explicitly at a campus antiwar teach-in on March 26, 2003, when he expressed his wish that Iraq would defeat the United States and that there would be "a million Mogadishus." This comment referred to the 1993 incident in Somalia when 18 U.S. soldiers were killed during a military operation. (In doing so, De Genova wished for the deaths of 18 million U.S. servicemen and the deaths of approximately 500 million to 1 billion Somalis.)

Yes, certain antiwar protesters *do* want us to lose the war in Iraq and the broader war on terror. Ask a war supporter what he thinks of antiwar protesters, and probably within a short time he will cite a banner at a March 15 demonstration in San Francisco, bearing the message, "We Support Our Troops, When They Shoot Their Officers." The banner was cited in more than 400 publications.

When far-left groups in western Europe organize a campaign dubbed "Ten Euros for the Resistance," aimed at sending "whatever is necessary, including weapons" to those fighting coalition troops in Iraq, then yes, it is fair to say they want us to lose. At this point, it even seems safe to question their patriotism.

And Moore's declaration that guys like Zarqawi are "the future, the minutemen, the revolution" constitutes a tribute to the moral superiority of those seeking to kill our troops and comes darn close to hoping we lose.

DEMS NEED SECURITY WONKS

It is a broad generalization, but generally, voters become Democrats because they care about abortion rights, gay rights, social spending/welfare/worker protections, civil rights, health care, and the environment.

Voters become Republicans because they care about lowering taxes, reducing regulations, preserving traditional values, punishing criminals, and killing foreigners who threaten Americans. That last one has always been big for members of the military and their families, and has only accelerated since 9/11. The young political science majors in colleges across the country tend to focus on the issues that matter to them the most. Young liberals focus, study, and specialize in their preferred topics; likewise for young conservatives.

The result is that when the issue at hand is, say, health care, Democratic lawmakers can call on the expertise and creativity of a small army of policy wonks, professionals, and people who have studied the issue inside and out for most of their lives. They have more intellectual capital to spend, more bright minds looking for new solutions, more people who can articulate their views and make the case for their proposals.

When the issue is terrorism, national security, and the military, it is the Republicans who have a staff advantage. There are hundreds of congressional staffers, think-tank experts, war college scholars, talking heads, armchair historians, and policy wonks on the GOP side who have spent their careers focusing on this issue. Whether the issue is terrorist ideology, recruitment methods, use of technology, terrain of countries they operate in, weapons systems, signals interception, tactics, or tracking, the Republican Party's lawmakers are surrounded by experts, and they have developed an interest and knowledge of these topics for years.

If Democrats want to be competitive on national security issues, they're going to need a lot more policy wonks who specialize in these issues. Unfortunately, at the moment when the party needs military expertise the most, the dovish wing of the party has done everything it can to make it inhospitable. Blogger Michael Totten writes:

> It is possible to be some kind of anti-Bush lefty and write thoughtful books and articles about national security without being a backseat heckler who opposes but offers no alternate vision. Paul Berman has managed to do it. But he labors away in an inhospitable left-wing environment that hardly has any room for him. For someone like me who doesn't have a lifetime's worth of street cred in the lefty press, I'm all but forced to play in the right's sandbox whether I like it or not. (But I don't dislike it as much as I did, and that's bad news for the Democrats. An entire genre of intellectuals like me exists and has a name—neoconservatives—because mine is all-too common a storyline.) These kinds of problems are self-reinforcing. The fewer intellectuals there are on the left who study military history and strategy, the less likely any otherwise left-minded person who is interested in such things will want or be able to work with or for liberals and Democrats. What has been happening is a nation-wide brain-drain from the left to the right—at least in certain areas.[7]

If they wish to be competitive before the war on terror ends, the Democrats have to play catch-up. Heather Hurlburt, a former speechwriter for President Bill Clinton and Secretary of State Madeleine Albright, puts it starkly:

> We will never learn to think straight about war until this generation of professional Democrats overcomes its ignorance of and indifference to military affairs. Many Democrats who came of age during the Vietnam War retain a gut-level distrust of the military. Younger staffers, who may not carry the same psychological baggage, have few mentors urging them toward military or security issues. The issues that drive most contemporary Democrats into politics are reproductive rights, health care, fiscal policy, or poverty, not national security.
>
> Even those young Democrats who are interested in foreign affairs tend to be drawn to "soft" subjects such as debt relief and human rights. Aspiring foreign policy wonks will often get pulled into military affairs by way of, say, their work on demining. But when these young people visualize exciting jobs in the next Democratic administration, they think State Department, not Pentagon. . . .
>
> Getting Democrats to take defense issues seriously will not be easy; it means changing the party's basic mode of thinking. But it can be done. After all, it took less than a decade for Democrats to go from being the party of deficits to being the party more trusted for fiscal responsibility. This transformation happened because enough Democrats got tired of losing elections and did the hard work of crafting innovative and effective ideas in areas like crime and economic stewardship that the party had previously ceded to Republicans. National defense is perhaps the last big area where Democrats have not really done this. And in a time of war, it's the one area where they can't afford not to.[8]

Learn the Distinction Between Making Specific and Helpful Policy Proposals and Bitching

In too many circles on the left, their idea of a winning argument on terrorism policy has been to ask, "Why haven't you caught Osama bin Laden, Mr. President?" As if they would have Osama in handcuffs in a matter of hours if they just had the reins of the Oval Office. It looks petty and small when the complaint comes from Al Gore or John Kerry; it insults our intelligence when the question comes from Al Sharpton.

Democrats can only do so much good by looking backward. John Kerry may have been right when he argued that more U.S. troops should have been used in Tora Bora in December 2001. But General Tommy Franks and the commanders on the ground said they did what they could with all the troops that logistics would allow, and the American people largely accept that—sometimes things go wrong in war. When you're forced to airlift troops in one helicopter at a time, you're just not going to have whole divisions marching around the mountains. The Pentagon bombed the hell out of the site and did the best it could.

Bush's critics look like Monday morning quarterbacks when they say he should have done this or should have done that, particularly when the discussion is about a decision made several years ago. Those arguments are wastes of oxygen. Democrats need to say, "We ought to do this" and "We ought to do that"—forward-looking recommendations that focus on what we can do now, not what we could have done then.

Democrats missed a brilliant opportunity in 2005 when former CIA director Porter Goss suggested that his agency actually has a solid idea of where bin Laden is. A *Time* magazine interviewer asked Goss when America would capture Osama bin Laden. "That is a question that goes far deeper than you know," he said. "We have some weak links" that make it impossible, for now, to get bin Laden, he explained, pointing to "the very difficult question of dealing with sanctuaries in sovereign states." Sounds like you know where he is, the interviewer pressed. "I have an excellent idea of where he is," Goss responded.

The proper Democratic response here is not to jump up and down and shriek that the Bush administration is letting Osama walk around free. The concept of the entire chain of command of the CIA, National Security Council, army, navy, marines, air force, and White House knowing where Osama is and not taking action strikes most Americans as unimaginable, and a lawmaker alleging a conspiracy of inaction will sound suspiciously like the smelly guy screaming on the street corner about UFOs and mind control.

The right move would have been to outhawk the usual GOP rhetoric. Picture some ideal Democrat speaking in the Senate:

> Since we've been in this war on terrorism, our stance has been to make no distinction between the terrorists and those who harbor them, a policy I fully support. In 2003, we put our national reputation on the line, crumpled up the concept of sovereignty like a piece of rubbish, invaded Iraq, and toppled Saddam's regime—all based on ties to terrorism that have been a lot less solid than we would have liked. I mean, I'm glad Abu Nidal, Abu Abbas, Uday, and Qusay are dead and that Saddam's in prison. But I'd rather have Osama's head on a stick. In fact, I would gladly trade Saddam to have Osama's head on a stick.
>
> From Director Goss's comments, we learn that apparently we know where Osama bin Laden is, but we're not going after him with everything we've got . . . *because he's in a sovereign state?* When did we suddenly decide we care about sovereignty again? Why were we junkyard dogs on Iraq, but

suddenly we have turned into yapping Pomeranians with this sovereign state standing between us and Osama?

I don't care whether the state that Goss is referring to is the hostile state of Iran or the cooperative state of Pakistan. I assume we're doing something behind the scenes, but frankly, the American people deserve to know that their government is doing everything it can to get this murderer dead or alive. And the Pakistani and Iranian regimes ought to know where we stand as well, and the consequences of standing between us and our prey. Mr. President, if some regime is protecting bin Laden or not letting us take the actions that we need to take, then call them out! Let the world know! If ever there was a good reason to confront another sovereign state, this is it. And go back to that appropriate and aggressive policy you declared on the evening of September 11, 2001. My party will stand shoulder-to-shoulder with any president who brings justice to our enemies. And for God's sake, if you won't, step aside for someone who will.

If we know where bin Laden is, then let's unleash the dogs, Mr. President."

This type of rhetoric would have flipped the usual image by forcing the Bush administration to defend a policy of either inaction or quiet behind-the-scenes action, and the Democrats would be in the position of calling for aggressive action. Imagine being a GOP opponent of the Democrat who gave this speech. How on earth do you paint this speaker as a hapless, indecisive dove?

Stop Looking for Ideal Option C's

There is a disturbing habit, mostly found among Democrats who don't face yes-or-no, up-or-down votes. The foul-mouthed yet keenly insightful blogger Ace of Spades puts it this way:

In a radio debate (actually, not much of a debate at all) between Katha Pollitt and the once-relevant Andrew Sullivan
shortly before the invasion of Afghanistan, Sullivan repeatedly asked Pollitt if she didn't support an invasion and expulsion of the Taliban, but also agreed that "something should
be done," what, on earth, was she suggesting that "something" be? And she continuously dodged the question.

Actually, she kept answering she wanted Option C: the
option where there is no invasion or military action (or even
sanctions!) and yet the Taliban agrees to not only turn over all
al-Qaeda suspects within the areas it controls but also peace-
ably departs to start a new organizational life as traveling
hookah merchants.

I don't remember any such "Option C" being readily
available in October 2001. And the left continues to choose
Option C on Iraq. Given that the French and Russians (and
to a lesser extent, the Chinese and Germans) were Saddam's
patrons and protectors (and business partners), we had only
two options.

Option A: defy the wishes of the pro-Saddam coalition of
the unwilling; destroy a corrupt and brutal regime, freeing
millions, but with limited support, and at the expense of
alienating world opinion and bearing most of the costs of
war ourselves.

Option B: join with the coalition of the unwilling, united
in opinion, and speak with a single voice, telling Saddam
"You can pretty much keep doing what you're doing and
we'll do absolutely nothing at all about it."

It's been two years since the process which led us to war in
Iraq began, and the left keeps refusing to answer the question.

They still want that g—ddamned Option C, and they're

not going to shut up about Option C until the sun flickers and fades and the earth freezes into a gray and lifeless rock.[9]

The Iraq war, the war in Afghanistan, and all U.S. military actions since 9/11 have seen mistakes and problems and setbacks. They happen in any human endeavor. If the task is worth doing, then it is worth the inevitable things that go wrong. And sometimes things go horribly wrong—innocents caught in the crossfire, Italian agents killed, or prison abuse. That doesn't mean you ignore those problems. You try to avoid them and fix them when you can. But there's no maturity or wisdom in a position that says, "I support the war, but only the good parts. I oppose it when it goes badly."

Stop Voting Against Defense Spending

If Democratic lawmakers don't like a particular defense program (and there are plenty of bad ones), then they ought to stand up and talk about the weapons systems they do like. The Bush campaign got plenty of mileage out of John Kerry's votes against increased defense spending. (Recall Zell Miller's accusation that Kerry wanted to command forces armed with spitballs.)

The Democratic argument on the defense budget can't just be for pay raises, better health care, and more day care centers on military bases (although those are all nice ideas). They have to find their own Predator drones, their own Joint Strike Fighters, their own gadgets and innovations and technological breakthroughs to endorse. They need to let out their inner geek and eagerly describe a future American military outfitted with weapons that were once the realm of science fiction. This is where the new defense policy geeks would come in handy.

When a Democrat runs for office, he needs to point out that he'll vote for weapons X, Y, and Z, and he needs to tout their advantages.

These will immunize Democrats from the accusation that they're defense-cutting doves.

Enforcement, Enforcement, Enforcement:
A big reason that Republicans and a good chunk of the center think Democrats are naive is their faith in verbal and written agreements with untrustworthy regimes. Carter trusted the Soviets until they entered Afghanistan; Clinton trusted the North Koreans on their nuclear deal; Clinton really believed that Yasir Arafat was seriously interested in a lasting peace deal. Today many Democrats continue to push for summits and treaties with an untrustworthy North Korean regime.

A treaty that doesn't get enforced is worse than nothing; it fools many people into thinking a problem is solved when it's actually getting worse. In the abstract, nonproliferation treaties are wonderful ideas. But in practice, the international community has mostly dithered about Iran and North Korea. The worst consequences are leaky trade sanctions for regimes that have demonstrated they don't care about their people's welfare.

Think of the "face" of these regimes: In the case of North Korea, Kim Jong-Il, whose best press in recent years may have been the rather cute singing puppet of his likeness in the movie *Team America: World Police*. Even then, he was portrayed as a megalomaniac out to destroy the world. The face of the Iranian regime for years was the sinister-looking, black-robed Ayatollah Khomeini; their new face and president is a hardliner alleged to have been one of the hostage takers back in 1979.

What politician in his or her right mind would stand before the American people calling for a treaty with these guys, declaring "trust them"?

Any politician addressing this issue has to recognize the American people's extraordinary (and justified) distrust of these guys. The rhetoric on Capitol Hill and on the campaign trail ought to reflect that.

The Futility of Purges

Immediately after the 2004 debacle, some Democrats concluded the defeat was mostly a result of Kerry's flaws as a candidate. But in some corners of the party, there were more discussions about purges than at a bulimic convention.

Writing on his Web site on January 27, 2005, Markos Moulitsas concluded the solution to the Democrats' woes was to . . . ditch Joe Lieberman. "Republicans love [Lieberman] for the same reason that Democrats love McCain—because they both spend a great deal of the time beating up publicly on their own party," Moulitsas wrote. "But for that reason, especially given our minority status (when the party needs to stick together for survival), Lieberman must go. I don't want another six years of him bashing Democrats on FOX News next to a fawning Sean Hannity."

The liberal blogger Atrios declared, "The problem with Lieberman isn't that he's too far to the right; it's that he's frequently willing to adopt and perpetuate Republican spin points. It's okay to criticize your own side, and it's okay to have some independence. What isn't okay is attacking your own side in a way which benefits the other guys, especially when it's most of what you do. It's a big tent, but not big enough for the FOX News Democrats."

And the liberal base of the party has responded. The Web site timetogojoe.com claims to be raising about $2,500 per day for Lieberman's Democratic opponent.

Bob Brigham of the left-of-center grassroots group the Swing State Project declares:

> The most important part of the battle to retake our party is giving Senator Joe Lieberman a giant s—tburger of a pri-

mary challenge. As far as I'm concerned, the junior Senator from Connecticut is a complete piece of crap that is only allowed in the Democratic caucus because Harry Reid is a gentleman. To be perfectly honest, I don't even care if we win. But we need to send a powerful signal that the appeasement days are over. Blanketing Connecticut with the nastiest ads ever created will go a long way towards forging a respect for solidarity in the Democratic Party. . . .

Twenty years down the road, if a resume crosses my desk from somebody who worked for Lieberman after today, that person will be rejected without any further consideration. If you want to work in Democratic politics, you do not want Lieberman or the DLC on your resume.[10]

Eloquence and reference to excrement sandwiches aside, notice the strategic brilliance at work here: "I don't even care if we win."

When Chicago mayor Richard Daley criticized Illinois Democratic senator Dick Durbin for making comments that appeared to compare the actions of U.S. soldiers at Guantanamo Bay to Nazis, Stalinist Russia, and the genocide of Cambodia, the Daily Kos blog turned the guns on Durbin's critic: "As for Mayor Daley, who cut off Durbin at the knees—a pox on his house. His time is coming to an end. I hope Jesse Jackson Jr. takes him on."

But the purge talk was not a one-way street. Beinart wrote in his essay, "A Fighting Faith": "The challenge for Democrats today is not to find a different kind of presidential candidate. It is to transform the party at its grassroots so that a different kind of presidential candidate can emerge. That means abandoning the unity-at-all-costs ethos that governed American liberalism in 2004. And it requires a sustained battle to wrest the Democratic Party from the heirs of Henry Wallace. In the party today, two such heirs loom largest: Michael Moore and MoveOn."[11]

As the intraparty debate continued, each side accused the other of calling for a purge and responded that the solution was . . . to purge out the other side.

When the Democratic Leadership Council's Will Marshall wrote in *Blueprint,* the group's magazine, "Democrats should have no truck with the rancid anti-Americanism of the conspiracy-mongering left," Kos accused the DLC of "demanding the party purge millions of supporters from its ranks." [12] He then began urging Democrats to disassociate themselves from the DLC, asking, "Do Hillary Clinton and Evan Bayh want to run for president with the DLC albatross around their neck? Do any of these people want to associate with an organization that is urging the eviction of millions of Democrats from the party's ranks?" [13]

Purge talk is pointless. Beinart and the Democratic hawks simply don't have enough allies to purge the MoveOn and Moore types from the party. And the MoveOn grassroots folks could purge the Liebermans and Bayhs and Daleys from their party, only to find themselves an even smaller and less relevant minority than they are today.

The answer is that blue-state Democrats can afford to be antiwar. Red-state Democrats—and frankly, ones representing "purple" states or districts—can't. Red-state Democrats need to not only support the war, but they have to criticize the Michael Moores of the world when they start comparing Abu Zarqawi to America's Minutemen. Obviously, these are not easy steps for Democrats to take. If they were easy, they would have taken them already.

The party faces a psychological crisis in that a large chunk of the Democratic base denies that they lost and refuses to even imagine that the voters rejected their policies. They think that the Republicans lied and stole the election. No need for the Democrats to change their positions, they just need to shout louder. This is akin to the company that concludes that its products are fine; it's the consumers who are wrong.

It's not just the base, frankly. Kerry, for one, refuses to believe his party has a credibility problem on national security. "The country had concluded that I was prepared to be Commander-in-Chief," he told the *New Yorker* in March 2005. "The bottom line is that, if you look at the data, the appearance of the Osama bin Laden tape had a profound impact. The fact is, we flatlined on that day. I presented stronger arguments, but there was a visceral unwillingness to change Commander-in-Chief five days after the bin Laden tape." [14]

DEMS NEED A SENSE OF OUR NATIONAL MISSION

At times, one wonders if today's Democrats played with action figures as children. For decades, the most popular toys and kids' entertainment has featured adventures of heroes and villains. G.I. Joe, Star Wars, Lord of the Rings. Almost any superhero, from Batman to Superman to Spiderman. This cultural telling and retelling of tales of good and evil is reinforced by other great, oft-repeated tales in our pop culture—the films of John Wayne, Star Trek, Indiana Jones. (Sometimes we import them, like James Bond.) Some are fictional, some silly, many aren't even American, but together they make up a national narrative, a hero's journey. The classic American story always features a hero who stumbles, who often tries to avoid his date with destiny, but who realizes the fight can't be avoided, and stands up against an evil force and ultimately triumphs after a great struggle. (Picture almost any character ever played by Humphrey Bogart.)

George W. Bush's life story fits this nearly universal tale. He represents the wayward and drunkard son who wasted 40 years before finding a purpose. Then, on the bloodiest day in American history, he transformed before our eyes from a mere caretaker president, elected with a popular minority, to a man called to great responsibilities by history. The short video at the 2004 GOP convention, narrated by the folksy former senator Fred Thompson, used his pitch at Yankee Stadium in late 2001 as a national metaphor:

> So George Bush took the mound. What he did that night, that man in the arena. He helped us come back. That's the story of this presidency. With the heart of a president, he told us, "You keep pitching." No matter what, you keep pitching. No matter what, you go to the game. You go to the mound. You find the plate and you throw it. And you become who you are.

The Republicans managed to take the most horrific blow to the national psyche since Pearl Harbor and turn it into another chapter of the American story—a heroic journey that will end with another corner of the globe liberated from oppression. Their message to the American people: We're guardians who have stumbled but who will ultimately triumph, following in the footsteps of the Greatest Generation.

Meanwhile, the Democrats have been left to make the case for the depressing and sometimes cynical harder questions of the Afghanistan and Iraq wars—the profits of Halliburton, rumors of a pipeline to Turkmenistan, the WMDs not found, and an opium trade left to flourish. Their message to the American people: "We're naive suckers who are being exploited by warmongers and corporations." Unsuprisingly, a majority of Americans prefer the former message to the latter. It can be argued that Americans reject it because the truth is hard to take, or because the argument is defeatist nonsense. But either way, voters aren't buying this message and aren't likely to warm up to it anytime soon.

Two weeks before Election Day 2004, I spoke with a longtime

GOP operative who has been around politics longer than I have been alive. I nicknamed him "Obi-Wan Kenobi," which brought the response, "He's not the funny-looking one, is he?" I assured him I was not comparing his appearance to Yoda.

Obi-Wan made the case that Kerry just wasn't going to win on Election Night. His confidence was tempered steel:

> If Kerry wins on Election Night, what is the storyline going to be, the economy? No way. The story is going to be the war on Iraq and the American people's reaction to terrorism. Bush has made this election a referendum on how he's fighting terrorism by taking the fight to them in Iraq. The anchors are going to say, "America sent a message to the president that they weren't happy with Iraq. They want to get back to the world before President Bush, before 9/11, before terror alerts and security lines and Fallujah and all of this fear and stress and drama. They want a return to normalcy."
>
> Does that sound like the America you know, Jim? In 1952, Harry Truman hadn't been aggressive enough in fighting the Korean war, they felt he was holding McArthur back, and the American people were so angry with him that he didn't run. They had a choice between Adlai Stevenson or the World War II hero Dwight Eisenhower. They picked Eisenhower, because they wanted to win the war, not the guy who could negotiate it.
>
> In 1972, the last wartime election, Americans had a choice between the candidate of the peace movement, Mr. "Come home, America," George McGovern, vs. Richard Nixon. Nixon wins in a landslide.
>
> In 1984, America again has a clear choice—Walter Mondale, the embodiment of the Democratic foreign policy establishment, Jimmy Carter's vice president, the man who is

determined to learn how to coexist with the Soviet Union, or the policies of Ronald Reagan, seeking to defeat the Soviets through strength. Again, they choose the fighter in a landslide.

Now, does that sound like the American people you know?

In the first horrific and shocking days after 9/11, America could have reacted by calling for the policies of John Kerry and the Democratic Party's foreign policy establishment—multilateralism, global tests, summits, treaties—looking at the threat as an intelligence and law enforcement problem.

But calls for that approach were few and far between. The overwhelming sentiment was to strike down on the Taliban with great vengeance and furious anger. "Bomb them back into the Stone Age" was a common phrase; when informed of how unadvanced Afghani society and the military was under the Taliban, the phrase was revised to "bomb them forward into the Stone Age."

The foreign policy vision of the Democratic Party's antiwar base—laden with the language of diplomatic nuance and with faith in the power of treaties against the homicidal—just isn't in the pugnacious American character.

THE GOP'S NEED TO APPEAR
AS RELUCTANT WARRIORS

While the Democrats need to assure the public that they're not too reluctant to use force, the Republicans need to assure voters that they're not too eager. While Americans will support the troops in Iraq until the job is done and the last soldier returns from Mesopotamian soil, something about Operation Iraqi Freedom stuck in the craw of the American public. Americans hated Saddam, saw the world as a better place with him in a cell, and despite bouncing poll numbers, are unlikely to leave that country to the tender mercies of Abu Musab al-Zarqawi.

But in this conflict, the United States shot first—or at least escalated a small-stakes conflict between Iraqi air defenses and coalition pilots enforcing the no-fly zone into a major land war aimed at toppling a regime. The American public will let it go this time, but the doctrine of preemptive attacks rankles at the nation's sense of fair play.

American (and Western) mythology is full of heroes who resisted a conflict until it was clear that there was no other option. Humphrey Bogart's Rick Blaine famously declared, "I stick my neck out for nobody." Frodo wants to live the quiet, comfortable life on the shire. Luke Skywalker resisted joining Obi-Wan Kenobi on his "damn fool idealistic crusade" until Imperial stormtroopers murdered his aunt and uncle. Indiana Jones doesn't want to look for the Holy Grail until he hears his father is missing. John McClane is an ordinary cop who just gets stuck in the wrong place at the wrong time (along with his wife) in the *Die Hard* movies; Jack Ryan keeps insisting he's just an analyst who writes reports in the works of Tom Clancy. Even the American icon who racked up the highest body count, Rambo, begins his third movie meditating at the mountaintop monastery, where he tells an army representative, "My war is over." Only when he learns that his old friend, Richard Crenna, has been captured by the Soviets does the veteran Green Beret go back into action.

In fact, the gradual goading of the reluctant hero is the nearly universal plotline of the most quintessentially American story, the western. Think of Shane, True Grit, or almost any character played by Clint Eastwood.

The hero of a western is a cowboy who would prefer to live on his ranch with his wife and spend his time clearing brush in his jeans and boots. (Judging by the standard landscape, it could be a ranch in

Waco or someplace.) But Black Bart and his gang ride into town and terrorize the people. Only reluctantly does the cowboy undertake the heroic task: agree to be sheriff, pin a tin star on his chest, and, in a showdown, attempt to arrest or shoot and kill all the outlaws.

When Europeans and foreign policy elites call Bush a cowboy, they think they're insulting him. But cowboys are heroes who cut a distinctive and valiant profile. For example, the most famous political poster in Polish history was created in 1989 by the Solidarity labor movement. The image is of Gary Cooper, in full *High Noon* cowboy regalia, walking. Above the image, it says "Solidarity" in Polish. Below the image, it says "High Noon" and the date. The date is the occasion of the first free elections in Central and Eastern Europe after World War II. Instead of a gun, Gary Cooper holds a ballot. And above his sheriff's badge is a Solidarity button. Lech Walesa, leader of the Solidarity labor movement, winner of the 1983 Nobel Peace Prize, and president of Poland from 1990 to 1995, had this to say about the poster:

> I have often been asked in the United States to sign the poster that many Americans consider very significant. . . . It was a simple but effective gimmick that, at the time, was misunderstood by the Communists. They, in fact, tried to ridicule the freedom movement in Poland as an invention of the "Wild" West, especially the U.S. But the poster had the opposite impact: Cowboys in Western clothes had become a powerful symbol for Poles. Cowboys fight for justice, fight against evil, and fight for freedom, both physical and spiritual. Solidarity trounced the Communists in that election, paving the way for a democratic government in Poland. It is always so touching when people bring this poster up to me to autograph it. They have cherished it for so many years and it has become the emblem of the battle that we all fought together.[15]

Of course, few westerns portray the hero as noticing that Black Bart is a "grave and gathering threat" and that "preemptive action" is necessary to eliminate him before he acts. And rarely does the hero have to take up administration of Bart's territories and organize a free, fair, and stable governing system for Bart's Sunni, Shia, and Kurd underlings.

The subsequent difficulties in Iraq have made it clear that the American people will have a limited patience or enthusiasm for a doctrine of preemption. If a future administration wishes to bring about regime change with military force, they are going to need a much more airtight case than the Bush administration had in 2003.

American public's support for the mission in Iraq has bobbled up with victories and slumped as the insurgents bomb American soldiers and Iraqi civilians. The nation's leaders need to continually make the case that not only is this struggle worth the price in blood and treasure, but that there is a strategy to win.

Did Americans really know what they were signing on for when they went to war in Iraq? While they clearly knew the fight could be tough, it's unclear that they signed on for a generation's worth of nation building.

No, the sense in March 2003 was that Saddam Hussein was a dangerous dictator who would never change his ways. When he first appeared to most Americans' eyes after the invasion of Kuwait, he was terrorizing a blond British boy labeled a "guest," effectively a hostage. He's gassed Kurds, tortured thousands, caused environmental disasters, paid terrorists, applauded 9/11, and is most memorably seen firing shots off of balconies in his public appearances. He is an evil S.O.B., and if there's something Americans are good at, it's giving evil S.O.B.s long-overdue ass kickings. This is where the failure to find weapons of mass destruction is so devastating.

Now that Bush has been safely reelected, conservatives can and ought to come out and say it—blowing the call on Saddam's WMDs was a travesty and did serious damage to our national credibility. Had the Clinton administration botched a call this badly, Republicans would have wanted to follow up an impeachment with a crucifixion. We don't have to blame Bush personally—he's a commander in chief, not an intelligence analyst, and he's not supposed to personally review satellite photos and determine whether dual-use technology is being used to assemble a forbidden weapon.

The Bush administration, its congressional allies, and Bush's successor need to remember that despite fluctuating poll numbers, Americans are determined and resilient and much braver and hardier than some talking heads would assume. After Somalia, the first reaction of Americans was not to pull out our troops; it was to send in as many as necessary to bring in Aidid, dead or alive.

Anthony Zinni, who served as commander in chief of the U.S. Central Command under Clinton and strongly criticized President George W. Bush's Iraq policies, saw the lessons of Somalia: "The lesson and the effect [of Somalia] as it relates to casualties isn't that the Americans can't take casualties, because I don't think that's true. I think it's they can't take casualties for causes and reasons that aren't understood and clearly laid out before you get in." [16]

It is worth noting that difficulties in Iraq are not necessarily good news for the Democrats. The party is split, again. On one side are elected officials who want either an increase in the number of troops sent there ("to do the job right") or a very gradual pullout, leaving a stable and well-trained Iraqi army and police to keep order after our departure. Representatives of this side would include Senators Joe Biden and Hillary Clinton.

On the other side is a passionate, angry, and uncompromising antiwar grassroots movement that wants U.S. troops pulled out immediately and damn the consequences (to us or to the Iraqi people). Representatives of this side would be MoveOn.org, ANSWER,

Nancy Pelosi, John Murtha, and Cindy Sheehan, the mother of a soldier slain in Iraq.

These antiwar voices will never pull the lever for the Republicans, obviously. But they are demanding that Democrats endorse a position that is not a winner with the majority: leave immediately and let Iraq devolve into chaos. Democratic candidates can either move left, adopt their position, and lose the middle; or they can stay where they are and endure the complaints of a grassroots movement that denounces them as only marginally better than Bush and the GOP.

REMEMBER YOUR MANDATE:
KILLIN' THOSE WHO NEED KILLIN'

A few months into Bush's second term, the president's postelection euphoria had dissipated, and his administration was bereft of momentum. His poll numbers dipped, he had a hard time persuading Americans of the merits of his Social Security reform plan, his nomination to be U.N. ambassador was held up repeatedly, he faced tough fights on judges, and congressional intervention in the legal fights over the Terry Schiavo case had proven unpopular.

Part of the president's problem came from the fact that his signature policy proposal of the first half of 2005—Social Security reform—was at best a middling part of his reelection campaign. No campaign ad focused specifically on it. He mentioned it for several lines in his convention address, but those weren't the lines that resonated. Few of Bush's regular supporters had voted for him primarily on that issue, and almost none of the middle found that topic decisive.

In fact, as a senior Bush campaign official observed at the 2005

Conservative Political Action Conference, no major constituency on the right had been clamoring for immediate action on Social Security. It topped the agenda solely due to presidential enthusiasm.

On Election Day 2004, voters concluded George W. Bush had done a good job of killing terrorists, and his contract was renewed for another four years to do the same job. Bush took office, offered an inspiring, far-reaching, and idealistic inaugural address about fighting terrorism by spreading freedom, . . . and then set about overhauling the nation's old-age income security program.

Surely, a good number of Americans response to this was *"wha?"*

This is not to say that the GOP's domestic agenda—adding private accounts to Social Security, creating an "ownership society," promoting a "culture of life," appointing "strict constructionist" judges—can never be enacted. A party needs ideas and policy proposals on both foreign and domestic issues. But the party's leaders need to remember the public likes them because they kill bad guys. The popularity and public confidence regarding the war on terrorism are not automatically transferable to other issues. During the Schiavo controversy, a significant number of libertarian-leaning conservatives were up in arms over what they saw as congressional meddling in tragic circumstances.

In the run up to the 2006 congressional midterm elections, Republicans will almost certainly return to their strongest and most unifying issue: the war on terror.

THE ELECTIONS TO COME

Some Republican strategists aren't sure that terrorism will be as dominant an issue in coming years. "Was terrorism a big deal in 2002? Sure. 2004? Absolutely. 2006 or 2008? Barring another attack, maybe not," Wszolek says. "If the problem seems 'solved,' then it won't be at the top of voters' minds."

Castellanos echoes that thought. "George H. W. Bush won the [Persian Gulf] war, and he lost the election," he says. "Churchill won the war, and he was out in two months. They were not needed anymore. We still are."

"Regarding the lingering 9/11 effect, had you asked me that question two weeks ago, I'd say it had largely faded away and was not a meaningful part of people's daily lives," Wszolek said in mid-July 2005. "Then came the London bombings. I think that brought all those fears crashing back into people's brains. And I think the fact that a bus was attacked really rattled people, because a whole lot more people ride busses than go to work in 100-story buildings. . . . A bus being blown up brought the fear into every town in the country because even though it was in London, it still felt close to home."

Despite the doubts of these gentlemen, it seems hard to imagine that in 2006 and 2008 the Republican Party will not be running on national security in some way, shape, or form. It seems probable that GOP strategists will find an equivalent of the Homeland Security Department labor protections or the "global test" philosophy of Kerry—a wedge issue that unifies Republicans and divides Democrats.

A few Democrats have foreseen this, but it's unclear that the party has any coherent strategy to deal with it. Stan Greenberg and James Carville Democracy Corps studied this angle intently in July 2005. If Republicans run on the message, "Democrats cut funding for intelligence and are not strong on defense. Republicans are committed to a strong national defense and keeping America secure," then 57 percent of poll respondents say they are more likely to support the GOP, and 38 percent say they are much more likely to support the GOP. If the message is, "The Democrats are now calling for a retreat and withdrawal of our troops from Iraq. The Republicans say we cannot leave without finishing the job," the numbers are similar: 55 percent more likely, 37 percent much more likely. As usual, Democrats did much better when respondents were asked about the economy, health care, stem cell research, and so forth.[17]

September 2006 will mark the five-year anniversary of 9/11 and with it will come all of the memorial services, television documentaries, and in-depth assessments of the war on terror that accompany that date.

"My hunch is that national security won't be as dominant an issue, but obviously this depends on facts and circumstances and what happens if events occur," says a senior White House strategist. "Every year you get away from the attacks, it seems to get farther away . . . then again, 2006 will be the five-year anniversary, and that will be big again. The media has made a conscious effort to play it down and to not show images of 9/11. At the end of the day, it's pivotal and people will remember it. Sometimes it is in the foreground and sometimes it is in the background, but it never disappears."

Fall 2006 will also mark the five-year anniversary of the anthrax attacks. The attacker, as of this writing, has not been identified or caught. In the years since, some have speculated that the mailer was a domestic terrorist, although there does not appear to be clear evidence pointing in either direction. It is worth nothing that CIA director George Tenet's first instinct was that the mailings were the work of al-Qaeda, perhaps with state assistance.[18]

THE DEMOCRATS' MOST UNLIKELY
HAWKISH ROLE MODEL:
SENATOR HILLARY RODHAM CLINTON

Other than an early misstep comparing hostility to her health care plan to terrorism, Senator Hillary Rodham Clinton's legislative and rhetorical record since 9/11 has been one of her party's most consistently hawkish. While the rest of the Democratic Party seems to act like Howard Dean's anger is universal, the junior senator from New York has been reading her polling data very closely.

Perhaps this is a natural repercussion of representing New York, the emotional epicenter of America's war on terror, and a reflection of Senator Clinton's walking the ruins of the World Trade Center and dealing with the invisible threat of anthrax in the Senate mail shortly thereafter. Perhaps her service on the Armed Services Committee has given her an understanding of modern warfare and the philosophies of the U.S. military that other Democrats haven't yet grasped.

Many on the right will see Senator Clinton's efforts as political maneuvering. But recall the phenomenon of the mothers in focus groups, and the lasting impact of how they felt that sudden sense of fear and biologically hardwired instinct to protect their children on the morning of 9/11. Now examine the senator's account of that morning.

SENATOR CLINTON: [Chelsea had] gone [to New York City], what she thought would be just a great job. She was going to go down to Battery Park, she was going to go around the towers. She went to get a cup of coffee and—and that's when the plane hit.

PAULEY: She was close enough to hear the rumble.

SENATOR CLINTON: She did hear it. . . . Of course, Bill was in Australia. And, you know, he was so upset by what he was seeing on television that I didn't want to tell him that I couldn't find her until I found her. I told him that, you know, everything's fine, don't worry. But I couldn't do it with the level of assurance that I needed until I could find her a couple of hours later.[19]

Hillary Clinton may well have been as scarred as the rest of us by her experiences that morning. Her opponents on the right ought to consider that her hawkishness may just be genuine.

"Senator Clinton fully supports the steps the president has taken to disarm Iraq of weapons of mass destruction," said Clinton spokesman Philippe Reines on the eve of the invasion of Iraq, shortly before visiting an upstate New York arsenal that makes military hardware such as mortars and howitzers for U.S. troops.

In November 2003, when presidential candidate Howard Dean and others raised the prospect of pulling out of Iraq, she argued, "We need a bigger presence."

On Thanksgiving 2003, the story of the day was the president's surprise visit to the troops in Baghdad. But Clinton was also touring Iraq, visiting soldiers, talking to troop commanders, and surveying the postliberation scene.

She supported the $86 billion supplemental appropriation for Iraq and Afghanistan in 2004, the one that Kerry voted for before he voted against it. During a February 2005 appearance on *Meet the Press*, she bluntly stated something that many in her party refuse to say: "It is not in America's interests for the Iraqi government, the experiment in freedom and democracy, to fail." She urged Congress to have "a united front . . . to keep our troops safe, make sure they have everything they need, and try to support this new Iraqi government."

Hillary has certainly criticized the Bush administration, but her arguments are more compelling than "Bush lied, people died." She has raised concern about the extended use of Guard and Reserve members, about the lack of body armor. She has called for pay increases for members of the military and argued forcefully against base closings. Those complaints are downright . . . sensible.

The Pentagon appointed the senator to a panel that meets behind closed doors at the military's Joint Forces Command in Norfolk, Virginia, to discuss improving military readiness. Peace activists have picketed Clinton's midtown office on multiple occasions.

A central argument of the antiwar crowd, as well as many Democrats, is that America's effort to topple Saddam Hussein is completely unrelated to the war on terror and is in fact a distraction from more pressing goals like finding Osama bin Laden. Yet in the summer of 2005, when the antiwar movement was calling for an immediate withdrawal and Senator Russ Feingold made his pitch to that crowd by calling for U.S. troops to leave Iraq by the end of 2006, Hillary Clinton called the effort in Iraq part of this country's "long struggle against terrorism."

Judging by the rhetoric of so many of her peers, Hillary Rodham Clinton may be the only Democrat who already understands the rest of this book. Presuming she runs in 2008, her Democratic primary cannon fodder—er, opponents—and Republican adversary will be in for the political fight of their lives. On the campaign trail, Senator Clinton won't casually utter idiotic attack ad material—for example, "I voted for the $87 billion before I voted against it"—like Senator Kerry did; credit either her hawkish transformation or simply greater discipline as a candidate.

While Republicans would fight tooth and nail to stymie the quasi-theocratic "Politics of Meaning" domestic agenda of President Hillary Clinton, they might be able to take some solace in her likely foreign policy choices.[20] In fact, she might manage to forge a broader and more lasting domestic political consensus endorsing hawkish stances in the war on terror.

The sad fact is that large swaths of the American media and the American public put partisanship above principle and will never back military action so long as it is led by a Republican president. Some of the media voices that have most relentlessly and harshly criticized the Bush administration's wartime leadership had no problem stirring resolve, encouragement, and optimism for antiseptic, low-risk, minimal-effectiveness aerial bombing campaigns in Iraq and Afghanistan not too long ago when a Democratic president was leading the fight.

Look back to President Clinton's action against al-Qaeda in 1998, the cruise missile strikes in Afghanistan. You'll notice a particular tone in the editorials reacting to that one-time-only military action.

"Bill Clinton has launched a battle against terrorism that promises to take the United States into unfamiliar intelligence, military, and diplomatic terrain," declared the editorial board of the *New York Times*. "The doctrine of self-defense invoked by the Clinton Administration is valid when American citizens and embassies have been attacked or face assault."[21]

The *Philadelphia Inquirer* editors declared, "The U.S. military strikes that set the night afire Thursday in Afghanistan and Sudan were justified actions against a mounting terrorist threat aimed at Americans and America's interests overseas."[22]

Syndicated columnist Robert Scheer, today a vehement critic of the Bush administration, wrote back then, "The missile attack was an appropriate response to the carnage [of the embassy bombings]. If our modern and very expensive weapons cannot be used against terrorists, what good are they in this post–Cold War world?"[23]

Then look back to December 1998 when Clinton bombed Saddam Hussein on the eve of the House of Representatives' vote on his impeachment. The *New York Times* editorial board again: "Viewed outside the prism of impeachment, the decision to launch cruise missiles against Iraq was fully justified. Just weeks after Saddam Hussein had yet again promised to give international inspectors unhindered access, Iraq barred them from sites suspected of housing chemical and biological arms. . . . Given the prospect that Baghdad would rebuild its arsenal of toxic weapons while United Nations inspectors were handcuffed, Mr. Clinton and Prime Minister Tony Blair of Britain had no choice but to use military force to destroy portions of Iraq's arms industry." [24]

The *Chicago Sun-Times* praised Clinton, declaring, "Clinton's swift and decisive order to send U.S. missiles to attack Baghdad showed precisely the sort of leadership and resolve Iraq no doubt hoped he was lacking." [25]

The *Boston Globe* agreed, stating, "Although there will be inevitable cries of 'Wag the Dog,' President Clinton had justifiable grounds for launching cruise missiles and bombing raids against Saddam Hussein's regime. Those grounds were provided by Saddam, who has repeatedly broken his promises to comply with the terms of the 1991 cease-fire that ended Desert Storm. At the heart of the current conflict is the deadly serious matter of Saddam's refusal to give up his chemical and biological weapons— the ultimate instruments of terrorism in the hands of a vengeful despot who has already used such weapons on his own citizens." [26]

Contrasting that past full-throated support with today's pessimism, skepticism, cynicism, doubt, and overall gloom and doom, you cannot help but suspect that a disturbing belief has taken root in American society—the concept that somehow the war on terror is "Bush's war." His, not ours. Certainly, the continued military operations in Iraq are seen by many as Bush's fight, not theirs.

This view is appalling, and history will not judge its adherents kindly. There is no "nevermind, we changed our mind, we don't really want to fight this" reset button in warfare. Once you're in it, you have to win it.

For hawkish conservatives disturbed by the thought of a second Clinton presidency, a silver lining would be that for many on the left, including the shrilly-whining harpies of the media, all of this—Afghanistan, Iraq, and any future battlefields—would finally become *their* fight, too.

No one can predict the future with perfect accuracy, but based on Hillary's rhetoric and voting record, many antiwar voices on the left are likely to be gravely disappointed with her presidency. And it's easy to imagine many voices in the media and many Democratic lawmakers suddenly jumping on the bandwagon and finding their long-atrophied hawkish muscles.

It may be worth wondering which option will bring victory sooner: For America's slim pro-war majority to soldier on, with a large chunk of the pouting in the corner and whining because they don't like the commander in chief? Or for a vast, bipartisan majority of Americans to be on board for continued military operations against Islamist extremists around the globe, led by a president of a different party?

Of course, Hillary's candidacy will still face serious problems, not the least of which is whether she can overcome the rest of her party.

Sure, Senator Hillary has sounded like a hawk, but would a second Clinton administration actually be hawkish? What concessions would she be forced to make to the dovish wing of her party? Could she overcome the objections of a party that, deep down, thinks Michael Moore is right?

To win in 2008, Democrats need a hawk. Of course, periodically a Democratic official or strategist will reveal how far the party is from recognizing this truth. Take, for example, this unfortunate quote to *The Hill* newspaper:

> [Joe] Biden's greatest strength, his supporters say, is his foreign-policy expertise. He is the ranking Democrat on the Senate Foreign Relations Committee and has served as its chairman.

"We're probably one terrorist act away from the Democrats' really focusing on a candidate who has unquestioned credentials on national security and terrorism," said David Wilhelm, who served as chairman of the Democratic National Committee during the 1994 election cycle and is an informal adviser to Biden. "Senator Biden brings that to the table. He is the go-to person in the Democratic Party on those issues." [27]

"One terrorist attack away"? What, 9/11 wasn't enough? Why does it take *another* terrorist attack to get Democrats to focus on a candidate who has unquestioned credentials on national security and terrorism?

THE CURSE OF INTERESTING TIMES

A strategist close to the Bush White House observes that the opposition party has devolved in two areas:

> If you look back at the history of the Democratic Party, there was a time when they were both strong on defense and strong on idealism. If you read the speeches of Kennedy and Roosevelt, you sense the themes of idealism and the need for a strong military. Then in the late 1960s, 1970s, and early 1980s, they became weak on defense, but still strong on idealism. Their critique against the Republican Party was that it wasn't standing up for American ideals. They focused on the corruption of South Vietnamese, on the need for sanctions on South Africa, on death squads in Central America. They made an idealistic case, even if they weren't willing to use military force.

Today the Democrats are weak on defense and weak on idealism. It is clear in terms of Iraq that they take no joy in the liberation of 25 million people from one of the most malevolent regimes in modern times. President Bush has seized the mantle of idealism that they have left, talking about the inherent dignity of man, human rights, and the rights of women.

Looking at the historical moment we find ourselves in, we are easily reminded of the Chinese curse, "May you live in interesting times." There is no doubt that we live in interesting times.

We have seen thousands killed in a day. We have seen our enemy declare that to end their attacks on the innocent, we must meet their demand that we completely change our culture and convert to their particular vision of Islam. We have seen many of the world's greatest and most cosmopolitan cities—New York, Washington, Istanbul, Madrid, London—turned into war zones, devastated by carnage. We have seen the beheadings of the innocent used as a publicity stunt.

We have also seen ordinary Americans foil a well-planned terrorist plot and save uncountable lives, just by rushing the cockpit of a hijacked airliner. We have seen U.S. Special Forces riding horseback to pursue the enemy. We have seen a terrorist mastermind get an early wake-up call from the Pakistani police, and have learned that he looks as groggy and unkempt when he first wakes up as we do. We have seen a once-powerful, ruthless dictator dragged out of a hole, looking like a disheveled and pathetic vagrant.

We have seen Afghani women take off their burqas, we have seen Iraqis voting and marking their fingers with purple ink, and we have seen Lebanese throw off a yoke of Syrian oppression. We have seen the dictator of Libya disarm and make a deal, because by his own words, he didn't want to take up residence in a spider hole.

Today is not September 10, 2001, and that day and all of its "normalcy" will not come again for a long, long time. The world we find ourselves in is not the one we would choose. It is one of fear; of anxiety; of painful choices; of blood, sweat, and tears; of never knowing what the next moment will hold, never mind the next day.

But the world we find ourselves in is also one of heroism, of ordinary citizens rising to the challenge and demonstrating extraordinary courage. It is one where an American Muslim World Trade Center survivor, after tripping on a street in lower Manhattan while running from the smoke, can find himself helped up by an orthodox Jew in sidelocks and yarmulke, telling him, "Hey, brother, let's get out of here."[28] It is one where we applaud ordinary guys doing the dirty work of clearing away wreckage, where sports stadium crowds sing "God Bless America" and mean every word, where a guy who lost a leg in Iraq or Afghanistan gets thanked by strangers on the street for his service and has a hard time ever picking up the tab at the bar or restaurant. It is a world in which every day we look at our loved ones and know what is worth fighting for.

Once-leftist, pro-war writer Christopher Hitchens acknowledged a bit of exhilaration on 9/11: "On the morning of September 11, I had in common with a lot of people a number of emotions: anger, disgust, solidarity. But there was another one that I couldn't quite place, and I hope I can say this without risk of indecency: it was exhilaration. Here is the enemy, in as plain and clear a view as it could possibly be: theocratic fascism, disclosed in its most horrific form. If that's the battle, if they want a clash of civilizations, they can have one, and I will never get bored with prosecuting it."

On that world-changing day, all of us suddenly learned what it feels like to be locked in life-or-death combat with a group and an ideology that earns the label "evil."

While it is easy to look back on the go-go 1990s with nostalgia, wishing for the days of easy dot-com money and predictable divided government, there was something small-minded about our politics then. In retrospect, we were only fooling ourselves into believing it was the end of history, and that the top issues of the era were school uniforms, lockboxes, obscure Arkansas land deals, tweaking the tax code, midnight basketball, and building a metaphorical bridge to a century that was going to arrive no matter what we did.

A great nation deserves great debates about great challenges. At this moment, one of our two great national parties has risen to the moment and offered a vision of great strength and great idealism. The policies and ideas of the Republican Party are not without their flaws, but they directly and squarely face the fundamental challenge of our time. Their friends on the other side of the aisle are a bit muddled. They have not risen to the moment yet; but that does not mean they cannot in the future.

The world changed. We have to change with it.

NOTES

One: Post-9/11 America

1. John Tierney, "Fantasies of Vengeance, Fed by Fury," *New York Times*, Sept. 18, 2001.

2. Ibid.

3. NBC News vice president Allison Gollust says the network "rarely permits" use of the video, because after an extensive internal discussion, "we chose to limit usage of these images because they are very disturbing and we feel that it isn't necessary to people watching be disturbed over and over again." At CBS News, there is a widespread understanding that the video can be used "only when it is really necessary." At CNN, the policy is to allow use of the video of the terrorist planes in flight but to "stop short of the moment of impact." Both MSNBC and Fox require the approval of a senior executive before showing the video again. The policies were detailed by Byron York in his article "Taboo: Abu Ghraib Images Are One Thing. But 9/11? Off Limits," *National Review,* July 28, 2004.

4. *Sophie's Choice* is a book and movie that features a young mother sent to Auschwitz because of her links to the resistance. The Nazis force her to make an unfair, unforgivable choice: Which of her two children will she send to the gas chamber? Which one will she save?

5. Bob Woodward, *Bush at War,* Simon & Schuster, New York, 2002, p. 17.

6. Remarks by Page at the Virginia's Center for Politics American Democracy Conference, Dec. 3, 2004.

7. Norton, New York, 2003, p. 48.

8. Karen Tumulty and Viveca Novak, "Goodbye Soccer Mom. Hello, Security Mom," *Time* June 2, 2003.

9. Ibid.

10. Richard Morin and Dan Balz, " 'Security Mom' Bloc Proves Hard to Find," *Washington Post*, Oct. 1, 2004.

11. Anna Greenberg, "The Security Mom Myth," AlterNet, posted Sept. 30, 2004.

12. Glenn Reynolds, "The Blogs of War: How the Internet Is Reshaping Foreign Policy," *National Interest*, Spring 2004.

13. Walter Russell Meade, "The Jacksonian Tradition," *National Interest*, Winter 1999.

14. Tulsa Kinney, "The Dinner Fight," *L.A. Weekly*, Dec. 12, 2002.

15. "Larry Clark Stands Up for U.S.," *New York Post*, Nov. 9, 2002, p. 6.

16. Lawrence K. Altman, "Donors Flood Blood Banks, But a Steady Stream Is What's Needed, *New York Times*, Sept. 18, 2001.

17. Rick Bragg, "U.S. Binds Wounds in Red, White and Blue," *New York Times*, Sept. 17, 2001.

18. Peggy Noonan, "We're All Soldiers Now," *Wall Street Journal Online*, Nov. 2, 2001.

19. Jeffrey Goldberg, "The Unbranding," *New Yorker*, Mar. 21, 2003.

Two: An Unpopular Position on Gay Marriage Is a Headache; An Unpopular Position on National Security Is the Ebola Virus

1. Steven Waldman, "Let's Talk about Faith," Slate.com, Nov. 5, 2004.

2. Carolyn Lochhead, "Gay Marriage: Did Issue Help Re-elect Bush?" *San Francisco Chronicle*, Nov. 4, 2004.

3. Cecilia Le, "No 'Monopoly on Morality': Clinton, at Hamilton, Tells Why Dems Lost" [Utica] *Observer Dispatch*, Nov. 9, 2004.

4. Carolyn Lochhead, "Gay Marriage."

5. Roemer's address at the Democratic Leadership Council's National Conversation panel on national security, July 25, 2005.

6. Margolis's remarks at the Virginia's Center for Politics American Democracy Conference, Dec. 3, 2004.

7. Robert David Sullivan, "Tote That Barge, Lift That Bale," *Commonwealth,* Nov. 2004.

8. Kilgore, "Lessons Learned, Part II," NewDonkey.com, Dec. 29, 2004.

9. See David Kilpatrick, "Some Democrats Believe the Party Should Get Religion," *New York Times,* Nov. 17, 2004; Peter Wallsten and Mary Curtius, "Democratic Leadership Rethinking Abortion," *Los Angeles Times,* Dec. 23, 2004; Andrew Sullivan, "The Case for Compromise on Abortion," *Time,* Mar. 7, 2005.

10. *Fox News Sunday,* Nov. 7, 2004.

Three: Yes, It Is That Bad, Democrats

1. All vote totals from CNN.com. Despite all the postelection focus on Ohio, several red states were much closer than that Midwestern battleground. In New Mexico, Bush's margin was 5,988 votes; in Iowa, 10,059 votes; in Nevada, 21,500 votes; and in Colorado 99,523 votes. These states didn't get the attention that Ohio did because Kerry would have needed to win three of the four to get 270 electoral votes.

2. Belisarius's essay was posted on Nov. 4, 2004.

3. Arianna Huffington, "Rethinking the Party," Salon.com, Nov. 11, 2004.

4. Jill Lawrence and Susan Page, "What Got So Many Counties to Shift from Blue to Red?" *USA Today,* Jan. 31, 2005.

5. Jann Wenner, "Why Bush Won," *Rolling Stone,* Nov. 17, 2004.

6. Speech by Republican National Committee chairman Ken Mehlman, Jan. 19, 2005.

7. Matt Bai, "Who Lost Ohio?" *New York Times Magazine,* Nov. 21, 2004.

8. McCurry's comments at the Virginia's Center for Politics American Democracy Conference, Dec. 3, 2004.

9. Carson's remarks at the Virginia's Center for Politics American Democracy Conference, Dec. 3, 2004.

10. The Pew Research Center's quadrennial postelection survey, conducted among 1,209 voters who were originally interviewed in October, finds that a third of all voters say they are very satisfied with their choice of candidates—the highest percentage expressing that view in postelection surveys dating to 1988. That reflects extraordinary enthusiasm among Repub-

licans, 68 percent of whom express a high degree of satisfaction with the candidates. As a polar of comparison, in 1996 just 34 percent of Democrats said they were very satisfied with the candidates after Bill Clinton's easy re-election victory. The dominant reaction to Bush's reelection among Kerry's supporters is disappointment (82 percent, but about a third (35 percent) say they feel angry over the election outcome. Liberals, in particular, express intense feelings as a result of the election. Roughly half of Kerry's liberal supporters say they feel angry (53 percent) or depressed (47 percent) because of Bush's victory. In contrast, large majorities of Bush voters say they feel reassured, relieved, and safer as a consequence of the president's reelection.

11. Roberto Suro, Richard Fry, and Jeffrey Passel, "Hispanics and the 2004 Election: Population, Electorate and Voters," Pew Hispanic Center, June 27, 2005, p. 14.

12. John Fund, "Bush Democrats," *Wall Street Journal*, Apr. 4, 2005.

13. Marc Danziger, "Terror & Liberalism, Will & Perspective," Command Post blog, Dec. 3, 2004.

14. Rove on *Fox News Sunday*, Nov. 7, 2004.

Four: It Takes Time and Effort to Build a Reputation as a Wimp

1. Historians debate whether Sirhan Sirhan's actions represent a precursor to today's terrorist attacks against Americans. The assassin was born to Palestinian parents and allegedly targeted Kennedy for his support of Israel. However, Sirhan was raised Catholic.

2. Daly believes history will repeat itself if Hillary Clinton or a similar "centrist" Democrat is nominated in 2008 and loses. The Democrats' antiwar grassroots will want to see a pure Howard Dean–type nominated in 2012.

3. Mona Charen, *Useful Idiots*, HarperCollins, New York, 2003, p. 96.

4. Discussion with Noonan, June 25, 2005.

5. James Robbins, a professor at the National Defense University in Washington, suggests that this was a defining moment in many Americans' lives; those who were outside the antiwar movement feel shame for not objecting to the abuse of returning U.S. troops at the time. He believes this shame explains the intense desire to "support our troops," whether supporting or opposing a specific military action, in American society today.

6. Frank Gregorsky, "What's Wrong with Democratic Foreign Policy?" (A paper by the House Republican Study Committee, 1984), p. 4.

7. Mona Charen, *Useful Idiots*, p. 66.

8. James Webb, "Sleeping with the Enemy," *American Enterprise*, May/June 1997.

9. David Broder, "Zigzagging in Search of Identity," *Washington Post*, July 15, 1984.

10. Mona Charen, *Useful Idiots*, p. 78.

11. James Traub, "The Things They Carry," *New York Times Magazine*, Jan. 4, 2004.

12. Mona Charen, *Useful Idiots*, p. 106.

13. PBS, *The American Experience: Jimmy Carter*, 2002.

14. Ibid.

15. "Iran Hostage Crisis," http://en.wikipedia.org/wiki/Iran_Hostage _Crisis; accessed May 1, 2006.

16. Richard Marcinko, *Rogue Warrior*, Simon & Schuster, New York, 1992, p. 233.

17. Andrew Bacevich, *The New American Militarism*, Oxford University Press, New York, 2005, p. 185.

18. Edmund Morris, *Dutch*, Random House, New York, 1999, p. 407.

19. Daniel Pipes, "Reagan's Early Victory in the War on Terror," *New York Sun*, June 15, 2004.

20. PBS, *The American Experience: Jimmy Carter*, 2002.

21. Martin Schram, "Carter's Hopes Held Hostage to the End," *Washington Post*, January 20, 1981.

22. Ibid.

23. Interview with Ed Moltzen, *Command Post*, Oct. 26, 2004.

24. Charles Krauthammer, *Reluctant Cold Warriors*, Nov. 12, 1999.

25. Douglas Brinkley, *The Boys of Pointe du Hoc*, HarperCollins, New York, 2005, p. 10.

26. Cowan interview with *PBS Frontline* for its report "Target America," aired Oct. 4, 2001.

27. Weinberger interview with *PBS Frontline* for its report "Target America," aired Oct. 4, 2001.

28. Lawrence F. Kaplan, "Old Allies," *New Republic*, Nov. 10, 2003.

29. James Eberle, "Europe Has Hardly Gone Soft on Terror," *Los Angeles Times*, Jan. 26, 1986.

30. Excerpt from Reagan's diary printed on RonaldReagan.com; Ronald Reagan, *An American Life*, Simon and Schuster, New York, 1990.

31. Judith Apter Klinghoffer, "With Us or Against Us: Why We Now Have to Put the Matter So Starkly," George Mason University's History News Network, Oct. 21, 2002.

32. Shockingly, the French denied the United States the right to fly over its airspace during the mission.

33. Reagan's televised Oval Office address to the nation, Apr. 14, 1986.

34. Carl Limbacher Jr., "Hannity Book: Kerry Objected to Reagan's Bombing of Terrorist Gadhafi," NewsMax.com, Feb. 18, 2004.

35. "Bonfire of the Democrats," *National Review*, Apr. 1, 1991.

36. Tom Webb, "Wellstone Keeps Distance This Time," *St. Paul Pioneer Press*, Sept. 26, 2002.

37. Don Kowet, "Desert Storm Hall of Shame," *Washington Times*, Mar. 19, 1991.

38. Max Boot, "Antiwar Ouija Boards," *Los Angeles Times*, Oct. 21, 2004. Carter, Kerry, and Brzezinski quotes appear in this column as well.

39. Department of Defense biography of Aspin, http://www.defenselink.mil/specials/seedef_histories/bios/aspin.htm.

40. Ibid.

41. Allard interview with *PBS Frontline*, Oct. 26, 2001.

42. Margaret Daly Hays and Read Admiral Gary F. Weatley, *Interagency and Political-Military Dimensions of Peace Operations: Haiti—A Case Study*, National Defense University Press, 1996, p. 4.

43. The lessons of Somalia travel fast, don't they? The Clinton administration could insist that the lack of overwhelming response in Mogadishu would not have negative repercussions for U.S. prestige and influence in the future. It's just too bad no one told the Haitians that.

44. Howard W. French, "Nations Block Landing of U.S. Forces," *New York Times*, Oct. 12, 1993.

45. This would be the Republican landslide of 1994. So Clinton's strategy apparently didn't seem to work so well.

46. Mark Helprin, "A Soldier of the Not So Great War," *Wall Street Journal*, Sept. 20, 1994.

47. Wesley K. Clark, *Waging Modern War: Bosnia, Kosovo, and the Future of Combat*, Perseus Books, Cambridge, Mass., 2001, p. 417.

48. Charles Krauthammer, "The Road to Hell: Clinton, Kosovo, and Good Intentions," *Washington Post*, Apr. 2, 1999.

49. Ibid.

50. Fareed Zakaria, "Keeping Kosovo: The Costs of Liberal Imperialism," *National Review*, Sept. 27, 1999.

51. Ibid.

52. Natasha Joffe, "At War with NATO," *Guardian*, Oct. 23, 2001.

53. Wesley K. Clark, *Waging Modern War*, p. 442.

54. Fareed Zakaria, "Keeping Kosovo: The Costs of Liberal Imperialism," *National Review*, Sept. 27, 1999.

55. Peter J. Boyer, "General Clark's Battles," *New Yorker*, Nov. 17, 2003.

56. Ibid.

57. Clark later claimed that the official who said this was Secretary of Defense Donald Rumsfeld.

58. Byron York, "Clinton Has No Clothes," *National Review*, Dec. 17, 2001.

59. Ibid.

60. Barbara Slavin, "Officials: U.S. 'Outed' Iran's Spies in 1997," *USA Today*, Mar. 29, 2004.

61. Byron York, *National Review*.

62. "Culture Crash," a web-only interview with William Langewiesche, *Atlantic Monthly Online*, Nov. 15, 2001.

63. Byron York, *National Review*.

64. Bob Woodward, *Bush at War*, Simon & Schuster, New York, 2002, pp. 6, 7.

65. Benjamin Soskis, "When America Liked the Taliban," *New Republic*, Oct. 22, 2001.

66. Bob Woodward, *Bush at War*, p. 35.

67. Byron York, *National Review*.

68. Lugar, interview with *Frontline*, Sept. 29, 1990.

69. Lawrence Kaplan, *New Republic*, Nov. 10, 2003.

70. *9/11 Commission Report*, p. 203.

Five: How Did Each Party React to 9/11?

1. Cheney's word choice prompted this exchange:

> Mr. Russert: Full wrath. That's a very strong statement to the Afghans this morning.
>
> Vice President Cheney: It is, indeed. It is, indeed.

2. Associated Press, "CIA Scrubs More Than 1,000 Informants," Mar. 2, 1997.

3. Bob Woodward, *Bush at War,* Simon & Schuster, New York, 2002, p. 45.

4. George Orwell, "Pacifism and the War," *Partisan Review,* Aug.–Sept. 1942.

5. "Oliver Stone's Chaos Theory," *New Yorker,* Oct. 22, 2001. Additional coverage can be found in Jeffrey Wells's column, "Oliver Locks the House, Reel.com, Oct. 10, 2001."

6. Elizabeth Auster, "Offer the Hand of Peace," *Plain Dealer,* Sept. 30, 2001.

7. Ethan Wallison, "War a Challenge for Peace Caucus," *Roll Call,* Oct. 1, 2001.

8. Lee's floor statement, *Congressional Record,* Sept. 14, 2001.

9. Jay Root, "A Race about Race," in *Midterm Madness,* Rowman and Littlefield, Lanham, Maryland, 2003, p. 173.

10. Clinton's remarks as transcribed by Georgetown University Office of Protocol and Events, Nov. 7, 2001.

11. James Carroll, "The War Is Not Just," *Boston Globe,* Nov. 27, 2001.

12. Lance Morrow, "The Case for Rage and Retribution," Time.com, Sept. 12, 2001.

13. Bob Woodward, *Bush at War,* pp. 52, 103. This comment by Black resulted in him receiving what must be the coolest nickname in the Bush White House, "Flies-on-the-Eyeballs Guy."

14. Noam Scheiber, "Exit Poll," *New Republic,* Feb. 24, 2003.

15. Juliet Eilperin, "Democrat Implies Sept. 11 Administration Plot," *Washington Post,* Apr. 12, 2002.

16. Frank Cannon and Chuck Donovan, "The Seriousness Gap: Why Voters Turned Republican," *Weekly Standard,* Nov. 18, 2002.

17. Chuck Todd, "Air Force Won," in *Midterm Madness,* p. 40.

18. Fred Barnes, "The New 9/11 Majority," *Weekly Standard,* Nov. 18, 2002.

19. Jay Root, "A Race about Race," in *Midterm Madness,* p. 174.

20. John B. Judis, "No Fault," *New Republic,* Nov. 18, 2002.

21. Martin Peretz, "Seventies Kitsch," *New Republic Online,* Nov. 6, 2002.

Six: Gaffes of Compounding Interest: The Terrorism Debate from 2002 to 2004

1. Gregg Herrington, "Senator Asks Students to Ponder," *Vancouver (Washington) Columbian,* Dec. 19, 2002.

2. Malie Rulon, "Lawmaker Compares Osama, U.S. Patriots," *Toledo Blade,* Mar. 6, 2003.

3. John Edwards, address on homeland security, Brookings Institution, Dec. 18, 2002.

4. Howard Dean, Children's Defense Fund forum, Apr. 9, 2003.

5. Gregg Easterbrook, "So What If You Told Us So?" *New Republic Online,* May 14, 2003.

6. Ryan Lizza, "One Step Forward, Two Steps Back," *New Republic Online,* May 23, 2003.

7. Clay Risen, "Kerry Shows Some Backbone," *New Republic Online,* June 6, 2003.

8. All quotes from *Meet the Press* transcript, June 22, 2003. The other hilarious, if off-topic, exchange that day:

> Mr. Russert: Well, you apologized to Bob Graham.
> Dr. Dean: No, I didn't.
> Mr. Russert: You called the AP and recanted the statement.
> Dr. Dean: I called the AP and said, "I'm sorry I said that."
> Mr. Russert: Well, that's an apology.
> Dr. Dean: No, it's not.
> Mr. Russert: "I'm sorry I said it" is not an apology?
> Dr. Dean: I didn't actually say I'm sorry.

9. Lawrence F. Kaplan, "Dean's Blind Eye," *New Republic Online,* July 7, 2003.

10. Michael Crowley, "Graham Prematurely Utters the Word 'Impeachment,' " *New Republic Online,* July 15, 2003.

11. Holly Ramer, "Dean Scolds Rivals about Belated Criticism of War," Associated Press, July 23, 2003.

12. Franklin Foer, "Not an Excerpt but a Scold," *New Republic Online,* Aug. 20, 2003.

13. Clay Risen, "Graham Gets Incomprehensible," *New Republic Online,* Aug. 21, 2003.

14. Byron York, "Do Democrats Really Care about Terrorism?" *National Review Online,* Oct. 27, 2003.

15. Michael Crowley, "At War With Himself," *New Republic Online*, Oct. 21, 2003.

16. Transcript of Democratic debate, WashingtonPost.com, Oct. 26, 2003.

17. Howard Kurtz, "Dean Assails Bush on Defense," *Washington Post*, Dec. 1, 2003.

18. Joe Trippi, *The Revolution Will Not Be Televised*, HarperCollins, New York, 2004, p. 177.

19. Lawrence Kaplan, "Impossible Promise," *New Republic Online*, Jan. 12, 2004.

20. Michael Crowley, "Kerry's Odd Book on Terrorism," *New Republic*, Feb. 9, 2004.

21. Michael Moore, "Heads Up," Michael Moore.com, Apr. 14, 2004.

22. George Soros, Remarks at Take Back America Conference, Washington, D.C. June 3, 2004.

23. John Mintz and Mike Allen, "Homeland Security is Politicized Issue," *Washington Post*, June 27, 2004.

24. Marc Sandalow, "Skeptics Wonder If Politics Motivated Warnings," *San Francisco Chronicle*, May 27, 2004.

25. Doug Donovan, "O'Malley Takes the Heat for Remarks about Bush," *Baltimore Sun*, July 1, 2004.

26. *Larry King Live*, CNN, July 8, 2004.

27. Associated Press, "Meek: Governor 'like bin Laden' in 2000 recount," July 10, 2004.

28. Al Hunt, "Bagging bin Laden," *Wall Street Journal*, July 15, 2004.

29. *Late Edition with Wolf Blitzer*, CNN, Aug. 1, 2004.

30. Jim Geraghty, "More McAuliffe and Zell," *National Review Online*, Aug. 2, 2004.

31. Matt Bai, "Kerry's Undeclared War," *New York Times Magazine*, Oct. 10, 2004.

32. Guiliani's connects on a Bush/Cheney 2004 campaign conference call, Oct. 13, 2004.

33. Dotty Lynch, remarks at the Virginia's Center for Politics American Democracy Conference, Dec. 3, 2004.

34. Steve Schmidt, remarks at the Virginia's Center for Politics American Democracy Conference, Dec. 3, 2004.

35. Arianna Huffington, Ariannaonline.com, Nov. 11, 2004.

36. Joshua Micah Marshall, "A Short Note," Talking PointsMemo.com, Oct. 30, 2004.

37. I asked Obi-Wan, "What does Osama bin Laden think he's doing here? What's his game? What did he hope to accomplish with this tape?" He replied, "The arrogance of evil," sounding a bit like his movie namesake. "He really thinks the American people will listen to him. Every dictator is like this, and Saddam used to do this all the time when he did interviews with Western media. He's arrogant enough to think that if he speaks to the American people, we will actually come around to his view."

38. Michael Moore, "One Day Left," MichaelMoore.com, Nov. 1, 2004.

Seven: Who Is Your Face?

1. Carter appearance on MSNBC's *Hardball,* Oct. 19, 2004.

2. Begala does slip up sometimes. He wrote a book entitled *It's Still the Economy, Stupid!* that was published in November 2002. Of course, the elections that occurred that month largely centered around national security, terrorism, and Iraq.

3. Michael Moore, "The Sad and Sordid Whereabouts of bin Cheney and bin Bush," from a free online chapter addition to *Stupid White Men,* MichaelMoore.com.

4. It is not merely "disingenuous filmmakers" who buy into this argument, based on bloodless mathematical calculations. Dean adviser Benjamin Barber: "Actual terrorist events are few and far between and, while devastating to those directly affected, are of less statistical consequence than say, a year's traffic fatalities or the mundane tragedies of people falling off ladders at home." *Fear's Empire,* p. 49.

5. CBS, *60 Minutes,* July 23, 2003.

6. Notice Moore uses the antiseptic, generic word *tragedy* to describe an act of mass murder. The Asian tsunami was a tragedy. Earthquakes and car accidents are tragedies. The 9/11 attacks were massacres, a deliberate act inspired by human thought and guided by human hands.

7. Niamh Slevin, "Moore Discusses Book, Blasts 'Bush of Arabia,'" *Michigan Daily,* Oct. 13, 2003.

8. Ed Koch, "Moore's Propaganda Film Cheapens Debate, Polarizes Nation," WorldTribune.com, June 29, 2004.

9. Christopher Hitchens, "Unfairenheit 9/11: The Lies of Michael Moore," Slate.com, June 21, 2004.

10. CyberAlert, Media Research Center, May 12, 2003.

11. "Nobles and Knaves," *Washington Times,* Jan. 11, 2003.

12. As Gregg Easterbrook noted in the *New Republic* on July 12, perhaps the first sign of Moore's politics to come can be found in his 1995 fictional comedy, *Canadian Bacon.* Much of the movie is an enjoyable comedy about a hapless president played by Alan Alda who decides to start a war with Canada to improve his poor approval rating. Easterbrook describes a disturbing scene: "The Clinton-like president sends a commando team into Canada. Needless to say, the elite U.S. commandos do nothing but bungle, comically. Then at one point, a commando falls and injures himself. The nearest other commando turns and, without hesitation, shoots his comrade repeatedly through the head. It's an ugly, sadistic scene totally out of place in what is otherwise a slapstick farce. Though it gets the message across: Michael Moore deeply, deeply hates the United States."

13. Darren Goodsir, "Infidels had Bali Coming, Not That I Did It, Says Samudra," *Sydney Morning Herald,* Aug. 12, 2003.

14. Viveca Novak, "Dean's Law and Order Views," *Time,* Oct. 30, 2003.

15. Mark Leon Goldberg, "Is Moore Less?" *American Prospect,* Feb. 4, 2005.

16. Those seeking a definitive list of *Fahrenheit 9/11*'s inaccuracies, half-truths, and lies are urged to read the list of Dave Kopel, research director at the Independence Institute, at davekopel.com.

17. Byron York, "The Vast Left-Wing Conspiracy," *Crown Forum,* p. 107.

18. Tina Brown, *Washington Post,* June 16, 2004.

19. Lieberman on *The O'Reilly Factor,* Fox News Channel, Nov. 10, 2004.

20. Cliff May, "Michael Moore, Hezbollah Heartthrob," Townhall.org, July 8, 2004.

21. United Press International, "UPI Hears . . . ," Sept. 14, 2004.

22. Mark Leon Goldberg, *American Prospect.*

23. Nicholas D. Kristof, "Time to Get Religion," *New York Times,* Nov. 6, 2004.

24. Mark Leon Goldberg, *American Prospect.*

25. Peter Beinart, "A Fighting Faith," *New Republic,* Dec. 13, 2004.

26. Michael Crowley, "Profit Sharing," *New Republic,* Sept. 6, 2004.

27. "Getting the Message," staff editorial in *New Republic*, Nov. 25, 2002.

Eight: Even If You Say Michael Moore Isn't Your Face, the Other Guy Is Telling People That He Is

1. Matt Bai, "Kerry's Undeclared War," *New York Times Magazine*, Oct. 10, 2004.

2. Richard Viguerie, "2004 Will Be First Election Decided by Alternative Media," ConservativeHQ.com, Sept. 10, 2004.

3. Michael Crowley, "Follow the Leader," *New Republic*, Nov. 25, 2002.

4. Patrick Ruffini, "Passion Does Not Equal Sanity," PatrickRuffini.com, Jan. 31, 2005.

5. David Frum, "Unpatriotic Conservatives," *National Review*, Apr. 7, 2003.

6. Stanley Kurtz, "The Vision Thing," *National Review Online*, Apr. 11, 2003.

7. Ryan Lizza, "Flip Side," *New Republic*, Sept. 27, 2004.

8. Hugh Hewitt, *If It's Not Close, They Can't Cheat*, Nelson Books, Nashville, Tennessee, 2004, pp. 17–19.

9. Ibid., p. 89.

10. Noam Scheiber, "Unified Theory," *New Republic Online*, Sept. 2, 2004.

11. Ronald Brownstein, "Race for Democratic Leader Entering Its Final Stage," *Los Angeles Times*, Jan. 31, 2005.

12. Markos Moulitsas Zuniga, "The Litmus Test," DailyKos.com, Aug. 3, 2005.

13. Chris Suellentrop, "Feel-Good Politics," Slate.com, Dec. 8, 2004.

14. It remains unclear as to just why one would bother having a rally after the election.

15. Hugh Hewitt, *If It's Not Close, They Can't Cheat*, p. xi.

16. Mark Steyn, "Facing the Music," *New York Sun*, June 20, 2005.

17. Senator Dick Durbin, Senate Hour, Statement, June 14, 2005.

18. John Leo, "It's All Our Fault," *U.S. News and World Report*, Aug. 8, 2005.

19. Ibid.

20. Mohammad-Mahmoud Ould Mohamedou, "Time to Talk to al-Qaeda?" *Boston Globe*, Sept. 14, 2005.

Nine: A Handicap Masquerading as an Advantage

1. J. Peter Mulhern, "Two Cheers for Media Bias," *Washington Weekly*, July 30, 2001.

2. Adam Nagourney and Janet Elder, "In Poll, Americans Say Both Parties Lack Clear Vision," *New York Times*, Nov. 3, 2002.

3. Chris Suellentrope, "The Other Incumbent Rule," Slate.com, Nov. 2, 2004.

4. Clanton's remarks at the Virginia's Center for Politics American Democracy Conference, Dec. 3, 2004.

5. Schmidt's remarks at the Virginia's Center for Politics American Democracy Conference, Dec. 3, 2004.

6. Mickey Kaus, "Did McCain-Feingold Actually Work?" Slate.com, Dec. 30, 2004.

7. Kevin Peraino, "Bush: 'Some Kind of Night,' " *Newsweek*, Dec. 27, 2004.

8. Michelle Cottle, "Hard Press," *New Republic*, Nov. 8, 2004.

9. Ibid.

10. Jim Rutenburg, "A Request to Partisans: Don't Shoot the Pollster," *New York Times*, Sept. 29, 2004.

Ten: You Can't Win If You're Angrier at Halliburton Than Osama bin Laden

1. T. A. Frank, "Left Out," *New Republic*, Feb. 7, 2005.

2. Thomas Friedman, "Let's Talk about Iraq," *New York Times*, June 15, 2005.

3. Thomas Friedman, "The Chant Not Heard," *New York Times*, Nov. 30, 2003.

4. FAIR Action Alert, "Is Thomas Friedman Even Listening?" Dec. 2, 2003.

5. Bill Whittle, "Deterrence (Part One)," www.ejectejecteject.com, Oct. 6, 2004.

6. Bob Woodward, *Bush at War*, Simon & Schuster, New York, 2002, p. 262.

7. Michael J. Totten, "They Ain't Studying War No More," Michael Totten.com, Nov. 13, 2004.

8. Heather Hurlburt, "War Torn," *Washington Monthly*, Nov. 2002.

9. Ace of Spades HQ blog, Mar. 5, 2005.

10. Bob Brigham, "The Rentalized Democratic Party," Swing State Project, May 24, 2005.

11. Peter Beinart, "Fighting Faith," *New Republic*, Dec. 13, 2004.

12. Was this an inadvertent confirmation from Kos that millions of the party's supporters in its ranks constitute the "conspiracy-mongering left"?

13. "Obama Still on DLC's List," dailykos.com, Mar. 15, 2005.

14. Jeffrey Goldberg, "The Unbranding," *New Yorker*, Mar. 21, 2005.

15. Lech Walesa, "In Solidarity," OpinionJournal.com, June 11, 2004.

16. "Ambush in Mogadishu," Zinni interview with *PBS Frontline*, originally broadcast Sept. 29, 1998.

17. Carville and Greenberg, "The Democrats' Moment to Engage," Strategy Memo, July 6, 2005.

18. Bob Woodward, *Bush at War*, p. 248.

19. Interview with Jane Pauley, *Today*, Sept. 17, 2001.

20. For the definitive look at Hillary Clinton's ambitious vision to overhaul American society and its connection to her deep-rooted Methodist faith, see Michael Kelly's essay, "Saint Hillary," *New York Times Magazine*, May 23, 1993.

21. "Taking on the Terrorists," *New York Times*, Aug. 22, 1998.

22. "The U.S. Raids in Sudan, Afghanistan," *Philadelphia Inquirer*, Aug. 23, 1998.

23. Robert Scheer, "Compelled to Attack," *Pittsburgh Post-Gazette*, Aug. 27, 1998.

24. "War and Impeachment," *New York Times*, Dec. 17, 1998.

25. "Strength at the Top," *Chicago Sun-Times*, Dec. 17, 1998.

26. "A Just Attack," *Boston Globe*, Dec. 17, 1998.

27. Alexander Bolton, " 'Uniter' Biden Says He Can Win in the Red States," *The Hill*, June 29, 2005.

28. Leander Kahney, "Amateur Newsies Top the Pros," Wired.com, Sept. 15, 2001.

INDEX

Soros, George, 179–82
Sorry, Everybody, 262–63
Soviet Union, 20, 56, 59–60, 68,
    314
    Afghanistan invasion of, 60,
    307
    collapse of, 79, 107
    puppet regimes of, 68, 69–70,
    71
SpaceImaging, 13
Spain, 8, 113, 178
Special Operations Forces, U.S.,
    243–44, 330
Specter, Arlen, 51
Stalin, Joseph, 106, 164, 309
State Department, U.S., 58, 105,
    110, 301
Statue of Liberty, 3–4
Steinem, Gloria, 125
Stephanopoulos, George, 146
Stevens, Ted, 118
Stevenson, Adlai, 313
Steyn, Mark, 265
Stockpile, Tara, 207
Stoll, Ira, 31
Stone, Oliver, 123
Strategic Arms Limitation Talks
    (SALT II), 60
Strategic Defense Initiative, 193
Straw, Jack, xii
Streisand, Barbra, 214, 269
Strickland, Ted, 285
Stupid White Men (Moore), 215, 218
Sudan, 102, 115
Sullivan, Andrew, 305
Sullivan, Robert David, 30
Sununu, John, 46, 146
Supreme Court, U.S., 52
Swift Boat Vets for Truth, 190
Swing State Project, 308
Syria, 68, 227, 244, 330

Take Back America, 162
Talent, Jim, 145
Taliban, 19, 105–6, 107, 108, 112,
    119, 121, 124–25, 127, 131,

132–33, 159, 172, 186, 223,
    305, 314
    fall of, 137, 140, 164, 171
talk radio, 38, 131, 248
Tanzania, 1998 bombing of U.S.
    Embassy in, 101–2
TargetPoint Consulting, 282–83
Tarrance Group survey, 82
Taylor, Gene, 46
Teixeira, Ruy, 37
Telluride Film Festival, 217
Tenet, George, 105, 118, 232, 322
Tennessee, University of, 12, 137
Tennyson, Alfred, Lord, 254
terrorism, xi–xii
    Clinton on, 136–37
    debate on, 155–209
    Democrats as weak on, 82–86,
    126, 245
    fear generated by, 3, 7–8, 18, 113,
    157–58, 323
    Iraq regime tied to, xiii, 146–47,
    167, 176
    Islamic, 61–66, 68–69, 73, 98, 99,
    216
    mass casualty, 1–21, 55, 97, 100,
    109–54
    Michael Moore on, 114–16, 119,
    139, 216–19, 220–21, 245
    natural targets of, 9
    state sponsors of, 72–79, 112
    U.S. accused of, 115, 120, 124
    U.S. responses to, 5, 6, 61–69,
    72–79, 111–12, 114, 117, 132,
    140, 168, 169
    war on, 10, 26, 29, 33, 77, 97,
    107, 142, 151, 156–58, 166,
    173, 176–77, 188–89, 201,
    207, 254, 327
Thatcher, Margaret, 81
Thompson, Fred, 312
Thurmond, Strom, 252–53
Time, 9, 139, 232, 238, 272, 302–3
Today show, 216
Toledo Blade, 160
"Tom the Dancing Bug," 142–43

ABOUT THE AUTHOR

Jim Geraghty grew up a rather hopeless political geek in Metuchen, New Jersey. His journalism career took him to the *Dallas Morning News, Congressional Quarterly,* and States News Service, where he covered Washington for the *Boston Globe, Washington Post, Denver Post,* and *Detroit Free Press.*

Jim joined the *National Review* in 2004 to cover the presidential election on a constantly updated blog called "The Kerry Spot." It quickly became must-reading for those following the campaign, marked by Jim's insomniac, obsessive-compulsive reporting with twenty to thirty updates a day and oddly nicknamed campaign sources like "Obi-Wan Kenobi" and "Middle Cheese." Washington Post.com readers voted the Kerry Spot as the site with the "Best Political Dirt" and his fellow bloggers named it the "Best New Blog of 2004."

On Election Night, Jim was among the first to note that Kerry was underperforming Gore's 2000 performance in the blue states, making Democratic victories in Ohio and Florida supremely unlikely, which prompted the *Times* (London) to praise his "killer insight."

In March 2005, Jim moved with his wife to Ankara, Turkey, where he is now a foreign correspondent and columnist for the *National Review, Philadelphia Inquirer, Washington Times, New York Sun,* and *New Hampshire Union-Leader.* He aims to return to the United States to start up "The Hillary Spot" in time for 2008. His blog can be found at http://tks.nationalreview.com, and he can be reached at jim inturkey@gmail.com.